To Elizabeth

Continued success in
your work to develop
leaders

Jack Zenger

Praise for *The Extraordinary Leader*

"I fell in love with *The Extraordinary Leader* on page one. From the moment I started reading I really got jazzed, and my enthusiasm only increased the more I read. You see, I'm just mad about books that attack cherished but unsupportable assumptions about anything, especially leadership. That's exactly what Jack Zenger and Joe Folkman do, and they do it persuasively, precisely, and professionally. *The Extraordinary Leader* is no hackneyed rehashing of tired nostrums. Through their exceptional research the authors demonstrate and prove that leadership *does* make a difference and that *you* can learn to lead. There are some profound insights in this book, and whether you've studied leadership for over twenty years, as I have, or you're brand new to the subject, Zenger and Folkman give you much more than your money's worth. And while their research gives the book distinctive credibility, their examples and practical applications give it life. This is a book that scholars and practitioners will be referring to for years to come. If your goal is to be a better leader than you are today, then you must read this book."

—James M. Kouzes
Chairman Emeritus, Tom Peters Company
Coauthor of *The Leadership Challenge* and *Encouraging the Heart*

"Joe Folkman and Jack Zenger have proven themselves to be extraordinary thinkers. In their new book, *The Extraordinary Leader,* they unfold the most intriguing and provocative new research on leadership that I have encountered in many years. This book is a 'must-read' for anyone faced with the day-to-day challenges of developing extraordinary leadership talent within an organization."

—Annie LaBombard
Director of Leadership
Fireman's Fund Insurance Company

"Read this book! Its approach to understanding leadership development is unique: It uses data, not opinion! Some of the insights are intuitive, but many are counter-intuitive. Extraordinarily readable, this book represents some of the best thinking on leadership I've seen in a long while."

—E. David Spong
President, Military Aerospace Support
The Boeing Company

"Ordinarily, I'd say the last thing we need is another book on leadership. But *The Extraordinary Leader* by Jack Zenger and Joe Folkman is refreshingly different. Rather than serve up yesterday's anecdotes, they've performed the heavy lifting of empirical data collection and analysis. The foreword promises clarity, simplicity, and utility in addressing the real-world challenges of developing leaders, and this book delivers that and more. This is a must read."

—Jon Younger, Ph.D.
Senior Vice President, Leadership Development
National City Corporation

"The authors' promise on page four to do their best 'to unravel the mystery of leadership through careful analysis and observation' of a huge database 'by emulating Sherlock Holmes,' grabbed my attention. Always an avid mystery reader, I found myself compulsively turning pages, devouring the entire book, like any good mystery, in one sitting. I especially appreciated the wisdom found in Insights #1–20, the non-obvious competency companions, and the distinctions between mattress and tent leadership models. By the last chapter (when all at last had been revealed) I had deduced a far better way to help my organization become a company of leaders than I've been able to figure out in the last twenty years!"

—Sallie T. Hightower, Ed.D.
Conoco University
Conoco, Inc.

"Finally someone has moved beyond theory and complicated models to tell us what great leaders really bring to the party. Zenger and Folkman have effectively summarized data on 20,000 leaders that help us understand what really makes leaders tick. Any serious student of leadership will both enjoy this book's journey and walk away with useful new insights that will help them and others."

—Ralph Christensen
Senior Vice President, Human Resources
Hallmark Cards, Inc.

"This book has changed the way I think! If you want to move from good to great as a leader, don't focus on a weakness; instead, take a strength and build on it. Jack Zenger and Joe Folkman have written an important book, full of insight and based on sound research. It will shape the way we help our clients develop executives."

—Douglas D. Anderson
Founder and Managing Partner
Center for Executive Development–Boston

"This is a 'must read' for coaches, leaders, and those who develop them. *The Extraordinary Leader* goes beyond anecdotes or 'war stories,' it builds upon comprehensive research. It is destined to be a classic in our field."

—Marshall Goldsmith
Named by *Forbes* as one of five top executive coaches and
one of *Wall Street Journal's* "Top 10" executive educators

THE EXTRAORDINARY LEADER

THE EXTRAORDINARY LEADER

Turning Good Managers into Great Leaders

John H. Zenger

Joseph Folkman

McGraw-Hill
New York   Chicago   San Francisco
Lisbon   London   Madrid   Mexico City
Milan   New Delhi   San Juan   Seoul
Singapore   Sydney   Toronto

The *McGraw-Hill* Companies

Library of Congress Cataloging-in-Publication Data

Zenger, John H.
    The extraordinary leader   :   turning good managers into great leaders   /
by John H. Zenger and Joseph Folkman.
        p. cm.
    ISBN 0-07-138747-1 (hardcover : alk. paper)
    1. Leadership. I. Folkman, Joe. II. Title.

HD57.7 .Z46 2002
658.4′092—dc21

                                                        2002005908

4 5 6 7 8 9 0   DOC/DOC   0 9 8 7 6 5 4 3

ISBN 0-07-138747-1

McGraw-Hill books are available at special quantity discounts to use as premiums
and sales promotions, or for use in corporate training programs. For more
information, please write to the Director of Special Sales, Professional Publishing,
McGraw-Hill, Two Penn Plaza, New York, NY 10121-2298. Or contact your local
bookstore.

 This book is printed on recycled, acid-free paper containing a
minimum of 50% recycled, de-inked fiber.

CONTENTS

FOREWORD

Today's business climate demands leadership throughout the organization. *The Extraordinary Leader* draws on data from over 200,000 individuals who have rated over 25,000 leaders to show how leaders can go from being good to being great, from being average to being extraordinary. The book focuses on the top 10 percent of leaders, as defined by their stakeholders. These leaders are exemplars and should become the standard to which others ascribe and aspire.

The Extraordinary Leader both complements and advances the work we began in *Results-Based Leadership*. In that earlier work, we argued that leadership is a combination of Attributes × Results, but we focused there on the "results" side of the equation; in this book the authors emphasize the "attributes" side of the equation and thus move toward a more complete picture of leadership. To this end, they are applying the logic from Jim Collins' excellent work on how organizations can go from good to great performance on the personal side of leadership. Rather than seeking quick fixes that don't last, this book proposes a leadership science that will offer sustaining and enduring leadership value. The book successfully links these two approaches together, showing how the attributes that make a difference to subordinates and peers are exactly the ones that produce better results for the shareholders.

Leadership requires both attributes and results. There are two ways to discover these attributes. First, find those attributes that drive financial and other results. Second, use "360-degree feedback" to define attributes that are right "in the eye of the beholder." Such 360-degree instruments help leaders determine what is expected from those they lead. They help leaders know the intended attributes that mean the most to those being led.

This book is informative because of its rich and thorough content, and it is useful because it contains ideas with impact, which will help leaders become seen as extraordinary by their associates. It links perceptual data with hard, quantitative business results, including unit profitability, retention statistics, customer satisfaction, and employee commitment measures.

An important message of the book is that leaders can change. Leaders can go from being good to being great, from being seen as adequate to being seen as extraordinary. The process for getting from good to great may differ somewhat for each person, but there is a pattern. This pattern enables leaders to discern what they need to do to deliver more value.

The book offers a plethora of content and new ways to think about leadership based on both research and experience. It gives the reader multiple perspectives of leadership, but amidst all that complexity the book promises simplicity. The authors give the reader a conceptual framework by which to understand leadership attributes. Their "tent" model is a powerful way to describe leadership. I believe most readers will appreciate this graphic depiction of an extremely complex (and sometimes obtuse) subject. Further, the model moves beyond simply describing leadership to also describing ideal leadership development methods—expanding strengths versus dithering about weaknesses. The authors emphasize that the best way to raise a tent is to extend the poles skyward, not to go looking for the drooping piece of canvas and propping it up.

One test of a business book is how it informs practice and action. The observations made in this book will have impact when they change how leaders think and/or behave. With this in mind, let me share what I would advise a leader to do, based on the ideas in this book. I assume that this leader wants to move from being good to being extraordinary, from being seen by subordinates, peers, and supervisors as average to being in the top 10 percent in a 360-degree feedback or similar exercise.

- *Display high personal character.* Everything about great leadership radiates from character. Personal character improves the probability of exhibiting strong interpersonal skills. Some of this perceived character is innate and based on a personal value set; but more is driven by the leader's self-awareness and interactions with others.

- *Start small.* Going from good to great follows an "S" curve of learning. Starting small means doing something now, something within your control that will have immediate impact. As small things cumulate, bigger things will happen. A leader should identify some quick, simple, and readily visible things that can be done along the "S" curve path.

- *Excel at something.* The worst leaders (34th percentile or bottom third) have an "average" profile, with no great strengths or weaknesses. They are vanilla leaders, not standing out on anything. The impact of one perceived strength moves leaders to the 64th percentile, and three strengths moves them to the 81st percentile. My advice to you as a leader is to figure out what you are good at and improve it to the 90 percent level. Be good at something, then a few things.

- *Connect competencies and leverage combinations.* You are a better leader when you connect competencies and see the power of combinations. For example, leaders who are highly competent at Focus on Results and Interpersonal Skills have a powerful combination. With a single strength in Interpersonal Skills, only 9 percent are at the 90th percentile. With a single strength in Focus on Results, only 13 percent are at the 90th percentile. With a combination (both Interpersonal Skills and Focus on Results perceived as strengths), 66 percent are at the 90th percentile.

- *Use a nonlinear approach to becoming a better leader.* For example, if you get lousy feedback on technical skills, the best approach may not be to work on improving your technical skills. The authors' proposal for competency companions suggests that it may be in your interest to improve your interpersonal skills as the best way to improve the perception of your technical skills.

- *Build on your strengths.* Figure out what you do well and magnify it. It only takes strength in a few (two to four) attributes while being average in the rest to achieve a high probability of being seen as a great leader. So, a leader needs to build on strengths. Find what you do well, then find the combination of competencies that you should do well to be seen as more effective.

- *Remedy fatal flaws.* The authors provide data showing that these are an inability to learn from mistakes and develop new skills; being interpersonally inept; being closed to new ideas; failure to be accountable for results; not taking initiative. Assess yourself and see how others assess you on these five fatal flaws. If any show up, work on them fast and furiously.

These suggestions are just the beginning of ideas with impact that you can draw from this book. However, these ideas represent the content that may help you as a leader to move from being good to being great. In the context of today's organizations, applying these ideas will not only help leaders improve, they will also help organizations become more competitive.

Dave Ulrich

ACKNOWLEDGMENTS

This book began several years ago as I was walking down the hall looking over some statistical output and bumped into Jack Zenger. Jack's question was, "Are you doing anything that's interesting?" My response was, "Funny you should ask, look at this data." What began as a fascination with some statistical analysis grew into a compelling body of evidence that modified substantially the conventional wisdom people have about what makes great leaders and how they develop.

To anyone who reads a number of books on leadership, it becomes apparent that over 90 percent of what you read has been said before. The packaging is different, the examples amusing, but fundamentally there is little that is new. I had no interest in writing that kind of book. Our approach was to do rigorous research and then formulate a theory to explain the results. In presentations on our findings to clients, we have been very pleased with the "Ah-ha's" that are apparent as we present the insights from our research. I am hopeful that readers of this book will have a similar experience.

One of the most interesting findings from our research is something called "powerful combinations." A powerful combination occurs when leaders combine two unique skills, which result in a substantial increase in overall effectiveness. In thinking about the process of getting this book written, I am very confident that neither Jack nor I could have accomplished this research and written this book alone. The combination of Jack's experience, knowledge, and conceptual skills with my research, measurement, and change management background created a very powerful combination. Working through the laborious and demanding process of writing this book with Jack has been an absolute delight. I am grateful for his patience, gentle persuasion, and persistence.

Many people contributed substantially by doing research and editing on the book. Thanks to Judy Seegmiller, Kerri Price, Brandon Folkman, Jason Wetherstone, Hayward Alto, Angela Bass, Heather Frandsen, and Brandon Driggs for their contributions.

As is always the case with projects such as this, it was impossible to produce record revenues, carry a full client load, write a book, and manage my responsibilities as a husband and father. It was my wife and family who gave up the most and voluntarily carried an increased load. I appreciate their willingness to do so very much. I recognize in them much that is extraordinary.

Finally, I would like to dedicate this book to my clients. I am extremely grateful to brilliant clients in a broad range of industries. Universally, they are dedicated to improving organizations and the individuals who work in them. They are continually looking for ways to make people more successful. The data, which is the foundation on which this book is built, came from them.

Joe Folkman

As a relatively young boy I worked in the hospital for which my father was the administrator. From him I learned much about leadership and the challenges of being the senior executive. His relentless pursuit of improvement and willingness to abandon systems that were working for the promise of something better were great examples to me.

My academic interests in leadership began at UCLA as a research assistant in the Human Relations Research Group. I appreciate the tutelage of Robert Tannenbaum and the late Irv Weschler. Then at USC came an association with Bill Woolf, who exposed me to a sociological and anthropological view of leadership. Many others influenced my thinking, including Mel Sorcher, the creator of behavioral modeling training in industry. Bernie Rosenbaum expanded my understanding of the elegance of this learning methodology.

I had many colleagues at Zenger Miller who influenced me, beginning with Dale Miller, Steve Mann, Ed Musselwhite, and dozens of others. Their association enriched my thinking about leadership and simultaneously helped build an extraordinary company. To them all I express appreciation. Later at Provant, I have worked with unusual colleagues, including Curt Uehlein, Herb Cohen, Marc Wallace, Dave Erdman, and Adam Senter. I recently worked with a team of people, creating a cutting edge, truly blended leadership development program. From Jeff Howard I learned new concepts and ideas about the role of leaders in developing people and from Rob Steinmetz, better ways of delivering learning.

The process of writing a book on leadership with Dave Ulrich and Norm Smallwood was another opportunity to expand my thinking. I greatly value their friendship and their wisdom. Marshall Goldsmith, Jan Katzenbach, Ed Lawler, and Frances Hesselbein have been others whose writings and dialogue have elevated my thinking. Doug Anderson, managing partner of the Center for Executive Development, has also provided important practical wisdom about leadership development.

I would never have imagined that I'd be writing a book with a statistically inclined organizational psychologist. Joe Folkman's academic interests have been quite opposite from mine, but the experience has been extremely positive. Differences were quickly and painlessly resolved. The book is something that neither of us could have done alone.

Finally, I extend my deepest appreciation to my combined family. From our children, their spouses, and many grandchildren have come great lessons in leadership, along with opportunities to apply some of what I have learned. To my wife, Holly, I express special thanks. Besides being a good critic of whatever I write, her organization of our life together creates the time and environment in which it is possible to write a book.

Jack Zenger

INTRODUCTION

"What will I gain from reading this book?"

"Will it be worth the effort I expend in plowing into its contents?"

"Will there be a good return on the time I invest in reading and studying it?"

"What is different about this book than other books on the subject of 'leadership'?"

Those are justifiable questions. The more you know about our objectives and the nature of this book, the easier it will be to arrive at good answers to those questions for you. Purchasing any book lightens your purse or wallet a tad, but the real investment is not dollars. Reading any book consumes an extremely valuable commodity—your time.

We had three primary objectives in writing this book. First was simplicity. We insisted that the book provide a clear, understandable message. Nothing is more irritating than to read a book on a topic of great personal interest, and then close the book and not be able to summarize the book's point of view or basic thesis. We do not expect everyone to agree fully with all the conclusions we put forth. But agree or not, this book contains a simple model of leadership, our answer about whether leadership can be developed, how leadership can be developed by individuals themselves, and what organizations can do to develop leaders. We present a case study of an organization that successfully transforms people into effective leaders. We present 20 insights, many of them new ideas, about leadership. These create the framework of the book.

Our second objective was that the contents be actionable. We do not expect that every idea in the book will be something you can implement immediately; but success for us will be your ability to take a great portion of our findings and be able to do something with them. We believe that real learning shows up in new behavior. If this book is a serious vehicle of learning, then the way to measure its value is via the new actions you take. In leadership development programs there is the perennial plea to the instructors for "What do I do on Monday morning?" Books on leadership should meet the same test. Most recommendations are ones that mere mortals can use comfortably—on Monday morning.

Our third objective was that the book be empirical. We insisted that it be based on hard data, facts, and statistical analyses. Huge sets of data were the touchstone to which we constantly returned. Frankly, we tire of books by executives and business writers that primarily express personal philosophies and beliefs, especially when they are so inconsistent. The discipline of leadership and those committed to developing leaders inside organizations surely deserve better. Our standard was to have every conclusion grounded in objective data. The combination of hard data and statistical analyses were to be the point of the spear. It then became our task to make sense of the data, and to put logical explanations around our findings.

We welcome feedback from readers. The topic deserves a great deal of dialogue from all of us who are concerned with the future of our great institutions—universities, schools, hospitals, government agencies, and businesses. These all need leaders in order to flourish. Our hope is that the information that follows will in some small way aid in the development of those much-needed leaders.

C H A P T E R

DEMYSTIFYING LEADERSHIP

> Leadership is one of the most observed and least understood phenomena on earth.
>
> *J. M. Burns*

> The aura with which we tend to surround the words leader and leadership makes it hard to think clearly. Good sense calls for demystification.
>
> *John Gardner*

THE MYSTERY REMAINS

While seated at a dinner table recently, it became known that we were writing a book. A dinner guest immediately inquired, "What is the book about?"

"It is about leadership," one of us replied.

Without hesitation the guest inquired, "Do you really think people can be developed into leaders? Aren't they born that way?" (We'd like to have a dollar for every time that question has been asked of us over the past decades.) The question seems as hardy as cockroaches or crocodiles. The general population has that query at the top of their minds, and so do a lot of CEOs and public organization leaders.

And the question is really in two parts. If the question is answered using the popular party line that says, "Of course you can develop leadership in people," the immediate follow-up question is, "How do you do that?" It is to those two basic questions that we address this book.

Does the world need anything more written on the subject of leadership? On the one hand, it could be argued that the answer is a loud "No!" Consider the fact that over 10,000 articles have been published about leadership in the past century. While some are based on research, most reflect the personal opinions of the authors regarding leadership, derived from their own experience or their observations of leaders. Many are written by successful business executives and reflect their own beliefs about what made them successful.

Add to that approximately a thousand research studies that have been conducted on leadership and published in scholarly journals. Then add nearly a thousand books that have been written about leadership over the past 100 years. Many of these were written by practicing leaders, while others were written by academicians and consultants who sought to explain this important role that some people perform. Given that immense body of literature, it would seem futile to add yet one more.

THE REASONS FOR ONE MORE BOOK

Despite that extensive literature, leadership remains shrouded in mystery. Rather than making the subject clearer, one recognized leadership expert, Warren Bennis, summed it up by saying "the more that is written about leadership, the less we seem to know."

Regarding the several thousand research studies that have been conducted, another respected scholar observed, "The results of many of these studies are contradictory or lack any clear conclusion."[1]

How Mysteries Are Solved
There is an astonishing description of one approach to solving a mystery in Sir Arthur Conan Doyle's classic Sherlock Holmes tale

The Sign of Four. Dr. Watson remarks to Sherlock Holmes, "I have a gold watch in my possession. Would you have the kindness to let me have an opinion upon the character or habits of the late owner?" Watson was testing Holmes and attempting to tone down his arrogant manner. Holmes then complained that because the watch had recently been cleaned, he was robbed of the most useful data. But after carefully examining the watch, Holmes then proceeded to tell Watson a series of hypotheses about the owner. These included:

- The watch belonged to his older brother, who inherited it from his father.
- He was a man of untidy habits.
- He had gone through a period of poverty, with intervals of prosperity.
- He had taken to heavy drinking before he died.

Watson sprang from his chair and accused Holmes of having made inquiries into the history of his unhappy brother and then pretended to deduce it from his observations of the gold pocket watch. He concluded by saying, "It is unkind and, to speak plainly, has a touch of charlatanism in it."

Holmes proceeded to explain how he had come to each of his conclusions by simply observing important data and seeing their implications. The initials on the watch's back, "H.W.," suggested a family member, and gold watches usually were passed from father to the elder son.

The watch was 50 years old. The initials appeared to be as old as the watch, and so it was most likely the father's watch, passed to Dr. Watson's brother. The owner's untidy habits were revealed by the dents and scratches that came from carrying this expensive watch in the same pocket with other hard objects such as coins or keys. Inside the case of the watch were scratched in pinpoint the numbers of a pawnbroker's ticket, suggesting that the owner had gone through a period of dire poverty. The fact that he regained possession of the watch would imply that he also had periods of prosperity. The owner's drinking problem was revealed by thousands of scratches around the keyhole where the winding key had slipped and scratched the case. Holmes noted, "That is characteristic of a drunkard's watch, not a sober man's."

Solving the Mystery of Leadership

Our hope is to take an enormous amount of data collected about and from leaders and, through careful analysis and observation, begin to unravel the mystery of leadership. We will do our best to emulate Sherlock Holmes. It would seem that if careful attention is given to the clues that lie inside huge databases, the continuing mystery of leadership might be penetrated.

Our objective is to provide the reader with an empirical analysis of leadership, a simple and practical conceptual model of what leadership is, and a practical guide to helping leaders develop "greatness." Our approach and understanding comes from our analysis of hundreds of thousands of leadership assessments from the direct reports of leaders, their peers, their bosses, and themselves. We let our findings guide our development of a practical theory.

Because together the authors have roughly three-quarters of a century of experience in leadership development, we were surprised that the research changed some long-held beliefs about the nature of leadership and how best to develop it.

THE COMPLEXITY OF DEFINING AND DESCRIBING LEADERSHIP OR WHY THE MYSTERY EXISTS

Everyone recognizes the challenge of trying to solve any problem that has multiple unknowns in it. That is precisely the problem in trying to solve the leadership dilemma. There are at once a significant number of unknowns, and many of them are constantly changing.

Sixteen of those variables are described below.

1. There are differences in the leadership behaviors and practices required at different levels of the organization. What we need from the CEO or Secretary of the Defense Department is different than the leadership requirements of a night-shift supervisor at McDonald's.

2. Leadership occurs in extremely diverse environments. Some leadership produces prescribed results in a relatively defined

and established organization. Such leadership may speed a product to market, or escalate the revenue from a sales force, but it is not conceiving new directions or strategies for the organization. Other leadership is exhibited in a start-up organization in which there is no structure or form, and the leader must create it from scratch.

3. Different skills are required at different stages in a person's career. The research on career stages shows that people's careers go through very predictable stages. Early on, people start as apprentices, learning some new discipline. They then move to become more independent in their work. From there, some people move into managerial positions in which they oversee the work of others or move from a narrow focus on their own work to a broader focus that involves coaching others to develop skill, and expertise. Finally, a handful of people become pathfinders and visionaries who lead broad-scale organization change and are the "statesmen" of their organization. Career stages are easily confused with organizational levels, but they are not identical. People who are promoted into managerial positions often continue to function as professional, individual contributors. They revert to the work they find most comfortable, and never take on the role of coach, mentor, or director of others. They continue doing technical work at which they are highly proficient. However, the stage of a person's career is another variable of the leadership equation.

4. Leadership is driven by major events. Mayor Rudolf Giuliani of New York was catapulted into the national limelight because of his handling of the terrorist attacks on the World Trade Center. Prior to that, his career had been waning. Churchill had sought several leadership positions, but it was not until the events of Dunkirk that his talents were recognized. Through World War II he was a premier leader, and then when the war was over, his countrymen voted him out of office.

5. The activities of leadership are not all the same. For example, not all leaders are required to "lead change." Some leaders spend a great deal of time on people development activities, while others are riveted to the operational or production elements of their role.

6. We confuse success and effectiveness as the general benchmark of leadership. If success is measured by dollars and titles, that is clearly not the same thing as effectiveness, or truly producing the results that the organization needs. We believe this is probably best measured by the feedback from subordinates who experience that leadership. Much of the research on leadership makes no distinction between success and effectiveness.

7. We lack agreed-upon measures, so it has been frustratingly difficult to get agreement on who is a good leader and who is not. We lack robust measures of leadership effectiveness, and especially have no comprehensive measures that track the leader's impact on customers, employees, organizations, and shareholders.

8. We have not taken into account the evolving nature of leadership. That is, we have analyzed leadership around the characteristics that are required for success or effectiveness today, but have not given much attention to the competencies that will be required in the future. Thus, much of the leadership analysis and development has been "looking in the rearview mirror" and not looking out over the horizon.

9. There has been no way to define the different constituencies of the leader. Thus, if a leader is in charge of "baby boomers" born from 1945 to 1955, this would call for some different values, motives, and skills than if the leader was responsible for a group of "Gen-Xers" born from 1975 to 1985.

10. Still another variable is whether the leader is operating alone versus acting as part of a leadership team. Clearly there are organizations in which one person plays an extremely dominant part and exercises control and influence over the big issues, along with the day-to-day tactics. Other organizations have a leadership team that acts in concert. In some cases a formal "office of the president" has people who act quite interchangeably in the organization.

11. A further dimension is the impact of technology. Effectiveness in some organizations would demand a high level of comfort with the latest computer and information technology, while

others would tolerate a leader who could neither send nor receive e-mail. New technologies exist to conduct virtual meetings, and in some organizations a comfort and familiarity with such technology would be a "must." A Dell Computer employee reported, "My boss spent the entire weekend retyping a 25-page proposal that only needed corrections. She claims the disk I gave her was damaged and she could not edit it. The disk I gave her was write-protected."

12. A new dimension of leadership is one of geography. Some leaders interact with a virtual team, while others have their staff all under the same roof in which they operate. This can be even further complicated by the fact that groups are often scattered across widely different time zones, thus making the leadership task even more complex. For example, holding meetings at one point in time can be cumbersome.

13. Another variable is the wide variety of leadership styles used within different organizations to motivate and inspire the frontline. Some of the best research in this regard comes from Jon Katzenbach and is described in his book *Peak Performance.*[2] In that he describes firms that were extremely effective and successful, but who used very different approaches to getting high performance from the people within. He described five of these:

   - *Mission, values, and pride.*   In this approach, the organization immerses everyone in the traditions, the spirit, the core values, and the mission of the organization. This in turn generates great pride, and people produce at high levels because of that pride in the organization. The Marine Corps is a good example of this.

   - *Recognition and celebration.*   Many organizations he studied practiced extensive recognition for their people, and went to great lengths to celebrate successes. Southwest Airlines is a classic example of this approach.

   - *Process metrics.*   Many organizations post detailed charts showing productivity and quality metrics for every department. People are trained to understand these metrics, and the organization's success is measured and rewarded by performance against these metrics.

- *Individual achievement.* Other organizations excel by allowing individuals to accomplish extraordinary things. Organizational effectiveness is the addition of all these excelling individuals. Professional service firms function this way, and McKinsey and Company is a good example.

- *Entrepreneurial spirit.* Still another approach to motivating people to high performance is to let them enjoy a huge financial stake in the potential success of the firm. Many high-tech start-ups have relied on this appeal to someone's entrepreneurial spirit, and this has enabled the organization to excel.

This is a good example of the complexity of leadership. All five of the above approaches work well. One is not right and the others wrong. What could end up being "wrong" is for a recognition and celebration leader to attempt to function that way in a process metrics organization. Chances are the organization would reject such a leader as the human body rejects any foreign substance implanted in it.

14. Who decides those who are good leaders? We have been unclear regarding who is in the best position to evaluate leadership effectiveness. Organizations have often relied on performance appraisals from the level above to evaluate the effectiveness of a leader. We have studies from several organizations showing absolutely no correlation between performance appraisals and their 360-degree feedback instruments. Yet the research for past decades has shown that subordinates were in the best position to appraise any leader's effectiveness. Research in the military proved that having the enlisted men select sergeants was more effective than having higher-ranking officers make those selections.

15. Several "companions" of leadership effectiveness have clouded the issue. For example, all of the following have been shown to have some correlation to leadership effectiveness:
- Intelligence, as measured by IQ scores
- Physical characteristics, such as height
- Emotional or personality characteristics, such as assertiveness and outgoingness

- Biochemical characteristics, such as testosterone levels in men

Because some correlation exists between these elements and leadership effectiveness, there has been a logical temptation to assume there to be a cause-and-effect relationship. At the same time, there was high interest in such conclusions from those responsible for leadership selection; the above elements did not help further the work of those concerned with development.

16. Language has an impact. Is the lack of adequate language partly responsible for the mystery that surrounds leadership? The Inuit (or as some call them, Eskimos) have some 23 words to describe snow. They can describe its hardness, texture, moisture content, color, age, and crystalline structure with their richer vocabulary. We, on the other hand, have roughly three words at best, as we talk about powder, slush, and corn snow. It is possible that if our vocabulary were more precise and robust, we could better succeed in describing what leadership is, and how to more effectively develop it? Given our current condition, leadership is still nearly impossible to define or describe in detail or specificity. However, as Professor Karl Weick has suggested, any idea can be "simple, general or accurate, but never all three."[3] We will strive to be general and accurate, but not specific. That appears to be the best way to improve our understanding of this most important topic.

RESEARCH-BASED BOOK

Our hope is to present a way for people to think about leadership in a highly practical and yet simple way. We will not review the past literature on leadership. Others have done that. Nor will we dwell on the theoretical. Nor will we attempt to describe all of the tasks or activities of leaders. Others have done that also. Instead, we want to present a way for you personally to think about your own leadership abilities and how you might go about increasing those, if you choose. And for those who have subordinates, we provide suggestions about what they and their organization can do to develop leadership in the people who report to them.

We believe this is best done by examining a huge body of data collected about leaders from their peers, subordinates, bosses, and themselves. Rather than describe our personal beliefs and prejudices about leadership, we will turn to more objective data. We think it enables us to discover some profound insights into the real nature of leadership. Where mysteries still remain, we call that to your attention and pass on our beliefs.

In order to answer intelligently the question, "Are leaders born or made?" and the sequel, "If they are made, then how do you do that?" we begin by providing the reader with a model of leadership that becomes our operational definition of a leader. That model then provides a workable vehicle with which to describe a practical way to make good managers into great leaders. Later in the book we present an example of an organization that has excelled at taking what some would describe as average people and transforming them into highly effective leaders. That organization is the U.S. Marine Corps.

This book examines the leader as seen through the eyes of those being led (subordinates), and influenced (peers), and those who manage the leaders (the bosses) and the leaders themselves. This process has become known as 360-degree feedback, because of its comprehensive view of a leader's behavior, looked at from above, the side, and below. Indeed, we later describe our database of some 200,000 responses, using 360-degree questionnaires. We focus on the question: What do these three groups (subordinates, peers, and bosses) notice? What do they see in "great leaders" that sets them apart from the average ones?

Of those three perspectives, we conclude that the best way to understand leadership is to examine the impact leaders have on the people they lead. It is the subordinates' view we value the most, because we believe they have the most complete and accurate data. Peers and bosses see slices of a leader's behavior, but there is good evidence to conclude that their perceptions are less accurate than those of the people who report to the leader.

We strongly believe that this comprehensive pool of data is far more powerful and accurate than information that would come from interviews of leaders themselves. As Michael Polanyi noted in his book *Personal Knowledge,* "most highly skilled performers in any activity, whether it be music, sports, or violin making, cannot accurately tell you what makes them so effective. Their behavior is often highly intuitive. You must actually observe them to accurately determine the true cause of their success."[4]

This database of approximately 200,000 questionnaires completed by subordinates, peers, and bosses, about leaders, collectively describes more than 20,000 leaders. They come from widely diverse industries. These leaders are from North America, along with many from Europe, the Pacific Rim, and South America.

To make our database and analysis more robust, we examined over 25 different leadership assessment instruments. Rather than depending on the same set of assessment items for all 20,000 leaders, we examined a variety of different assessments, each built on different assumptions. This provided us with a database rich in diversity and helped give us a much clearer sense of what makes effective leadership and what doesn't. All together we included in our analysis over 2000 unique assessment items.

Research Methodology
We began our analysis by identifying the top 10 percent of managers as seen through the eyes of their subordinates, peers, and bosses and compared them to the bottom 10 percent. The top 10 percent, with the highest aggregate scores, became a high-performing group, and the 10 percent with the lowest aggregate scores were placed in the bottom group. Next we asked the question: What were the competencies or attributes that separated these groups?

We were surprised by the results that came from analyzing all of these data. It opened our thinking to some highly promising new ways to look at leadership, as well as providing new directions in the ways we go about developing leaders.

MOVING COMPLEXITY TOWARD SIMPLICITY

If you and 10 colleagues were asked to describe a computer, there would be some general consistency among the answers, but the answers would most likely focus on what a computer does, not what is going on inside it. Indeed, for most people, what goes on inside a laptop or desktop computer is a complete mystery. Most have never looked inside one. What's more, you don't need to. The output from the computer is all you care about; that can be spreadsheets, computer graphics, design simulations, e-mail, or simple word processing.

Many people know that there is a hard drive inside and roughly know its capacity. They also know there is a microprocessor, and they have some idea about its speed. They know there is some memory capacity and approximately what the RAM of their computer is. In short, they know some general things about it and what it produces.

That is the level of understanding that practicing leaders need to have about leadership. They do not need to know the details, but it is helpful to have some general understanding of the components that come together to make a great leader.

THE LEADERSHIP TENT—A CONCEPTUAL FRAMEWORK

We propose approaching leadership in the same way. We will not add one more description of the inner character traits or thought processes of great leaders. The conceptual model we propose is rather simple, and involves five elements, which we will compare to the poles in a tent.

Our empirical factor analysis of huge amounts of data collected on leaders' competencies reveals that all vital and differentiating leadership competencies can be grouped into five clusters. For the sake of ease in remembering and analysis, we have created a diagram in the form of a tent floor (Figure 1.1) that shows the relationship of these building blocks to each other.

Character
Our model in Figure 1.1 starts with a center pole representing the "character" of an individual. There is a huge body of writing on this subject. Indeed, some writers and researchers have argued that leadership is totally about character or integrity. We do not share that

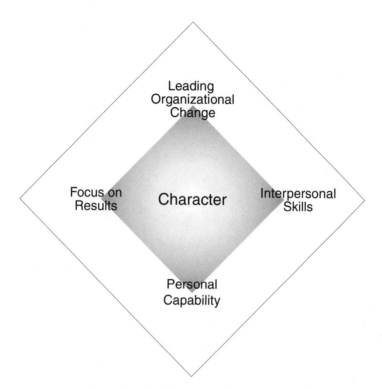

FIGURE 1.1   The leadership tent floor.

view, but we do agree that personal character is the core of all leadership effectiveness. We strongly concur that the ethical standards, integrity, and authenticity of the leader are extremely important. With a strong personal character the leader is never afraid to be open and transparent. In fact, the more people can see inside, the more highly regarded the leader will be. Without that personal character, on the other hand, leaders are forever in danger of being discovered. They are like a Hollywood set that from one side looks attractive, but after walking around it, the illusion is dispelled and the hollowness is obvious.

Personal Capability

On one side of the tent floor is the pole of personal capability. This describes the intellectual, emotional, and skill makeup of the individual. It includes analytical and problem-solving capabilities, along with the technical competence the person possesses. It requires an ability to create a clear vision and sense of purpose for the organization. Great leaders need a strong collection of these personal capabilities. Leadership cannot be delegated to others. The leader must be emotionally resilient, trust others, and be self-confident enough to run effective meetings and speak in public.

Focus on Results
The third tent pole of leadership represents the behaviors that can broadly be described as "focusing on results." It describes the ability to have an impact on the organization. It means being capable of getting things accomplished. We fully subscribe to the main thesis in the book *Results-Based Leadership,*[5] which argues that leaders may be wonderful human beings, but if they don't produce sustained, balanced results they simply are not good leaders. We will later examine the interplay of these three elements as a powerful predictor of leadership effectiveness.

Interpersonal Skills
The fourth tent pole of leadership puts into one cluster all of the interpersonal or people skills. There is an enormous body of evidence that says leadership is expressed through the communication process and is the impact that one person (the leader) has on a group of other people. It is the direct expression of the character of the individual and is often the window by which people understand the personal character of the leader. (Note, however, that leadership does not equal any one competency. It is expressed in a result. Yes, the competency is the tool or the manners in which that result are obtained. As such, it is worthy of understanding, but a competency is never an outcome, and leadership is ultimately about outcomes.) We have arbitrarily separated the leader's impact on people from the leader's ability to obtain good results in other arenas, such as financial outcomes, productivity improvement, enhanced customer relations, or greater organizational capability.

Leading Organizational Change
Fifth, as noted earlier, another expression of leadership comes in the ability to produce change within an organization. The highest

expression of leadership involves change. Caretaker managers can keep things going on a steady path, but leaders are demanded if the organization is to pursue a new path or rise to a significantly higher level of performance.

A key point here is that for many leadership roles, the first four tent poles may be all that are required. It is not until a person gets into leading broad, strategic change that the final tent pole is required.

AN OVERVIEW OF IMPORTANT IDEAS IN THIS BOOK

There are 20 insights presented in this book. The following chapters present further analysis of these ideas.

Insight 1.   Great leaders make a huge difference, when compared to merely good leaders.

We have known for some time that huge differences exist between top performers and average performers in any job category. One meta-analysis (a synthesis of some 80 well-conducted studies on productivity) showed that for high-level jobs (and leaders certainly fit that category) the productivity difference between the top person out of 100 and the great majority is huge. For example, the top person performing high-complexity jobs is 127 percent more productive than the mean average person, and infinitely more productive than the 100th person in that curve. The researchers said "infinitely" because the number was so large that it would be lacking precision to say anything other than "infinite."

Our research with a large mortgage company showed that the leaders in the top decile of ratings (90th to 99th), as rated by their managers, subordinates, and peers, produced twice as much net revenue to the organization (their term for profitability) as managers in the 11th through 89th percentiles. So the difference between really great leaders and the others is extraordinary. We have found strong statistically significant relationships between leadership effectiveness and a variety of desirable business outcomes such as profitability, turnover, employee commitment, customer satisfaction, and intention of employees to leave. In almost every study where we have undertaken to understand the impact of various dimensions of organizational effectiveness, leadership effectiveness has consistently had substantial impact. This is discussed in Chapter 2.

Insight 2. One organization can have many great leaders.

Being a great leader can be defined by selecting the top 5 or 10 percent from any distribution, but this is artificial. It was done for the sake of ease and objectivity in our research. However, greatness should ultimately be defined against a standard rather than merely comparing people against each other. There is no reason why half the leaders in an organization could not be great if they were developed properly. Better still, why not all? Great leadership is not a competitive activity in which one person's success detracts from another's success.

Four great golfers can play together and all four can come in 10 strokes or more under par on the course. If anything, playing with other great players elevates the play of each individual. Likewise, an organization can have large numbers of leaders performing at a high level and having positive impact on their people, and producing excellent business results. The goal should be to have all leaders performing at an extremely high level, and there is no reason why this cannot occur.

Jack Welch's legacy at GE was a strong emphasis on developing a large number of great leaders, many of whom went on to lead major divisions of GE, and some who left to head up other major corporations. Somehow we must change the mentality that holds that any organization can have only a few really good leaders in it. Chapter 2 covers this topic.

Insight 3. We have been aiming too low in our leadership development activities.

We contend that one of the major failings in leadership development programs has been the tendency to aim low. Michelangelo said, "The greatest danger for most of us is not that our aim is too high and we miss it, but that it is too low and we reach it."

We have often set the target as "getting a little bit better." We have not set our sights on getting people to become outstanding leaders. The more great leaders an organization develops, the more it will become an outstanding organization. There is no reason to accept mediocrity in leadership any more than in software programming, customer service, or selling. This is more fully covered in Chapter 2.

Insight 4. The relationship between improved leadership and increased performance outcomes is neither precisely incremental nor is it linear.

After evaluating a variety of different assessments comparing leadership effectiveness with outcomes as mentioned above, a distinct pattern emerged in almost all of our studies. Poor leaders (those up to the 20th percentile) had poor results, while leaders above the 80th percentile achieved exceptional results. Looking at only those two data points, the relationship appears fairly linear, but in each case where we examined those leaders with good results (20th to 80th percentiles), they achieved approximately the same level of outcomes even though their effectiveness ranged from the 20th to the 80th percentile. The concept that leadership effectiveness is not precisely incrementally related to performance outcomes means that incremental improvements in leadership will not create incremental improvements in performance outcomes. Perhaps if it did, people would be more focused on improvement. They would see that a slight improvement in their leadership ability created improved job performance. Leaders whose effectiveness ratings are at the 40th or 50th percentile end up achieving about the same performance as leaders at the 60th or 70th percentile. Those at the 40th or 50th percentile and who choose to conserve the energy involved in change might ask themselves, "What's the point? My results are the same as others who are working to improve their leadership." The lack of incremental movement of leadership and performance makes it difficult for people to make the jump to extraordinary performance. And so most choose to be satisfied with good performance rather to move forward to higher levels. Some organizations as well appear to be satisfied with leaders that are good. Chapter 2 presents further evidence and information on this issue.

Insight 5. Great leadership consists of possessing several "building blocks" of capabilities, each complementing the others.
We have described the "building blocks" of:

- Character
- Personal capabilities
- Focus on results
- Interpersonal skills
- Leading organizational change

Each of these consists of several fairly distinct competencies or sets of behaviors. These are described in some detail later in the book, but a key insight is that possessing only one of them is not likely to have you perceived as an effective leader. In fact, leaders possessing one competency as a strength at the 90th percentile would not be rated at the 90th percentile in terms of overall leadership effectiveness. Chapter 3 elaborates on this concept.

Insight 6. Leadership culminates in championing change.
The highest expression of leadership involves change, and the highest order of change is guiding an organization through a new strategic direction, changing its culture, or changing the fundamental business model. Thus, change is an important and ultimate criterion by which to measure leadership effectiveness. Chapter 3 discusses this.

Insight 7. All competencies are not equal. Some differentiate good from great leaders, while others do not.
There has been an enormous amount of money spent, mostly by large corporations, to define competencies. The implication of these lists has often been that all of these were of equal importance, and that the wise manager would devote time to being good at all of them.

Our research, on the contrary, suggests that some competencies tower above others, and which ones are most important often depends on the organization. For example, in one organization we studied the data showed that the single most important competency for a leader was to be seen as technically competent. Conversely, the quality that put leaders into the bottom rung was their lack of technical competence. This one characteristic was far more important than the second or third distinguishing capability.

The point is that if people seek to be perceived as great leaders, it behooves them to know which competencies really make a difference in their organization. Our research identified 16 competencies that actually separated the top 10 percent of all leaders from the rest. We believe these are the competencies on which most leaders should focus. This comprises Chapter 4 of the book.

Insight 8. Leadership competencies are linked closely together.
While an effort has been made to make them appear unique and specific, the fact of the matter is that leadership competencies are highly intertwined. Several forces appear to be at work to make this happen. One is that becoming good at one competency appears to make people better at another. This is the "cross-training effect." The second way they become linked appears to be from "attribution" or the creation of a "halo effect." If a leader is perceived as being highly effective in working with people, then it is easy to attribute to that person the skills of being committed to the development of subordinates. See Chapter 4.

Insight 9. Effective leaders have widely different personal styles. There is no one right way to lead.
Military leaders provide some of the clearest contrasts in leadership behavior. Eisenhower was an able administrator and builder of coalitions, and generally self-effacing. MacArthur was strategically focused, sensitive to the culture of the enemy, and highly flamboyant. Patton was impetuous, passionate, and a "lone-ranger." We now have solid research evidence of these widely different styles, especially viewed from one organization to the next.

In our research we tried diligently to discover the one, two, or three capabilities that were common for all extraordinary leaders. We failed. Our research confirms what has been suggested from clinical studies of organizations and leaders. There clearly is no one pattern that covers all organizations, nor leaders within any one organization. Our data support the conclusion that effective leadership is incredibly complex and diverse. Providing one simple key to leadership is just not workable.

Our inability to find these universal issues was in many ways one of our most profound findings. The research suggests that extraordinary leaders come in all shapes and sizes. Some have strengths in some competencies while others complement them because of their strengths in different competencies. For an organization to have exceptional leadership ability it needs to assemble the right team with ample diversity and talent to maximize the collective influence of the team. Chapter 5 elaborates on this principle.

Insight 10. Effective leadership practices are specific to an organization.

Countless leaders who were successful in an organization switch to another and then fail. This is compelling evidence that leaders must fit the organization.

Our research showed wide variations between organizations regarding the specific competencies that were valued most by each one. Leadership always occurs in a context. See Chapter 5 for further information.

Insight 11. The key to developing great leadership is to build strengths.

When people are challenged to improve their leadership effectiveness, they almost automatically assume that the best approach for improvement is fixing weaknesses. In fact most leadership development processes result in leaders developing an action plan that focuses primarily on weaknesses. Our research has led us to conclude that great leaders are not defined by the absence of weakness, but rather by the presence of clear strengths. Great leaders, as seen through the eyes of subordinates and peers, possess multiple strengths, and our research shows a relatively straight-line progression. The more strengths people have, the more likely they are to be perceived as great leaders. For example, one large group of managers had this pattern:

- No strength puts them in the 30th percentile of all leaders in that group.
- One strength placed them at the 60th percentile.
- Three strengths put them at the 80th percentile.
- Five strengths catapulted them into the 90th percentile.

These strengths are not always the same ones. Of the 16 competencies that we discovered, great leaders did not have the same four strengths. However, these strengths cannot all be from the same cluster. They must be distributed among the various building blocks described earlier.

In general in examining all of our data, it is clear that the greater the number of strengths you have, the more likely you are to be considered a great leader.

This has enormous implications for executive selection processes, which seem often to be seeking people who possess no flaws. It seems that the emphasis should be on seeking people with remarkable configurations of strengths. Proven track records of accomplishment stemming from competencies appear to be the key to finding great leaders.

This also has enormous implications for leadership development. In the past we have often focused our efforts on patching over weaknesses. When executives are given a 360-degree feedback report, the consistent reaction is to ignore the pages describing their strengths, and immediately focus on weaknesses, which in most cases are simply behaviors that are rated as less positive rather than real fatal flaws. It is as if strengths are givens, and the thing to work on is weaknesses or less positive areas. Increasingly we are convinced this is a mistake. It is far better to magnify strengths, or create strengths out of those characteristics that are in positive territory but not fully developed. Leaders who are moderately effective and preoccupy themselves with incremental improvement of less positive issues will never move from good to great. Chapter 6 expands this idea.

Insight 12. *Powerful combinations produce nearly exponential results.*

Being good at one thing is sufficient for some athletes or musicians, but seldom for leaders. Our research confirmed that a combination of competencies is the key to being highly effective. For example, the person who is focused only on getting results often fails to obtain those results. Why? It is akin to a person attempting to row a boat with one paddle. Instead, good results come from a combination of skills, especially those joining the emphasis on results with strong interpersonal behavior and relationships with people. Neither one, by itself, takes you very far. Together, they produce spectacular outcomes. In one study we found that if you are in the top quartile in Interpersonal Skills but rated poorly on Focus on Results, the likelihood of you being perceived as a great leader is only 9 percent. If you are in the top quartile on Focus on Results but given low ratings on Interpersonal Skills, the likelihood of being perceived as a great leader is 13 percent. But if you possess both strong Interpersonal Skills and a Focus on Results, then your probability of being perceived as a great leader jumps to 66 percent. It is the powerful combination of those factors that makes a huge difference.

Whether you are working with complex organizations or with one subordinate, there is seldom any one thing responsible for producing a positive outcome. Instead, it is the combination of several forces that produces desired outcomes. In general, leaders are most effective when they possess strengths in each of the major clusters of competencies. Chapter 6 provides further insight into this finding, along with empirical evidence for this conclusion.

Insight 13. Greatness is not caused by the absence of weakness.
Our data reveal that a large percentage of leaders, approximately 84 percent, do not possess any severe weakness, and yet they are not perceived as strong leaders. They are "blah." Subordinates do not single out any one weakness as the root cause of the leader being weak. Instead, the combination of being in the "mid-range" on a number of dimensions is the pattern of the mediocre manager. In sum, the absence of weaknesses combined with the absence of any pronounced strengths commits you to being no better than average.

Our research shows that the self-evaluation of most leaders in this category is highly distorted. They feel like they are good leaders. Possibly because they are not really bad at any one area of leadership, they come to believe that they are good. But rather than trying to convince them that they are bad leaders, we think it far more valuable to help this group see what they can do to become outstanding in several areas, and that when they do that, they will in all likelihood be perceived as highly effective leaders.

Our research indicates that good leaders are, in fact, producing better outcomes than leaders who are bad. Good is better than bad, but neither they themselves nor their leaders appear to recognize the substantial contribution they could make by moving from being merely good to great.

An example of the focus most executives have in fixing weaknesses was demonstrated in the following consulting engagement: We conducted an organization-wide study to determine the key factors influencing the success of 100 field offices. We submitted a report that found the issue that was the most powerful factor influencing the success of field offices was the effectiveness of the office manager. After studying the report carefully, the executive team came out with a recommendation to "find the bad managers and fix them." However, after finding the "bad" managers, it was determined that there were not enough of them to explain the organization's overall poor performance. The executives came back doubting the validity of our study. With further analysis, however, we collectively came to the conclusion that the organization's poor performance problem was not because of bad managers, but was the result of having a large number of mediocre ones. Their performance paled in comparison to the few exceptional managers, and the key to raising the overall performance of the organization was to help facilitate the improvement of the mediocre managers to the level of the exceptional ones. Greatness is driven by strengths, with "the more the better" being the simple fact. Chapter 6 elaborates on this important idea.

Insight 14. Great leaders are not perceived as having major weaknesses.

One of the common bits of folk wisdom about leaders is that great leaders have great strengths, but that strengths taken too far become weaknesses. Furthermore, no one is perfect, so great leaders must have highly visible flaws. We were fully expecting to find that notion confirmed by our data.

To our surprise, there is no hint of that. Instead, our data describe the leaders who are seen as highly effective by their subordinates as not having flaws. Their scores across all competency categories were remarkably similar on the high side. Frankly, we wondered if there was not a pervasive halo effect that caused people who are really effective at a few skills to be perceived as being good at everything. We fear the converse may also be true: that leaders who are not seen as standing out on several dimensions are perceived as not standing out on any dimension.

In recent decades our political leaders have seemed to display great strengths that are accompanied by serious flaws. (Notable examples are Richard Nixon and Bill Clinton.) Whether private- and public-sector leaders really differ from elected leaders, or whether there is just more intense public scrutiny placed on elected political leaders, is the subject of a good deal more research. (Chapter 6 covers this.)

Insight 15. *Fatal flaws must be fixed.*
While our focus will be on developing strengths, there are some circumstances when a focus on weaknesses is warranted. This often happens when the nature of the weakness jeopardizes the center pole of the "leadership tent," character. If a person is not honorable, does not keep promises, does not tell the truth to people, or if this person places personal gain above the needs of the organization, then that flaw will cause the person to be ineffective.

There are other "fatal flaws." These begin with an inability to learn from mistakes, and include poor interpersonal skills, unwillingness to accept new ideas, lack of accountability, and a lack of initiative. Chapter 7 covers this.

Insight 16. *Leadership attributes are often developed in nonobvious ways.*
Our research has helped us uncover a new approach to behavioral change that we have arbitrarily called nonlinear development. We will argue that the vast majority of action plans created by leaders use a linear philosophy regarding behavioral change. But, the perception of competency may be strengthened in nonobvious ways. We will argue that competencies are not reality, but are the perceptions of others about a given leader. There may be nonobvious ways to improve how leaders are perceived. We have called these "competency companions," and these are behaviors that always rise or fall with another competency. While it is impossible to prove

cause and effect between the two, the fact that they are laced so tightly together suggests that something important can be learned from them.

The practical implications of this are huge. For example, assume that a leader in an organization receives the following feedback: "Your subordinates do not see you as highly motivational or inspirational. They do not feel energized after they interact with you. They do not feel that their horizons are expanded after meeting with you."

The common and seemingly practical way to address this message and change these perceptions would be to do the following:

- Enroll in a public-speaking course in order to learn how to be more compelling in presentations.
- Read good texts or articles on human motivation.
- Deliberately display more enthusiasm by speaking louder and more rapidly, and with more gestures.
- Attend motivational seminars where prominent, nationally known motivational speakers team up to present their messages. Your hope would be to get good content, and also learn from their style of presentation.

Our research, however, on the competency companions to "inspires and motivates others" reveals some different ways to improve people's perceptions on this competency. When people score high on "inspires and motivates others," they also receive high scores on "communicating clear expectations." And when people receive low scores on "inspiring and motivating others," they receive low scores on "communicating clear expectations." There is obviously something about being clear that is closely linked with people feeling motivated and inspired. So, managers who receive this feedback might want to work hard at being extremely clear about the expectations they convey to others. Further, they may want to check with others periodically to see if their message is coming across with simplicity and clarity. A manager could ask questions such as, "Is there anything that is not clear about this request?" "Would it help if we went over this project description one more time?"

Another somewhat nonintuitive "competency companion" is the practice of "creating a learning environment." Leaders who figure out ways for their colleagues to discover for themselves how important something is, or to have colleagues determine for themselves the best way of doing something, are the leaders described as most motivational and inspirational. So, rather than give an impassioned "locker-room" speech to your team about the importance of better customer service, a more effective approach could be to ask your team members to listen in to customer complaint calls, or to call 10 customers who had ceased purchasing from your firm. That technique could be far more "motivational" than any speech delivered.

Another nonobvious competency companion is the practice that some leaders have of setting extremely high standards and stretch goals. Some people might assume that leaders inspire and motivate their troops, and having done that, then fail to present to them a challenging goal. They might assume that properly motivated people will figure out the goal for themselves. Our research, however, suggests that the very process of setting a stretch goal is motivating and inspiring for the recipient.

Our message is not that reading a book on motivation, or taking a class in public speaking, or deliberately showing more energy and enthusiasm is a bad thing to do. Instead, the message is that many behaviors and practices come together to create the perception on the part of subordinates that their leader is motivational and inspirational. Understanding the competency companions gives the leader additional ways to improve that perception. It appears that the more of these a leader displays, the more likely the leader is to be perceived as a highly effective "motivator and inspirer" of others.

The more linear, "hit-it-straight-on" development seems best geared for moving people from bad to neutral. It may also be of some help in moving people from neutral to the "good" range. The competency companions seem especially helpful for those who desire to move from "good" to "great" or "extraordinary." They open up many new doors for development. Some would perceive these as side doors, maybe even back doors. But for those who have difficulty in following the traditional, linear development process, we believe that competency companions provide exciting new paths to explore. Chapter 8 elaborates on this idea and gives examples of competency companions for each of the 16 competencies that make a difference.

Insight 17. Leaders are made, not born.
This controversy continues. The question has not gone away. We attest that leaders are made. While this is certainly not a new point of view, we go on record declaring this to be a fact. We contend that strong evidence exists to support this conclusion. We readily acknowledge that some people start with advantages of intellect or personality, but the case for leaders being made can be confirmed by finding just one organization that does it successfully.

Chapter 9 presents a case study of an organization that many consider the epitome of effective leadership development. The U.S. Marine Corps has for the past 226 years been developing leaders. We present the argument that from their long experience they have adopted many practices that are only now being confirmed by research.

Insight 18. Leaders can improve their leadership effectiveness through self-development.
Finally, in Chapter 10 we discuss the implications of our research to leadership development undertaken by the individual. These ideas apply to any people in leadership positions who desire to improve their own leadership skills and effectiveness.

Insight 19. The organization, with a person's immediate boss, provides significant assistance in developing leadership.
In Chapter 11 we present some ideas about how any corporation or public agency could incorporate these ideas into their own leadership development offerings.

Insight 20. The quality of leadership in an organization seldom exceeds that of the person at the top.
In analyzing our many sets of data collected from multiple organizations, we observed that the scores of leaders in the organization rarely exceeded the scores of the most senior leader. That person was the cap on leadership effectiveness. See Chapter 11 and Chapter 2 for further analysis of this observation.

CONCLUSION

Leadership has been shrouded with a "woo-woo" quality that drives our desire to make less mysterious something that has seemed so hopelessly baffling. Obviously, many more books on leadership will be written. We hope our research will help to push the study and understanding of leadership attributes and leadership development to the next rung on the ladder by removing some of that mystery.

2

GREAT LEADERS MAKE A GREAT DIFFERENCE

Good is the enemy of excellence.

Leadership is the challenge to be something more than average.

Jim Rohn

GOOD AND BAD LEADERS

In our research we found conclusive evidence that leaders with poor leadership skills generate poor results. That finding will not come as a shock to anyone. It is quite intuitive to anyone who has worked in an organization for more than a few weeks. And our research is equally clear about the fact that good leaders tend to produce good results for their organizations.

What's more, most individuals do not need sophisticated measurement tools to tell the difference between good leaders and bad leaders. They feel the difference. They have experienced the effects at a very personal level. In general, good leaders are more effective than bad leaders in almost every dimension, including improving productivity, reducing turnover, enhancing customer service, and creating high levels of employee commitment.

GREAT VERSUS GOOD LEADERS

Our research, however, shows that there is another, even more dramatic, level of difference between good and extraordinary leaders. This is the central theme of this chapter and a major surprise finding of our research. We had failed to appreciate fully just what a significant difference there is between "good" and "great."

In examining the relationship between leadership effectiveness and desirable outcomes, the consistent finding in all our research was the impact of the best and worst leaders on achieving bottom-line results. Figure 2.1 isolates the results on an employee commitment measure (high scores indicate greater commitment) by the results of individual leadership effectiveness broken into 10 levels. Each level represents 10 percentile points on the leadership effectiveness measure. Note the dramatic change involving leaders at both the top and bottom of the rankings. In addition, note how the results in the middle are nearly flat.

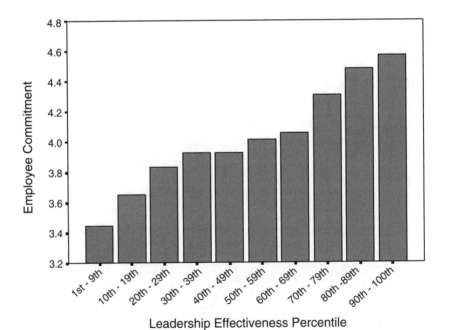

FIGURE 2.1   Employee commitment.

The characteristics of the graph in Figure 2.1 are extremely significant in describing the relationship between leadership effectiveness and bottom-line outcomes. We see poor results at the lower deciles, substantially more positive results at the higher deciles, and flat results in the middle. This graph presents several important findings:

1. Leaders have a dramatic impact as they move from "bad" to "good."

2. Poor leaders have an adverse impact on the groups they attempt to lead.

3. The important characteristic of the middle deciles is that results remain relatively consistent from the 30th to the 70th percentiles. Making small, incremental improvements in leadership effectiveness for a leader at the 50th percentile is clearly not going to have much impact on employee commitment.

4. In order to achieve the next level of impact on employee commitment, a leader would have to move to the 70th, 80th, or 90th percentile. The results of several other studies demonstrate the relationship between leadership effectiveness and additional desirable outcomes.

Impact on Net Profits in a Mortgage Bank

From measures on subordinate commitment to the organization, we now turn to measures of financial performance. In a mortgage bank we collected data on their measure of profitability, or net profits, for a series of leaders. Figure 2.2 shows the results of our study.

What we found in this study was that the poor leaders actually lost money for the company. Their performance was so ineffective that it appeared to drive customers away. The good leaders, on the other hand, made a reasonable profit for the company. Their performance, compared with the bad leaders, represented a substantial change. However, the extraordinary leaders nearly doubled the profit generated for the company by the good leaders. Imagine the impact of transitioning 10 or 20 percent of leaders from the "good" to the "extraordinary" category. It would add 10 to 20 percent to the bottom line of the entire company.

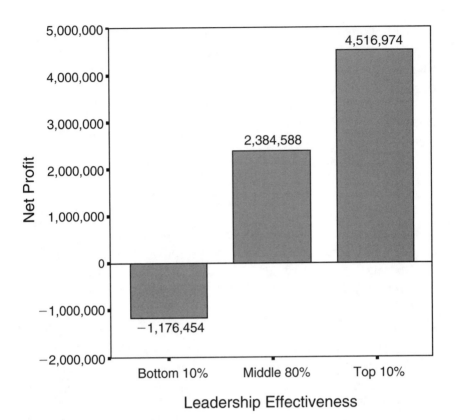

FIGURE 2.2   Net profit.

In a related study, Rucci, Kim, and Quinn found what they called "the employee-customer-profit chain" at Sears."[1] Their study found that employee behaviors affected customer behaviors, which in turn affected company financial performance. When customers enter a store where employees are frustrated and unmotivated, it affects their buying habits and their willingness to return and purchase more items. Pleasant, considerate, and knowledgeable sales associates had a positive effect on customers. These sales associates encouraged customers to buy more and to come back. In their research, Rucci et al. found that a five-point improvement in employee attitudes resulted in a 1.3 percent improvement in customer satisfaction, which in turn increased revenue growth 0.5 percent.

The implications of our research are that another link needs to be added to the chain; e.g., it should be "the leaders-employee-customer-profit chain. Figure 2.1 showed the impact that leaders have on employee commitment and satisfaction, which ultimately translates into the direct impact of leaders on profitability.

The new chain of cause-and-effect events is:

$$\text{Leaders} \rightarrow \text{Employees} \rightarrow \text{Customers} \rightarrow \text{Store Profits}$$

One should also keep in mind that the additional insight this research adds to the profit chain of events is that great leaders have even more impact on employees, who affect customers and therefore create even greater profits for the organization.

Impact on Turnover in an Insurance Company

Turnover costs companies millions of dollars every year. John Sullivan, chief talent officer at Agilent Technologies in Palo Alto, California, put the cost of turnover for a software engineer at $200,000 to $250,000 per departing employee. He went on to say that, "One firm I work with just calculated the cost of an engineer vacancy in lost revenue at $7000 per day."[2] Although there are many reasons for turnover, our research consistently bears out that the relationship an employee has with his or her manager substantially influences the employee's decision to stay with a company or move on.

Figure 2.3 shows the results from a study conducted at a large insurance company. Leadership effectiveness was determined and matched up with yearly turnover rates within each leader's group. In this study, higher turnover (19 percent per year) was created by leaders in the bottom third in terms of their leadership ability as seen by their subordinates and peers. These leaders presumably did nothing to force people to leave, but their style and approach did not encourage them to stay. Better achievement came from good leaders, who experienced 14 percent turnover. However, extraordinary leaders cut the average turnover rate in their groups by another 5 percent. Reduced turnover had a direct impact on profitability, customer satisfaction, and claim resolution speed.

Intention to Stay with the Company

In another study with a high-tech communications company, we looked at the relationship between leadership effectiveness and intention to stay with or leave the company within the coming year.

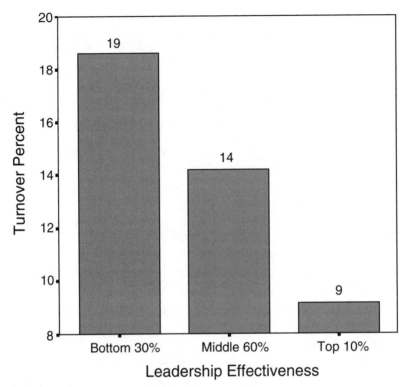

FIGURE 2.3   **Turnover percent.**

(These results were extremely consistent with the organization's actual turnover data.) In this study, low scores indicated a greater intention to leave, while high scores indicated a greater intention to stay. As is apparent from Figure 2.4, the employees of the extraordinary leaders were significantly more committed to stay with the company. The intention to stay then translates into lower turnover for those who work with the best leaders.

Impact on Customer Satisfaction

In a study done with a high-tech communications company, we looked at the relationship between leadership ability and customer satisfaction (Figure 2.5). Once again, extraordinary leaders have substantially better ratings on customer satisfaction. In this study, high scores indicate higher customer satisfaction. Again, we assume

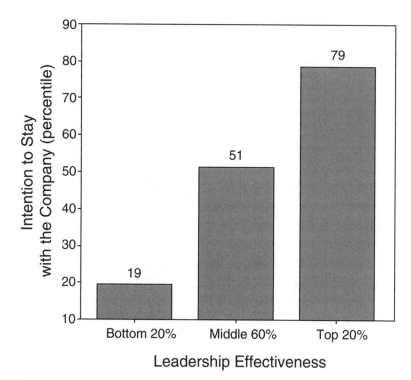

FIGURE 2.4   Intention to stay with the company.

that the leader does not have direct contact with most customers, but it is the leader's influence on the level of commitment of the front-line employees that makes the dramatic differences in customer satisfaction.

In a related study conducted by our colleague Larry Senn, he was asked by a retail client to change the behavior of store employees to be more customer service oriented. The company began an intensive program aimed at changing the behavior of store employees. After months of work it became apparent that some stores were being successful in creating a more customer-friendly atmosphere, while other stores were not. Employees in both the successful and unsuccessful stores had received the same training, and the employees did not appear to be any less capable or experienced in unsuccessful stores. As they studied the unsuccessful stores to understand the reason for their failure, they found that managers

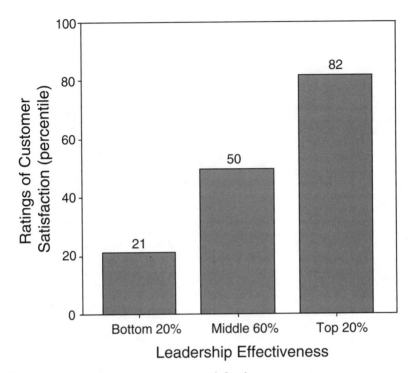

FIGURE 2.5   Ratings of customer satisfaction.

in unsuccessful stores tended to be operationally oriented, whereas successful store managers were customer oriented. The operationally oriented store managers reinforced the importance of tracking money and time. Customer-oriented store managers, on the other hand, reinforced the importance of customer satisfaction. After going through the experience the researchers came to the conclusion that efforts to change employee behavior had to start by making sure that their managers' behaviors were in alignment.[3]

LEADERSHIP HAS AN IMPACT ON THE BOTTOM LINE

Our purpose in presenting these studies is to impress on the reader that the impact of leadership:

- Affects every measurable dimension of organization performance
- Is large, not trivial
- Is extremely consistent
- Has highly interrelated areas of impact

Poor leaders have a substantial influence on an organization's success. They consistently achieve less effective results, create greater turnover, discourage employees, and frustrate customers. Good leaders will achieve good results. A good leader will have fewer turnovers, higher profitability, and more employee commitment.

Incremental improvements in good leaders will not, however, show up in improved bottom-line results. The next jump does not occur until the 70th, 80th, or 90th percentile. Extraordinary leaders will consistently achieve results that far exceed those of the good leaders. They will create even less turnover, motivate employees to a much higher degree, and satisfy customers to a much higher level.

These studies clearly demonstrate the significant difference an extraordinary leader makes on bottom-line results and confirm that if leaders can move from the "good" level to the "extraordinary" level at a reasonable cost to the organization, the return on that investment will be substantial.

Jim Collins conducted fascinating research in which he and his research team examined results from 1435 companies from 1965 to 1995. This research found 11 companies that made significant transformations from "good to great." The 11 companies had an average stock return of 6.9 times higher than general market. These companies held that rate for 15 years after the point of transition. In looking at a variety of variables about the cause of this success, Collins gave specific instructions to researchers to downplay the role of senior executives. Collins' researchers looked at every possible variable that might affect the success of each company. Over time, his researchers found that they could not ignore the contributions of senior executives. Collins indicated that "There was something consistently unusual about them." Collins and his research team found that all 11 companies consistently had a leader whom they labeled a "Level 5 executive." "Level 5 executives built enduring greatness through a paradoxical combination of personal humility plus professional will." The leadership was not the only factor that differentiated the 11 companies, but it was one of the critical variables. The researchers identified five other factors, but effective leadership plays a critical role in the execution of each one.[4]

IS "GOOD" GOOD ENOUGH?

While the results for extraordinary leaders are much better than for poor leaders, the current problem is that too many good leaders feel that being "good" is good enough. They are satisfied that they are not poor leaders, and, therefore, remain unchallenged to go to the next level. Many of these good leaders do not recognize that continued improvement in leadership would make a substantial difference in the outcomes they are attempting to produce. Many "adequate" leaders stay where they are because they fail to understand the differences between good and extraordinary leaders.

WHAT CAUSES GOOD LEADERS TO BE UNCHALLENGED TO CHANGE?

1. When you mention that there is a leadership effectiveness problem, many people automatically believe that the problem is poor leaders. There exists a natural human tendency to blame problems on low performers. We like to assign a scapegoat as the source of any problems. This can turn into witch-hunts for the "bad" leaders. Frequently many of the "bad" leaders are new, inexperienced supervisors who need time and training to develop. It is more tempting to ferret out the bad leaders than to face a different reality. This troubling tendency was most aptly expressed by Walt Kelly's comic strip character, Pogo, when he often observed, "We have met the enemy and he is us."[5]

   Blaming bad leaders is a simple solution. It is much more difficult to accept that the problem with leadership is the need for everyone to undertake some level of improvement. Those who are good could have a substantial positive impact on the organization if they moved from good to great. In the year 1999, John Thornton, co-president and COO of Goldman Sachs, announced to 500 top executives of the firm, "We're not as good as we need to be." Their performance appraisals and peer feedback processes showed serious deficiencies in people management skills and overall leadership strength. The growth objectives of the firm were clearly not going to be met unless the overall quality of leadership was ratcheted to a new level.[6]

2. Training programs often send a false impression. When organizations sponsor training programs positioned to take bad leaders and make them into good leaders, it unwittingly sends the signal that those leaders who are currently in the "good" category can coast. Beyond that, most supervisory and management training courses are designed to develop basic leadership skills. The focus is on acquiring and understanding the fundamental skills required in a leadership role. Many leaders act as if the introductory course in a series is the only course that exists or is necessary for them. We are aware of only a handful of corporate development programs targeted specifically to make good people great.

3. Many 360-degree leadership assessments compare leaders' results and show how they compare to the average. The unintended message that most leaders get from the assessments is that if you are in the mid-range, "You are okay and okay is good enough."

    Figure 2.6 shows the results from a typical 360-degree assessment. The dark background area is the norm, which is the average of all others taking this assessment. Looking at the results for Pat Brown against the norm gives the impression that Pat is viewed in a generally positive light by the respondents, and is a good leader. The results for Pat are more positive in several areas than the norm. Even after informing leaders that a norm is the average of the best and worst leaders, most people continue to look at areas where they are slightly more positive than the norm as areas that are strengths; only areas considerably less positive than the norm are viewed as serious weaknesses requiring any remedial action.

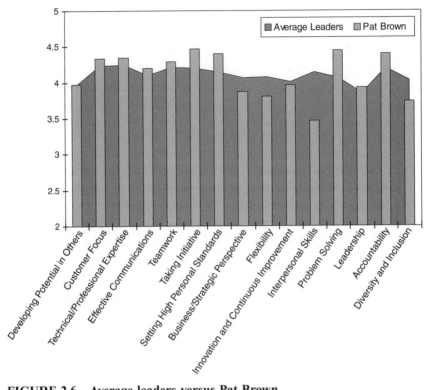

FIGURE 2.6   Average leaders versus Pat Brown.

Figure 2.7 depicts the same results for Pat Brown, but this time the standard represents the 90th percentile score on each of the competencies. Showing this new target tends to change the focus of the feedback. Pat Brown is doing well but still has a long way to go to move from a good leader to an extraordinary leader. By contrasting results to a mean average, the message communicated is, "The goal is to be better than average." Contrasting results to levels of extraordinary leaders shows people the distance that they need to achieve in order to move to a higher level.

4. Good leaders often fail to appreciate and understand the differences between good leadership and great leadership.

It is always interesting to watch diving competitions during the Olympics. When observers witness the first dive, most are

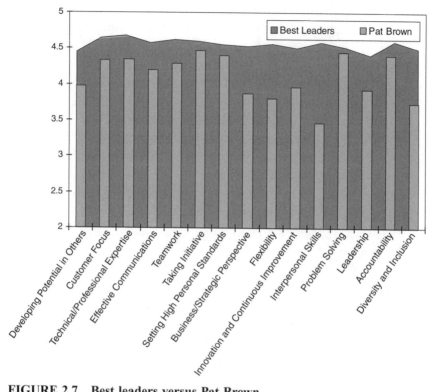

FIGURE 2.7 Best leaders versus Pat Brown.

usually impressed. Your point of comparison is often amateur diving, and compared to amateur competitors, this dive is beautiful, graceful, and executed precisely. Then the scores come up and they are "5," "6," "6," "5," "7," and the commentator says, "Did you see that splash?" or "Notice how the knees were bent and the feet pointed in different directions." You are often surprised and chagrined because you had not noticed any of those problems. As the competition continues, the judges and the commentators train everyone on the finer points of competition diving. After an hour of watching diving competition, people's ability to judge great diving skills has moved from nonexistent to rudimentary. If a diver makes a huge mistake you notice it, but you are still frequently surprised when you judge a dive as excellent and the judges mark it down because of a fine detail that you missed.

Judging leadership is much the same way. Too many have remained casual observers of leadership rather than trained judges. They experience leadership from others and feel the effects (that was great leadership or that was terrible) but lack the insight of how the effect was created or what its longer-lasting consequences will be.

People frequently confuse personality traits for leadership. They assume that assertiveness, or the ability to make a compelling speech or giving people crisp orders, is leadership. It is not.

In order for people to improve their leadership ability they need to become astute observers of leadership. They need not only to understand some basic concepts and be reasonably well read, they need to be able to judge everyday interactions and understand what is missing.

5. Many good leaders believe that extraordinary leaders are prodigies, having been endowed with some unusual gifts from birth. Most recognize that people with exceptional leadership talents exist, but it is difficult for others to understand the path in their development that brought them from being good leaders to being extraordinary leaders. The bar set to achieve extraordinary leadership seems too high to achieve, and the path to develop extensive skills is not clear. This is akin to watching a great concert pianist and aspiring to play the same way she does. The fantasy is fun, but given the reality of looking at what it would take to accomplish such a feat, most don't even start. One music student described her experience completing her degree in music pedagogy. She indicated that there were a few students who had exceptional natural ability but lacked discipline. Watching the professors interact with these students, she observed that the professors were not very excited about working with these students with natural talent but poor discipline. Professors chose to mentor students with strong discipline. When asked about their choices regarding which students they chose to mentor, one of the professors commented, "Discipline is always more important than some natural ability. With some dedicated practice those with discipline will surpass those with natural ability in a

few semesters. Without discipline and the ability to learn, those with natural ability will never progress above their current ability."

A great deal of research has been done on individuals who achieve high levels of individual performance. The researchers, Anders Ericsson and Neil Charness, described having exceptional ability or talent as "expert performance." These researchers have produced a great deal of empirical research on the question of whether people are born with "innate talent."[7] Most people believe that there are individuals possessing superior intelligence and aptitude who distinguish themselves and are referred to as gifted. The philosophy of gifted individuals dates back to periods of time when kings and rulers were called "royalty." The implication of royalty is that there is some genetic or inherited difference between individuals. The idea that many individuals can develop exceptional ability is inconsistent with the idea that only my son is qualified to be king. A review of the literature reveals that appropriate training can have a dramatic impact on performance. Research in music performance revealed that children who showed little sign of musical talent but who were trained with the Suzuki method achieved equivalent levels to musical prodigies. A common conception is that most child prodigies show innate abilities at a young age. Research into the backgrounds of those with exceptional talent show a great deal of evidence in the interest of children, but very little evidence in any innate ability.

The reality is that people who are considered prodigies in music, chess, athletics, or other areas all had a very consistent pattern. All showed interest in their talents, and all practiced from between two to four hours a day for 10 years. The 10-year mark was an amazingly similar finding regardless of musical, mathematical, or athletic talent. There is very strong research to show that expertise as a violinist correlated almost exactly with the number of hours of practice. Experts practice over 10,000 hours, the next level about 7500 hours, and the next level 5000 hours. Ericsson and Charness concluded their analysis by stating, "The traditional view of talent, which concludes that successful individuals have special innate abilities and basic capacities, is not consistent with the reviewed evidence." They went on to say that more plausible explanations of individual differences "are factors that predispose individuals toward engaging in deliberate practice and enable them to sustain high levels of practice for many years."

Another characteristic of expert performers was that they typically had coaches who encouraged them to practice intensely. Suppose that a person decides she wants to learn to play golf. She begins by signing up for several lessons and then she hires a personal coach to play with her. After a few months of lessons she is performing at an adequate level and so she begins to "play" golf with friends. Playing is inherently more fun than intense practice, but the learning curve goes down considerably. In order to continue to improve, people need to take the time regularly for intense practice, and that is most effective when accompanied by an experienced coach.

Most individuals, as they become managers for the first time, go through an intense learning period. They receive a great deal of training, personal coaching, and are open to ideas and suggestions from experienced managers. They take time to plan meetings, performance reviews, and how they will give feedback to direct reports. They also pay close attention to others, watching to understand techniques and skills. They are practicing leadership with an intent to get better. Their learning curve is high. Once they get reasonably competent at being managers they do something very similar to the above example of golf. They switch from practicing to playing. While playing, the intensity of their learning goes down. Playing leadership is inherently more fun than practicing leadership, but skill development is very slow and sometimes stops altogether. In a recent meeting at a large oil company we asked a group of executives if they were focused on playing or practicing leadership. The consensus of the group was that everyone was busy playing and nobody was practicing to get better.

One implication of this research is that some great leaders are not born with, but acquire at an early age, the desire to make things happen with other people. We believe that other leaders can acquire increased leadership ability with practice at any age. The real key is that they engage in intense practice. Bad leaders assume that deliberate practice makes no difference, so they continue to perform but never improve.

6. Leaders are only willing to be as effective as those who in turn lead them. Tom Watson, Jr., is often credited as the key architect of IBM's culture. One manifestation of that culture was that men wore white shirts, dark suits, and wing-tip shoes. He once remarked that if he wore a pink shirt to work, he was sure that the following day he would see hundreds of executives wearing pink shirts.

Leaders cast a significant shadow in the organizations where they work. A colleague, Paul McKinnon, did some research several years ago to measure the shadows of leaders with several of his clients. In a follow-up study we conducted to analyze the shadow of leaders, we found that employees who have worked for the same boss for several years tend to share not only the strengths but also the weaknesses of their boss. In the study we examined the 360-degree results for a manager and identified areas of strength and opportunities for improvement. The 360-degree results were then analyzed for all of the direct reports of the manager (who were also managers). Managers with a large shadow showed the exact same list of strengths and opportunities for improvement as their direct reports. The analysis calculated the percent overlap between managers and all of their direct reports. The percentages varied from a small shadow (e.g., 25 percent overlap) to a large shadow (100 percent overlap).

This "shadow" can cut both ways. If you work with an extraordinary leader, the tendency is that your leadership effectiveness will be close to your leader's. On the other hand, if your boss is an ineffective leader, the tendency is that you won't be much better. In the study we found the length of a leader's shadow to vary. The length of time people spend with the same boss can increase the size of the shadow.

In the study we found that some leaders and their direct reports had a 100 percent overlap between strengths and weaknesses. By their nature, people think their approach to work is best, and bosses tend to hire employees who have a similar style. Over time bosses reinforce their positive as well as negative traits by unconsciously rewarding some employee behaviors while discouraging or ignoring others. As a result, employees are conditioned to mimic those to whom they report.

For example, assume a leader who is very detail oriented, task focused and technically proficient, but not sensitive toward coworkers reporting to him. More often than not this person's subordinates generally share his skills and are also not regarded as especially considerate of others. Most of the time, bosses do not actively encourage brusqueness, but the managers saw their boss get away with it and felt they could too. The process of mimicking the strengths and weaknesses of one's boss is an unconscious process. Possibly one of the most startling pieces of research that validates these findings is the study of child abuse. It is well established that children who are abused have a high likelihood of becoming abusive parents. It seems almost impossible to comprehend why children who detest and suffer from the way that their parents treat them, often treat their children exactly the same way. Many adults have exerted great effort to successfully break their child-rearing practices from the past and start a new legacy of positive child rearing. Many parents have had the experience as a child of promising themselves that they would "never treat their children that way," only to find themselves doing exactly the same thing to their children.

A by-product of the phenomenon is that employees are rarely more effective than their bosses. That is good news if the boss is an extraordinary leader. The direct reports tend to rise to that level. But we observed over and over that employees are only as good as their bosses. Bosses set the standards, high or low. The findings have implications.

- The extent to which leaders merely encourage subordinates to be their clones becomes problematic. Indeed, it may demonstrate a lack of appreciation for different styles and approaches, which ultimately may be detrimental to the organization's goals.

- Leaders in the organization should be made cognizant of the ways they reinforce their own behaviors in their direct reports. Superiors should think more consciously of the role they play in people's lives and careers, and the legacy they will leave once they are gone.

- Superiors need to be reminded to recruit employees with a diversity of skills and work styles that would enrich and contribute to the organization.

- Organizations seeking a culture change should begin with an intervention at the senior level, since the best way to bring real change is usually to change the leaders.

- It takes great leaders to develop great leaders. The idea of "Do as I say, not as I do" just won't work with leadership.

Imagine the impact on any organization if 20 percent of the good leaders could move on to become excellent. Fast forward in your mind to the organizational results that would produce. Consider the profound impact on culture and the motivation level of employees. Imagine the transformed work experience of all inside the organization.

The research is clear regarding the impact of leadership on desirable outcomes. Good leaders are substantially more effective than bad leaders, but great leaders make a great difference.

THE PROPER MEASURE OF "GREATNESS"

For the sake of convenience, we have selected "great" leaders by examining the top 10 percent from a population of leaders from well-respected organizations. However, we are the first to acknowledge that this is merely for convenience. The proper measure is against an objective standard, and there is no reason why an organization could not have 90 percent of its first-level managers or supervisors who were great, versus the arbitrary 10 percent that we analyzed. Indeed, our definition could probably be reverse engineered. When you could identify a leader who produced

- High productivity
- Low turnover
- High customer satisfaction
- High profitability
- Innovation
- Positive relationships with suppliers

then you could, by definition, say this was an extremely effective leader. Effective leadership is best defined and measured by the results produced, not by simply taking a certain number from the top of a distribution.

The Organization's Objective

The more "great" leaders an organization can develop, the stronger it will be. This is true for multiple reasons, but some of those are the following:

- The contribution these leaders make to the units they manage
- The example or role model they set for the entire organization
- The cumulative impact their performance has in creating an entirely new culture for the organization
- The elevated standard of performance that is set within the organization

We have advocated strongly that individuals focus on their strengths. By doing that, they greatly increase the likelihood of being perceived as great leaders. That same principle applies to the organization. By increasing the number of high-performing leaders, the organization gains great strength. It is always tempting to attempt to fix the low-performing ones, but the greatest gain appears to come by helping more leaders become truly excellent.

The only downside of any organization doing that is the target they become for headhunters. Just as GE has become the spawning ground for corporate CEOs, so will any company that produces great leaders. However, that is a relatively small price to pay for the enormous gains to be achieved by successfully developing great leaders for the firm.

GOOD VERSUS BAD THINKING

As a teenager, one of the authors had the opportunity to hear an astronaut describe the challenges of going to the Moon. His analogy was that the accuracy of going from Earth to the Moon was equivalent to shooting a bullet in New York and hitting a gumball in Los Angeles. It was a very dramatic example of the importance of correct aim and mid-course corrections. If the aim was off just a little in New York, the target would be missed by a state or two barring major corrections. The more we work with individuals and organizations, the more it becomes clear that small, even barely noticeable, actions can have huge consequences over time.

One of the small, barely noticeable philosophies that most people hold today is binary thinking about good versus bad. We are constantly amused that when trying to uncover problems in organizations, there is a search to identify the "bad people." One of the most common tendencies is that when a mistake occurs in an organization and there is a search for the cause, frequently a person or group is sought to be the source of the problem. The "fall person" is blamed for everything. This is rarely the truth, but most people find it much more convenient.

On the other side, we have the search for "good." Having conducted a variety of studies to identify characteristics of high performers, what inevitably becomes a difficult task is to determine the criteria for identifying high performers. This would appear to be a simple task, but as the different measurements are laid out it becomes a challenge. Organizations search for some simple criteria to easily and quickly pinpoint the good from the bad.

In this chapter we have presented a new philosophy about leadership. This philosophy expands a person's thinking from "Leaders are either good or bad" to "Leaders are bad, good, and great." This is a small change from what many currently believe, but we believe this small philosophical difference can have a huge impact on the success of both individuals and organizations.

For individuals this philosophy should help good leaders understand that good is not great. It never was and never will be. Good is good, but the ultimate target is extraordinary leadership. We hope this helps people not to be satisfied with good performance.

For organizations this philosophy ought to clarify the competitive advantage of great leadership. When discussing their leadership talent, executives will sometimes state, "I don't think we have a problem with our leaders" (which when translated means, we don't have bad leaders). The problem is not an abundance of bad leaders; the problem is the universal acceptance of good leaders, and assuming that they cannot be any better.

3

SIMPLIFYING LEADERSHIP

> I wouldn't give a fig for the simplicity this side of complexity but I would give my right arm for the simplicity on the other side of complexity.
>
> *Oliver Wendell Holmes*

O UR OBJECTIVE IN THIS CHAPTER is to provide some of the "simplicity that lies just on the other side of complexity." In Chapter 1 we presented many of the dimensions that create the extremely complex nature of leadership. In this chapter we wish to reduce that complexity to a model of leadership that is more easily understood.

MATTRESSES AND TENTS

Mattresses

For decades, researchers and observers have tried to find the competency, trait, knowledge base, personality dimension, or thought process that make a person a good leader. The analysis was extremely granular, breaking leadership into as many discrete competencies as possible. The outcome was to describe leadership behaviors or competencies as highly specific, discrete, individualized acts. Each trait or characteristic was made separate and distinct from all the others.

One metaphor compares this approach to understanding leadership as a "coil-spring mattress." This approach to leadership assumes that these traits or characteristics are like individually encased coil springs in an expensive mattress. The advertisements for these mattresses show a glass of water standing on the mattress, and someone dropping a bowling ball adjacent to the glass of water, all without spilling a drop.

In understanding leadership, if that theory were true, a leader could be extremely technically competent without that affecting the relationships in a team. Or the leader could be a highly effective motivator or inspirer of people, but totally lacking the ability to make things happen inside the organization. To the extent that competencies are definable, specific behaviors, independent from all other behavior, this belief has great logic. And we acknowledge that this happens in selected instances.

The major defect with this entire theory is that it simply does not fit the empirical data we have available. We will present compelling evidence in Chapter 4 that:

1. Not all competencies are equivalent to each other. Some are far more powerful in separating highly effective leaders from the rest.

2. Leadership behaviors are all knit together, much like the complex network of the human brain. There is a great deal of interdependence between them. Each of the 16 competencies that were most powerful in separating leaders was on average correlated (with statistical significance) to half of the other competencies. One competency was correlated significantly with all but one of the 15 others.

3. Effective leadership demands a balance of competencies from five different sectors.

4. Combinations of competencies, not any single one, produce great leaders.

5. The more people have of the 16 competencies that truly make a difference, the more likely they are to be perceived as great leaders.

Tents

Instead of a mattress with individual springs, a more accurate picture of leadership is represented by a large tent, as depicted in Figure 3.1, with the three-dimensional space under the canvas representing the leadership effectiveness of the individual. The best leaders have the greatest number of cubic yards of space under their tent. We think this view helps to understand the true nature of leadership and how it is developed.

The distinguishing characteristics of this model are:

1. Leadership behaviors are clustered into five areas.
2. Strength in a cluster becomes a "tent pole" that lifts the leadership of that person to a higher level.
3. Effective leaders possess skills in each area; so multiple poles are necessary to lift the tent.
4. Statistically significant correlations exist between most of the important competencies (the canvas is in one piece).

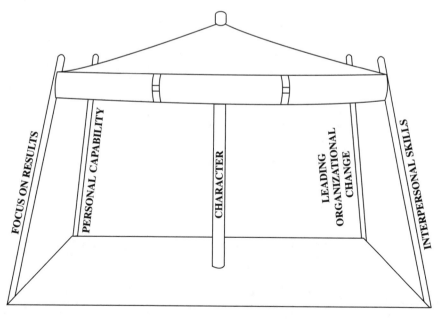

FIGURE 3.1 Leadership tent.

The key to lifting more of the tent (becoming a more effective leader) is to get multiple poles high in the air. If you have only one tent pole, it pulls the entire tent around the center of the pole. Our metaphor unfolds as follows. Allow us the liberty of having modern tent poles that extend themselves like the antenna on a car. As a pole is extended, one section of the tent is lifted up, and in doing that a broad expanse of canvas is raised. The more the pole is extended, the higher the canvas is lifted. (Remember, the tent pole is the degree of strength, and the number of competencies with great strength in one area that an individual possesses.) So, assume that this first tent pole comes up from the cluster we have labeled "Character."

A second pole (assume this one is created by the cluster "Focus on Results") elevates a new section of the tent, and in so doing, raises the canvas that is directly above it, but also raises the canvas that is between this new pole and the first one. The canvas that was initially around the first pole moves closer to the full height of both tent poles. With each succeeding tent pole, large expanses of canvas are lifted until ultimately there is a huge volume of space under the tent.

The poles in our metaphor represent key "strengths" of the individual leader, especially those that have been shown to make a difference in separating the great from the good. The canvas represents all of the behaviors and competencies possible to be displayed by a leader. (We have seen competency models from some organizations in which there were 173 behaviors defined for the leaders to assess themselves against. That seems to us to be a few more behaviors than most humans can keep track of on a daily basis.)

MAKING A LEADER

We will now more thoroughly describe these five major elements of leadership attributes.

Character—The Center Pole of Every Leader
We begin with the component that is indeed at the core. Everything radiates from it. It is the center pole of the tent (see Figure 3.2). It

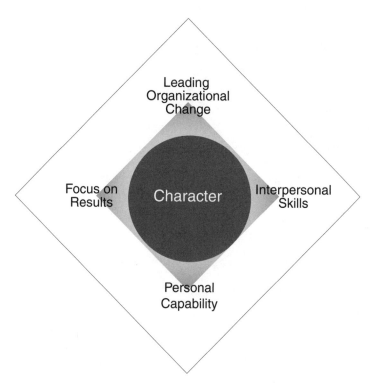

FIGURE 3.2   Leadership tent floor: Character.

is so important that some authors have written about it as if it were synonymous with leadership. For example:

- Warren Bennis, one of the most respected writers and researchers on leadership, has talked about leadership being all about integrity.
- Max De Pree, the CEO of Herman Miller and a frequent writer on leadership, has equated leadership with personal character.
- Jim Kouzes and Barry Posner have written a book entitled *Credibility,* and defined personal credibility as the foundation of all leadership.
- Jim Shaffer writes about leadership being defined by "telling the truth."

- Stephen Covey has written about the importance of leaders following principles in their daily behavior.

These are just a sampling of the many writings about leadership that emphasize the role of personal character in leadership. Our research confirms that personal character is absolutely at the heart of effective leadership.

Here are some of the ways character gets defined:

- Making decisions with the organization paramount in their mind, versus allowing a personal agenda to influence decisions
- Keeping commitments that are made
- Practicing self-development; constantly learning
- Being receptive to, and specifically asking for, feedback from others
- Being approachable by anyone
- Treating everyone the same—no "smiling up and kicking down" behavior
- Treating the waitress and bellhop with dignity, as well as people of high status
- Trusting other people; assuming they have good intentions
- Working collaboratively with others, versus seeing everyone as a competitor
- Not acting in an arrogant manner toward others
- Being tenacious and not giving up because something is difficult
- Having emotional resilience; adjusting rapidly to changing environments

Many organizations have learned that finding people with the right character is the absolute requirement for long-term success of the organization.

A colleague asked a senior executive of Louis Vuitton, the maker of high-end luggage and personal accessories, how they went about getting people to produce such high-quality products. The executive's answer was, "You look for people who seek quality in their personal life, and in all the things they use and possess. You can't train that into people."

The retailer Nordstrom is currently working to regain the position that it once held as the leading provider of excellent service. Again, when the executives are asked about how they plan to do that, their answer is: "Hire nice people." It is much easier to teach a nice person selling skills and how to use "point of sale" equipment than it is to teach "niceness" to someone who knows how to complete the paperwork for a sales transaction.

However, our research shows that when people receive high scores on this important dimension of leadership, but this is all they score highly on, then the likelihood of them being perceived as outstanding leaders is approximately 6 percent. And if people are given low marks on these "character" dimensions, they will absolutely not be perceived as great leaders.

We concur, therefore, with the people who have written of the importance of leaders being persons of high character. Without it, long-term failure is certain. Where we part company with some is our conclusion that character is a necessary, but not sufficient, element for great leadership. To complicate the matter even further, there are some people who are perceived as effective leaders yet who seem to possess major character flaws. This will probably be known in leadership literature in decades to come as the "Clinton phenomenon." It seems more often to be reserved for political leaders than for those in business and industry, but we do not pretend to fully understand that anomaly.

In the aftermath of the attack on the World Trade Center on September 11, 2001, Mayor Rudolf Giuliani stepped in to orchestrate the City of New York's response to the situation. Giuliani rose to the occasion with hands-on, calming, decisive behavior that earned him extremely high marks from citizens and the media. One commentator on National Public Radio said that "it was as if the situation erased all the negative images that had surrounded Giuliani." He had been through a sordid divorce, had been accused of racial slurs, been tagged as "Mussolini on the Hudson," and was in general disfavor. Then, suddenly an event and the way he handled it transformed him into a hero.

Personal Capability

The second important tent pole of leadership is the personal capability the individual possesses (see Figure 3.3). This cluster of abil-

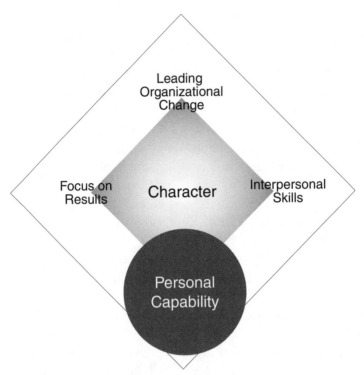

FIGURE 3.3   Leadership tent floor: Personal Capability.

ities comprises skills or competencies that are absolutely crucial for people to be highly regarded by peers, subordinates, and bosses. These are not skills that would typically be described as leadership skills, and yet our research proves they must be in place for any individual to be perceived as a strong leader.

Some of these individual capabilities are:

- *Technical knowledge.*   Research with a large natural resources products company showed that the quality or attribute that had the highest correlation with being perceived as a great leader was technical competence. Those who were perceived as the best leaders always scored high on this dimension. Conversely, those in the bottom 10 percent of the overall scores scored low on technical competence.

- *Product knowledge.* A thorough understanding of what the organization produces and why it is superior to competitive products.
- *Problem-analysis and problem-solving skills.* The ability to define a problem, analyze it, and come up with solid recommendations for resolving it.
- *Professional skills.* These include the ability to write an intelligent, concise report or memorandum; the ability to comfortably make a compelling presentation in front of a group; and the abilities to organize one's work in an efficient manner, to monitor progress, and to act without being told by someone in authority.
- *Innovation.* This refers to the ability to have a fresh outlook in approaching a problem, to shake loose of old methods and processes and see new possibilities. Innovation means being able to climb out of ruts and do things in a different fashion.
- *Initiative.* This describes the person who sees something falling in the cracks between one department and another, and who immediately steps in to make certain it is handled. It involves volunteering when something needs to be done and no one currently is doing it.
- *Effective use of information technology.* This person sets an example in the consistent use of e-mail, powerful software applications, and any technology that escalates performance.

One of the most useful frameworks by which to understand how people contribute in their careers is the *four stages model,* originally developed by Gene Dalton and Paul Thompson.[1] This model describes four stages of career growth through which people may move. In many cases people become locked into one stage because they do not possess the necessary skills and behavior to move forward. In other cases people stay at a particular stage because it fits their needs and aptitudes. The four stages are:

- Stage I: depending on others
- Stage II: contributing independently
- Stage III: contributing through others
- Stage IV: leading through vision

Stage I.   The first stage of careers has been described as *depending on others.*[2] In Stage I, people willingly accept direction from others. People in Stage I demonstrate some competency on a portion of a larger project but tend to focus on performing detailed and routine tasks. Stage I individuals show some directed creativity and can be depended on to deliver on time and on budget. Stage I is an important career step. It is that time when people learn the ropes and gain an in-depth understanding of technology and organizational dynamics. Most individuals spend limited time in Stage I at the beginning of their career or when they take on a new assignment. Because the major psychological focus of Stage I is *dependence*, no leadership is exhibited in this stage. People in Stage I are led; they do not lead. Research with hundreds of organizations has uncovered that some people never leave Stage I. They continue to rely on others for direction. Other people make a transition from Stage I early in their careers but then, because they are out of date or lack skills, transition back later in their career.

Stage II.   The second stage is *contributing independently.* This describes a series of behaviors that enable a person to assume responsibility for a definable project, not to rely on a supervisor but, instead, to work autonomously. This person produces significant results, and in so doing, develops greater technical expertise, along with a strong reputation. This person also builds a strong network of personal relationships. This stage of career growth is an absolute gateway to further progression. If people cannot perform well in Stage II positions, they cannot move on successfully to roles in which they will be responsible for a group of people.

Having a proper set of personal capabilities is another way of saying that the excellent leader must have moved successfully through Stage II. Leaders cannot skip this stage; if they do, they pay a price as they move upward in the organization and then have to go back and acquire skills that should have been acquired earlier in their careers. This is the time when self-confidence must be developed, and trust in one's own perceptions of situations.

Moving too fast through Stage II is also dangerous. In moving too rapidly, people do not develop self-confidence or build credibility with others in the organization. Our analysis of the research data on leaders shows that effective leaders learned professional skills during this stage of their careers. Without these skills, further progress is severely limited. Leadership in Stage II is sometimes described as personal leadership.

Stage III.   The third stage is about *contributing through others,* and every effective leader of others is at least in Stage III. Many people who have the title of "Manager," however, are not in Stage III, but remain locked in Stage II, even though they are surrounded by the trappings of a Stage III leader. These are managers who continue to process claim forms, or design a new part, because it is more comfortable to function as an individual contributor than as a leader. Frequently they will "cherry-pick" the best assignments and compete with their direct reports for recognition and rewards. They are unable or unwilling to leave their comfort zone of being personally productive using some technical tasks.

Stage III behavior requires people to develop others, to represent the organization to clients and external groups, and to build strong internal and external networks. Stage III contributors achieve positive results as they work with and through others. They have organizational impact by mentoring others, by heading up a project team, and by taking on responsibility for much more than their own performance. (What this means, of course, is that there are many Stage III people who do not have the words "supervisor," "manager," or "director" in front of their names. The creators of this useful framework by which to understand career growth have done research that shows there to be five times as many people in Stage III who do not have a managerial title as there are those who have a formal role and title.)

Stage IV.   A small number of people move beyond Stage III and become Stage IV leaders. Research shows that only 5 percent of the working population ends up in Stage IV functions. That means, obviously, that 95 percent of everyone working in organizations ends up having perfectly satisfactory careers without moving to Stage IV. For that group, there is one more tent pole that must be erected to

TABLE 3.1 "Personal Capabilities" for Stages II, III, and IV

Stage II Contributing Independently (Personal Leadership)	Stage III Contributing through Others (Local Leadership)	Stage IV Leading through Vision (Organizational Leadership)
• Knows the job well • Many people seek his or her opinion • Is considered an expert in his or field • Integrates large volumes of data into a logical and coherent structure for analysis • Demonstrates the ability to solve problems under conditions of uncertainty and ambiguity • Creates new opportunities or overcomes obstacles by rethinking situations	• Demonstrates a breadth of technical/ functional knowledge outside of his or her core specialty • Is not threatened by the technical competence of others • Clarifies complex data or situations so that others can comprehend, respond, and contribute • Assists others in interpreting and tolerating ambiguous information • Coaches others on how to present interpretive results • Provides support and encouragement to others when they attempt to innovate— even when they fail	• Shapes organization direction to reinforce the continual need for technical excellence • Ensures that the organization has access to technical/professional resources that allow employees to remain cutting edge • Identifies and helps to quickly resolve ill-defined, complex problems that cross organizational boundaries • Requires accurate and crucial information as a basis for sound organization-wide decisions • Communicates the importance of clear, critical thinking in all jobs throughout the company • Fosters an organizational environment that encourages others to question their usual way of looking at things

make them complete leaders. First, let's examine what they must accomplish.

Stage IV leaders are that group of individuals in the organization who:

- Create the overarching vision for the organization
- Define the strategic direction of the firm
- Exercise strong influence over the critical decisions that are made
- Represent the organization to the outside world, including customers, suppliers, and trade associations
- Are the antenna to the outside world, collecting information and scanning the horizon for change
- Shape the culture
- Allocate resources among competing groups
- Translate the strategic direction into personal objectives for people

For each individual at each stage, leadership looks different. Table 3.1 describes the necessary elements of personal capability for Stage II, Stage III, and Stage IV leaders.

Focus on Results
Our model for effective leadership now takes on a new dimension (see Figure 3.4). It would be ideal if we could erect these next two tent poles simultaneously. These two elements, Focus on Results and Interpersonal Skills, require that Character and Personal Capability be in place, but it appears to make no difference which of these two components comes after that. Indeed, there exists a remarkable relationship between these two components of leadership.

How do leaders focus on results? Here are some of the ways:

- Establish stretch goals for their people
- Take personal responsibility for the outcomes of the group
- Provide ongoing feedback and coaching to their people
- Set loftier targets for the group to achieve
- Personally sponsor an initiative or action
- Initiate new programs, projects, processes, client relationships, or technology
- Focus on organization goals and ensure that they are translated into actions by their department

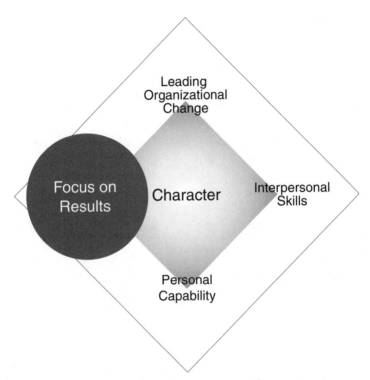

FIGURE 3.4   Leadership tent floor: Focus on Results.

- Operate with speed and intensity; accelerate the pace of the group
- Champion the cause of the customer
- Balance long-term and short-term objectives

Table 3.2 shows how Focus on Results differs for Stage II, III, and IV leaders.

Producing results is a key outcome of effective leadership. As Dave Ulrich, Jack Zenger, and Norm Smallwood noted in their book, *Results-Based Leadership,* leadership is ultimately about producing results.[3] What we have described in this section are some of those behaviors, skills, and competencies that lead directly to the production of positive results in an organization. The authors of *Results-*

TABLE 3.2   "Focus on Results" for Stages II, III, and IV

Stage II Contributing Independently (Personal Leadership)	Stage III Contributing through Others (Local Leadership)	Stage IV Leading through Vision (Organizational Leadership)
• Can be counted on to accomplish his or her job without close supervision • Bounces back from setbacks; does not lose confidence or become discouraged • Overcomes difficult challenges that interfere with getting the job done	• Builds commitment in others for their individual and team objectives • Accepts responsibility for the results-based outcome(s) of group efforts • Holds others accountable for results • Promotes a strong, sense of urgency for reaching goals and meeting deadlines	• Establishes key result areas for the organization • Communicates the key or "vital few" performance indicators that measure organizational results • Leads or champions efforts that increase productivity and goal accomplishment throughout the organization

Based Leadership described these as the "attributes" necessary to produce spectacular results.

In one study of just over 1000 managers of a large corporation, we analyzed the behaviors that separated the top 10 percent of their leaders from the rest. Here are some of the items:

- This person brings ideas into action.
- This person pushes to "take the next step forward."
- This person brings energy, enthusiasm, and urgency to his or her work.
- This person looks for ways to improve his or her job and overall function.

Notice the pattern of taking action, causing things to occur, pushing forward, and continual improvement. The image that comes to mind is a leader in the driver's seat with his or her foot on the accelerator—most of the time, pressed to the floorboard.

Interpersonal Skills

The companion set of skills to Focus on Results required for effective leaders is "people" skills or Interpersonal Skills (Figure 3.5). These are extremely important to the success of any leader, especially since the demise of "command and control" styles of leadership. This tent pole, along with the one in the center, supports the most canvas. Interpersonal Skills includes more "differentiating competencies" than any other cluster, and they are the most frequently correlated with all of the other "differentiating competencies."

What are the specific skills required of a Stage III leader with strong interpersonal skills? Here are the competencies:

• Communicating powerfully and prolifically

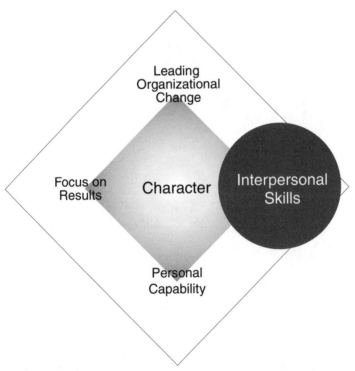

FIGURE 3.5   Leadership tent floor: Interpersonal Skills.

- Inspiring others to high performance
- Building positive relationships with others
- Developing the skills and talents of subordinates
- Working in a collaborative manner with others
- Being an effective team member
- Recognizing and rewarding the contributions of others
- Being open and receptive to new ideas
- Responding positively to feedback
- Effectively resolving conflicts within their own department, and with other groups outside
- Influencing people upward in the organization, in addition to peers and subordinates
- Building the self-esteem of others, giving positive indications of their ability to succeed
- Teaching others in a helpful manner

Table 3.3 shows how Interpersonal Skills differ for Stage II, III, and IV leaders.

Some writers on the subject of leadership have suggested that interpersonal skills are the major determinant of leadership effectiveness, and that 80 percent of all organizations' lists of crucial competencies for success would be included in the dimension of interpersonal effectiveness. Our data show, however, that if leaders are good only at interpersonal relationships, they again have a fairly low probability of being in the top 10 percent of all leaders in a firm.

The Power of Combinations. From an experience of his professional life, one of the authors recounts the following story. "Upon returning from a trip, I noticed that my administrative assistant had a severe rash on the inside of her arm. We worked for a pharmaceutical company, one of whose specialties was dermatology. I jokingly said, 'Kathy, you aren't a very good advertisement for our products.' She explained that she had been to three dermatologists, who had each prescribed different medications. Nothing had helped. I said, 'Well, we have a consulting dermatologist downstairs who is considered to be one of the best in the world—let's go see him.' So,

TABLE 3.3 "Interpersonal Skills" for Stages II, III, and IV

Stage II Contributing Independently (Personal Leadership)	Stage III Contributing through Others (Local Leadership)	Stage IV Leading through Vision (Organizational Leadership)
• Establishes rapport easily • Is interested in what other people have to say • Adjusts his or her interpersonal approach to meet the interpersonal style and needs of others • Deals effectively with people in order to get his or her work accomplished • Helps others find their own answers rather than telling them what they should do • Considers the opinions of other team members • Challenges proposed team actions in such a way as to create constructive discussion of alternative views	• Represents the work group's ideas and interests to others • Helps others learn the interpersonal skills needed to network effectively • Encourages people to say what they think • Is generous in recognizing the contributions of others • Demonstrates confidence and trust in other people's ability • Proactively coaches and/or mentors others • Knows when to let go of the details in order to help others learn from experience • Delegates tasks or assignments that provide developmental experiences • Keeps the team informed about current and upcoming issues • Fosters a climate of trust and respect within the team	• Maintains and utilizes relationships outside the company through which he or she can generate resources or information • Builds and/or supports mutually beneficial relationships with other organizations, professional associations, and community contacts • Actively and generously shares his or her extensive network of internal and external contacts to accomplish organizational goals • Influences or leads organizational efforts (e.g., succession planning, key assignments) that support employee development • Identifies and sponsors developmental opportunities for others that help them gain wide exposure and experience • Models teamwork by working effectively with other leaders in the organization • Plays a leading role in integrating and orchestrating the operations and activities of key business teams

this eminent dermatologist looked at it, took a culture from it, and when I returned from another business trip Kathy's rash was gone. I asked what had happened, and she said, 'Dr. Scholtz discovered that I had both a fungal and bacterial infection on my arm. The previous doctors had treated one or the other. He treated them both simultaneously and it cleared up.' I learned from this experience that doing two things together can work magic, while doing one alone often accomplishes nothing."

In a study, we looked at managers who were in the top quartile on Focus on Results but were not in the top quartile on Interpersonal Skills. The likelihood of being perceived as a great leader was 13 percent. Contrasting people in the opposite position (e.g., in the top quartile on Interpersonal Skills and not in the top quartile on Focus on Results), there was a 9 percent probability of being perceived as a great leader. When we found leaders who were good at both Focus on Results and Interpersonal Skills, the likelihood of that person being perceived as one of the top 10 percent leaped to 68 percent. This fact powerfully reinforces the idea that effective leaders are not one-celled people, who focus maniacally on just one thing. To the contrary, we have learned that great leaders do many things well.

Steve Frangos described his efforts to transform the black-and-white film division of Kodak in his book, *Team Zebra*.[4] One powerful message in the book was that success in changing the culture of the organization came from doing several things simultaneously. No one thing, by itself, did much. But the combination of training programs, surveys, team building, quality circles, and coaching initiatives was extremely powerful.

Leading Organizational Change
What are the specific skills required for leading organizational change (Figure 3.6)? Here are the competencies:

- Has the ability to be a champion for change in the organization
- Leads projects or programs, presenting them so that others support them
- Is an effective marketer for his or her work group's projects, programs, or products
- Has a strategic perspective

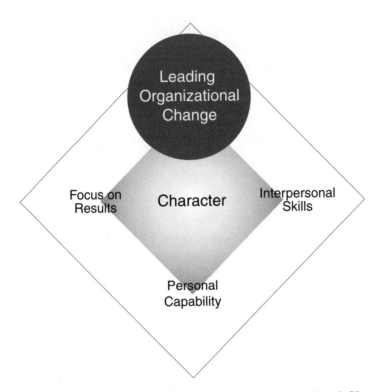

FIGURE 3.6 Leadership tent floor: Leading Organizational Change.

- Knows his or her work relates to the organization's business strategy (line-of-sight connection)
- Translates the organization's vision and objectives into challenging and meaningful goals for others
- Takes the long view; can be trusted to balance short-term and long-term needs of the organization
- Connects the outside world with internal groups
- Represents work group to key groups outside the group or department
- Helps people understand how meeting customers' needs is central to the mission and goals of the organization

Table 3.4 shows how Leading Organizational Change differs for Stage II, III, and IV leaders.

TABLE 3.4 "Leading Organizational Change" for Stages II, III, and IV

Stage II Contributing Independently (Personal Leadership)	Stage III Contributing through Others (Local Leadership)	Stage IV Leading through Vision (Organizational Leadership)
• Is quick to recognize situations or conditions where change is needed	• Energizes others to want to change by pointing out the need for change	• Energizes others to want to change by pointing out the need for change
• Adjusts work objectives, activities, and tasks to align with and support achievement of change	• Encourages people to let go of old ways so the new ways can begin	• Encourages people to let go of old ways so the new ways can begin
• Aligns his or her business objectives with the organization's strategic plan or objectives	• Helps others overcome their resistance to change	• Helps others overcome their resistance to change
• Uses information about the market and competitors to provide input into the organization's strategic planning process	• Clarifies how changes will affect jobs, work groups, and/or the organization	• Clarifies how changes will affect jobs, work groups, and/or the organization
• Thinks beyond the "day-to-day" to take a longer-term view of the business	• Coordinates team and cross-functional activities to assure strategic alignment	• Sets and articulates a compelling vision for the organization
• Understands how his or her work relates to the organization's business strategy	• Proposes initiatives that become part of the organization's strategic plan	• Continually communicates the highest priority strategic initiatives to keep the leadership team focused on the right things
	• Clarifies vision, mission, values, and long-term goals for others	• Ensures that all systems in the organization are aligned toward achieving the overall strategic goals
	• Consistently communicates "the big picture" business implications to others	• Ensures that the organization has people skills and resources to meet the strategic challenges of tomorrow
	• Explains to others how the changes in one part of the organization affect other organizational systems	

MEASURING YOUR CHANGE LEADERSHIP EFFECTIVENESS

One study we conducted involved the different techniques that leaders use to introduce a specific change into a work group.

Assessing Your Change Leadership Style
Take a few moments to complete the following short questionnaire on your usual approach to introducing a change in your organization.

MAKING TACTICAL CHANGE

Listed below are behaviors describing different approaches a person could use to help create organizational change. Circle the letter beside the action you would most likely take. Even if you were likely to do both, select the one answer that you feel would have the greater impact of a successful change effort.

1. A. Make the tough decision necessary to help implement the changes.
   B. Encourage people to express their ideas and opinions about the changes openly.
2. A. Communicate effectively so others see how these changes fit into the picture.
   B. Involve people in problem solving and decision making regarding the changes.
3. A. When people are not clear about how to move forward on a change, get them to consider alternative approaches to implementing changes.
   B. Actively seek out information about people's thoughts and perspectives regarding the changes.
4. A. Closely monitor, against clear standards, the progress people are making on the change.
   B. Seek examples of the impact of the changes.

5. A. Let people know clearly what is expected of them regarding the changes.

   B. Help people understand the rationale behind decisions regarding the changes.

6. A. Keep people focused on the changes to be made.

   B. Provide support when people take risks making changes, even if they fail.

7. A. Follow up with people on individual commitments they make to bring about changes.

   B. Encourage people to share information about what's working and what's not.

8. A. Clarify individual tasks and responsibilities associated with the change effort.

   B. Find ways to create and utilize development opportunities associated with the change effort.

9. A. Find ways to push through the changes regardless of unanticipated problems.

   B. Encourage people to reveal their true feelings, even on highly emotional concerns regarding the changes.

10. A. Keep people focused on the changes, despite any frustration or opposition.

    B. Ask people to present their point of view even when it differs from your own regarding the change.

    Total "A" _____   Total "B" _____

Count up the number of times you marked answer "A" and answer "B." As you probably already discerned, this questionnaire is measuring two basic approaches to initiating any change.

- The first is directing, monitoring, and pushing to make certain the change process is moving forward in a satisfactory way.

- The second approach describes the way in which the leader creates a climate of participation and involvement for all concerned.

We invite the reader to answer the question, "Which pattern of leader behavior produces the most positive outcomes?"

1. Largely directive?
2. Highly involving and participatory approach?
3. A 50/50 mix of the two?

A: Directing Change

Behaviors associated with directing change are:

Making tough decisions in a timely fashion

Providing vision to help employees see how the group's work fits into the big picture

Monitoring programs against clear standards

Actively encouraging people to find new and better ways to do the job

Ensuring departmental/work unit goals are consistent with strategic business goals

Leading by example

Monitoring performance against clear standards

Letting employees know what is expected

Generating new ideas about how to create the change

Following up with people to ensure implementation

B: Involving Others in Change

Behaviors associated with involving others are:

Encouraging people to express their ideas and opinions openly

Promoting a spirit of cooperation among members of the work group

Involving employees in problem-solving and decision-making activities that have an impact on them

Encouraging and facilitating resolution of conflict within the work group

Actively seeking out information about others' thoughts and perspectives

Motivating and encouraging employees

Providing feedback in a constructive manner (i.e., giving specific examples)

Helping employees understand the rationale behind their decisions

Creating development opportunities by assigning appropriate and challenging work

Providing support when employees take risks, even if they fail

Interpreting Your Scores. This assessment measures your favored tendency when you approach change. It is similar to which hand you favor (e.g., right handed, left handed, or ambidextrous). A score of 6 on either "A" or "B" indicates that you probably have a slight tendency to favor that approach. A score of 7 or more indicates a strong tendency toward that approach. It does not necessarily mean that you would not ever use the other approach, but you would probably lead with your favored actions.

EFFECTIVE LEADERS CHAMPION CHANGE

With most organizations today in a constant state of change—from dramatic growth to downsizing and restructuring—a critical skill for leaders is leading successful change efforts. A turbulent business environment puts leaders to the test: excellent leadership can turn a significant change into a pleasant journey, while poor leadership might be better described as a "trip to hell."

We know that the best leaders inspire their troops to rally around a change, whereas poor leaders have to push, persuade, or even threaten employees to accept change. Top-performing leaders become effective marketers of projects, programs, or products, gaining support for them along the way. Conversely, poor leaders fail to engage or commit others to the change.

Too Much of a Good Thing
A key learning from our research on leading change was that either of the two approaches actually can be detrimental if used exclusively. Effective leaders used both approaches in a careful balance.

The metaphor that comes to mind is a person rowing a boat. For maximum control and speed, you need both oars. One oar alone causes you to go in circles, no matter which oar you choose.

For example, while directing may be a great way to maintain control, leaders who significantly favor directing change may end up with employees feeling that changes are being done to them but not with them. Consequently, employees may become resistant to change and begin to distrust management.

Additionally, those who have strong directing tendencies typically have a well-organized plan and communicate the change plan and provide feedback about what needs to be done differently. However, they often fail to have open discussions with their team about the impact of the change.

Those who favor involving others in change often fail to provide enough direction, leaving employees confused about next steps, what their roles are, and what they need to do to keep the change moving forward. Also, a high involvement tendency may indicate an unwillingness on the leader's part to take risks or to take a decisive position.

Our research shows clearly that these two sets of behaviors are both necessary in order for a leader to manage change effectively. Leaders who direct change help their people know the specifics involved in the change. Involving others in the change efforts increases employee commitment rather than emphasizing employee compliance.

The more significant the change, the more of both is needed in order for a change to work effectively. Maybe this explains when a strength becomes a liability: it is when people use it to the exclusion of other balancing skills.

LEADERSHIP AND CHANGE

One of the complexities of leadership is the issue of change. Some have made a compelling argument that what separates "management" from "leadership" is that leadership has to do with change. We have traditionally defined the manager's role as preserving the stability of organizations and leaders as instruments of change. But we agree with John Gardner when he wrote:

> Many writers on leadership take considerable pains to distinguish between leaders and managers. In the process leaders generally end up looking like a cross between Napoleon and the Pied Piper, and managers like unimaginative clods. This troubles me. I once heard it said of a man, "He's an utterly first-class manager but there

isn't a trace of the leader in him." I am beginning to believe that he does not exist. Every time I encounter utterly first-class managers they turn out to have quite a lot of the leader in them."[5]

The bigger issue is that all change is not the same. All change is not created equal.

Tactical Change

For want of better terminology, we describe some change as tactical. For example:

- A new work process
- A higher sales quota
- Moving into a new facility
- Introducing new technology
- Implementing new payroll procedures
- Changing the employee benefit plan
- Introducing a new training initiative
- Revising the compensation plan
- Hiring from the outside to fill positions requiring unique new skills
- Changing the firm's organization structure

Tactical change includes a sales manager implementing new reporting procedures to track sales activity better; or a customer service manager implementing a series of meetings to better inform a group who will be responsible for the implementation of new processes for tracking customer requests and complaints.

Strategic Change

On the other hand, there are strategic changes that we look to leaders to bring about. Included in that category are:

- Creating a new vision for the organization
- Redefining the fundamental focus of the business (changing from a product-focused business to a service business, or from a production capability focus to a consumer marketing focus)
- Orchestrate a new strategic initiative (such as the implementation of Six Sigma throughout the organization)

- Change the culture of the organization (from a "command and control" organization to one with higher involvement and participation from everyone)

We define strategic change as the change that sets the institution off in a new direction. It means a Kimberly-Clark divesting itself of its forests and production plants and becoming a consumer marketing organization. A commercial bank that changes from a product-focused strategy (a variety of unique products, each driven through a separate department) to a customer strategy (the bank needs to identify the unique needs of different groups of customers and deliver all products through one point of contact with the customer). Strategic change is Ford declaring itself a consumer marketing organization, not a car company.

Strategic and tactical changes are both important. Both are "real" change efforts, but they differ in scope. Strategic change takes the organization in new directions, whereas tactical change targets make the organization perform better in its current sphere.

We conclude that the combination of the four building blocks that have been described so far is fundamentally all that 95 percent of all leaders need. Mixing leadership competencies required by different stages has greatly complicated our understanding of leadership.

Bringing in the leadership requirements of 5 percent of the organization, and stirring those in with the leadership requirements for all the rest, compounds the complexity of leadership research and understanding.

Our objective again is to find the simplicity that lies just beyond the necessary complexity. We hope that by separating out the kinds of change that different leaders must bring about, and by separating them out by stage, we can begin to discover that wonderful simplicity that lies just beyond complexity.

HOW THESE FIVE ELEMENTS OF THE MODEL
INTERRELATE WITH EACH OTHER

As we have noted earlier, much of past thinking about leadership has been the quest to find out, "Is the key to leadership having high integrity, or is it ambition? Is it developing trust in people, or is it being a good problem solver?" We hope that the reader will be permanently disabused of this thinking, and will cease to view leadership in "or" terms, but will instead think about it in "and" terms. We will attempt to describe why these leadership elements logically go together, and why development efforts in one area is like flooding the pond and lifting all boats at the same time.

1. Character is at the heart of our model, and everything radiates out from it. It ties strongly to Interpersonal Skills. A person of questionable character is not usually effective interpersonally. In eyeball-to-eyeball conversations you cannot help seeing inside the other person. We recoil from phonies. We do not enjoy being with toadies who butter up people in authority and abuse everyone else. Most people avoid those who are arrogant or condescending. Relationships with such people are distant and strained. If someone has broken her word to us, we deal with her in a cautious and tentative way. The link between Character and Interpersonal Skills is an extremely strong bond. So is the link between self-development (personal character) and developing others (interpersonal skills). It is also clear that the ability to inspire and motivate others is strongly linked to how people perceive the integrity of the leader.

   We return to the question, "If leaders can be made, then how do you make them?" The linkage between character and interpersonal skills is a good example. Social psychologists confirm that the easiest way to change people's character, as expressed via their attitudes, is by getting them to behave in a new way. People make their attitudes conform to their behavior.

   Consider the case of an older supervisor in a manufacturing plant. He has received no training on how to manage people effectively. His behavior is patterned after the way he was treated by his supervisors. When an employee makes a mistake this supervisor chastises him, sometimes in public. Often the erring employee may be threatened with potential discipline or termination if such mistakes continue. If a change needs to be implemented, the supervisor says what must now be done, but with no explanation of why. This supervisor would never solicit ideas and opinions from the employee group. Turnover is higher in this supervisor's area, productivity is below average, labor grievances are more frequent, and upper management recognizes that this supervisor must change. But how? Isn't this behavior part of this supervisor's character? Short of extensive psychotherapy, how could this be changed?

Our experience is that the most sure-fire way to bring about behavioral change is to have this supervisor participate in a training process that provides a new mind-set or way of thinking and then teaches new behaviors and skills. The supervisor is not told how he must think and feel, but simply is told that there is good evidence of a better way to behave. He learns how to describe a problem in a calm, rational way to an employee, ask for the employees' ideas about how to solve it, and to agree jointly on the best way to proceed. The supervisor discovers that this works wonders. The same or better results are achieved with a great deal less anger. His relationships with his employees improve significantly. They greet him like a friend, not the enemy. His attitudes toward his subordinates become less adversarial. He is open to new ideas that previously would have been instantly rejected. His character changes. Why? Because his behavior changed, and people make their attitudes conform to their behavior. That principle is extremely well documented in social psychology research. It is also true, however, that it becomes a circular phenomenon. As attitudes improve, behavior begins to change as a result.

2. Character also affects the cluster labeled Focus on Results, but possibly in a less obvious way. People around the leader are often sensitive to perceived motives for doing things. If the focus on results is for reasons of self-aggrandizement, to look good to a boss, to further a political career in the firm, or for any other perceived selfish reason, then personal character detracts from any successful drive for results.

David McClelland, a Harvard psychologist, did extensive research on the need for achievement and its role in people's behavior and effectiveness. His research showed that the success of nations depends on the presence or absence of this need for achievement. He developed ways to measure this quality, but many assumed that it was something with which people were born. McClelland decided to experiment with ways to increase people's need for achievement. One test he used was the game of quoits. Quoits is a children's game involving a wooden peg on a base, and several 8-inch hoops of rope called quoits. The game consists of attempting to toss the quoits over the peg from a distance of several feet. Participants were asked to place the peg anywhere they chose in a large room and then get the quoits onto the peg. People with low levels of need for achievement would either put the peg near their feet and drop the quoits onto it, or they would put the peg at a huge distance and fling the quoits toward the peg with little hope of success. People with high need for achievement would put the peg a reasonable distance away, so that a careful toss of the quoits would have a reasonable chance of success. McClelland took the people who had displayed little or no need for achievement, and had them perform this exercise the "right" way. Over time, these people from Third World countries developed stronger motivations to achieve. By giving them an experience in feeling the success of attaining a positive result, their attitudes and character began to change.[6]

3. Personal Capability links to Interpersonal Skills. The respect and esteem with which anyone in the organization is viewed begins with his or her Personal Capability. We noted earlier that it is at Stage II ("contributing independently") that people develop a wide range of personal relationships. The time when people are developing their professional and technical skills is the time when they should also be developing skills that will enable them to work effectively with others. Technical and professional expertise is tightly linked to developing others and building relationships.

4. Personal Capability links to Focus on Results. One of the key roles any leader plays is that of role model. When the leader is personally effective and highly productive, that example is viewed by everyone involved. Leaders cannot ask others to do what they are not doing.

5. Focus on Results is linked to Interpersonal Skills. We have earlier noted the unusually close link between these two characteristics. Many leaders think that the linkage between Focus on Results and Interpersonal Skills is an *or* rather than an *and.* They believe they can be one or the other but not both. While each is highly desirable by itself, they are like a voice being amplified by a great sound system when they are combined together. The combination of the two ignites a power that catapults a person into the highest realms of effective leadership. Focusing on results and setting stretch goals have multiple links to the interpersonal skills of "inspiring and motivating to high performance" and to "collaboration and teamwork."

6. Character links to Leading Organizational Change. Organizations follow a leader who is perceived as being of high character. The greater the "connection" that is felt with the leader, the more likely the organization is to support the change being proposed. That support is tied to perceptions of the genuineness, caring, and integrity of the leader.

7. Focus on Results links to Leading Organizational Change. Leading organizational change is most often a long-term objective, and effective leaders are always balancing short-term and long-term objectives. A focus on results is a necessary balance to the longer-term emphasis on strategic change.

8. Interpersonal Skills links to Leading Organizational Change. Nowhere is there a higher requirement for consummate interpersonal skills than in the introduction of strategic change within the organization. Whether it is an attempt to change the culture or to implement a major new initiative, trust from others and the communication skills of the leader are absolute requirements for success.

C H A P T E R

THE COMPETENCY QUEST

Many writers on leadership take considerable pains to distinguish between leaders and managers. In the process leaders generally end up looking like a cross between Napoleon and the Pied Piper, and managers like unimaginative clods. This troubles me. I once heard it said of a man, "He's an utterly first-class manager but there isn't a trace of the leader in him." I am beginning to believe that he does not exist. Every time I encounter utterly first-class managers they turn out to have quite a lot of the leader in them.

John Gardner

Not the cry, but the flight of the wild duck leads the flock to follow.

Chinese Proverb

THE MOST PREVALENT APPROACH to leadership development in recent years has been the competency movement. The fundamental premise is simple. Identify and define the competencies of effective leaders in a specific organization. (Competencies are the combination of knowledge, skills, traits, and attributes that collectively enable someone to perform a given job.) Then, when selecting leaders, choose people who possess those competencies because they will have a much higher likelihood of success. If you want to develop leaders in the organization, design activities that directly expand or strengthen those competencies for the leaders in the organization.

For example, if Ajax Manufacturing decided to embark on a competency based system, it would need to study its leaders to determine what the best leaders had in common. To accomplish this, Ajax might retain a firm experienced in this research, and that firm would follow one of several paths to determine the appropriate competencies. Alternatives could include:

- Conduct extensive field research within the firm by analyzing the requirements of various leadership positions, studying 360-degree feedback reports, and observing leader behavior.

- From their extensive experience, provide the organization with a list of competencies, basically derived from past work they had completed in other similar organizations.

- Assemble a group of senior executives in the organization and elicit their views of the competencies required to succeed.

- Assemble groups of people who work with leaders and obtain their collective views about the knowledge, skills, traits, and attributes required for success in Ajax.

After having followed one or more of those avenues with the help of the outside consultants, Ajax might conclude that the best leaders commonly share the following competencies:

1. A high level of self-understanding
2. Good problem-solving skills
3. A strong set of personal values
4. Extensive technical knowledge of the industry
5. Assertive interpersonal behavior in group meetings
6. Willingness to make decisions despite great ambiguity
7. Ability to juggle several projects/activities simultaneously
8. Comfort in dealing with adversarial behavior by colleagues
9. Broad strategic thinking that goes beyond tactical issues
10. Willingness to make decisions that cause others discomfort
11. Flexibility and agility in finding new ways to accomplish tasks

12. Formation of strong bonds of trust with others in the organization

This list of competencies then becomes the "touchstone" by which further leadership is selected and around which all development programs are structured.

This competency approach swept through human resource departments. It has been estimated that at least 80 percent of companies have created such competency lists. The competency movement promised to bring scientific objectivity to employee selection and development. Indeed, we think it brought greater rigor than previously existed and helped to improve the hiring process. And for the past two decades, companies have focused their people development efforts around these defined competencies. In sum, the approach has impeccable logic to it.

WHY HASN'T IT WORKED?

So, why has the competency movement not borne more fruit? Why has it not been successful in helping organizations produce higher-caliber leaders? As John Gardner wrote, "Why do we not have better leadership? The question is asked over and over. We complain, express our disappointment, often our outrage; but no answer emerges."[1]

We think the competency movement had several major flaws.

1. It was too complex. Leadership, along with everything else in life, has to be reduced to some manageable simplicity. The competency movement pushed in exactly the opposite direction.

2. It was based on some faulty assumptions. Most of the problems with the competency movement stem from these questionable beliefs. Once recognized and corrected, we believe the basic premise is sound and has the potential to make a much more useful contribution.

3. It produced several unintended consequences. Many worthwhile programs and projects in organizations produce unintended consequences. The competency movement has produced a number. Again, if they are identified, and ways are found to remedy those consequences, the competency movement should go forward.

4. It suffered from poor execution. As with most initiatives, the strategy can be sound, but if the execution is flawed, it does not succeed. A big portion of the problem with the competency movement has been a lack of execution on the fundamentals that began the movement.

Our objective is to help the reader understand what has gone wrong, but more important, how this basic approach can be fixed and made more effective.

1. Complexity

One large public-sector organization had an outside consultant create a list of competencies for each of three pay bands in the organization. Each pay band (or salary group) had 173 to 175 specific behaviors defined for it, which in turn were organized into 15 general competencies. Imagine a list of 175 behaviors that you were expected to understand and somehow apply to your work. It is patently ridiculous. Few people could ever comprehend the meaning of this amount of complexity, let alone put it into action.

While that is an extreme example, it is not unusual to see organizations with lists of 30 to 50 competencies for their leaders to be evaluated and developed against. Complexity has become a major deterrent to effective implementation.

2. Some Faulty Assumptions about Competencies

There are several important assumptions underlying the focus on competencies. They were seldom stated overtly, so let us try:

1. Each organization possesses its own unique set of attributes or competencies.
2. Competencies within each person are distinct and separate from each other. They can be isolated and studied as if they were separate chromosomes in a person's genetic makeup.
3. The more similarity or congruence between an individual and the organization's unique pattern, the better leader he or she will be.

4. Competencies are all of roughly equal importance.

5. The best way to develop any competency is to focus directly on that specific trait or behavior. Working harder and longer at it will make you better at it, and therefore make you a better leader.

Unfortunately, it now appears that most of these assumptions do not coincide with the current reality, nor are they reinforced by our current research.

Correcting the Assumptions

Assumption 1. Competencies are unique to each organization.

Fact: Despite the efforts to create distinctive lists of competencies, there is a remarkable sameness about them from one company to another. Several explanations for this come to mind. The first is that the requirements to work in one company or public organization are not that different from those in another. People are people wherever they work. What makes for success in one firm is a carbon copy of what causes success in another.

The authors have long felt that the differences between people within any one organization are certainly as large or larger than those between organizations in the same industry, and probably between all organizations. That is, the differences between the people who work for Ajax Manufacturing in quality assurance and sales, or those in accounting and marketing, or between the people in research and development in contrast with those in maintenance—those differences are usually large, and every bit as large as the differences between the people from Ajax Manufacturing and those from its competitor, Behemoth Manufacturing. And these differences are probably as large as the differences between Ajax and the Carthage Corporation in the neighboring state.

Another explanation is that the same consulting firms are doing the competency analysis, and their processes ferret out the same things wherever they go. Much of the research on competencies has been done by a relatively small group of consulting firms.

Finally, it is probable that there are a handful of factors that will always account for overall leadership effectiveness. Lyle Spencer writes in his book, *Competence at Work,* "that the competencies of achievement orientation, influence and personal effectiveness will likely account for 80–98 percent of all competency models."[2]

Assumption 2. Competencies are unique and distinctive traits or qualities possessed by an individual.

Fact: One of the most dramatic discoveries of our analysis is the massive linkage between competencies. The linkage we are talking about does not consist of a handful of competencies that are slightly linked to each other. Instead, nearly every competency we studied was highly correlated with many others. Rather than being separate and distinct, each organization's competencies were like a three-dimensional spider web, in which any place you touch is linked to countless other strands in the web.

It appears that the researchers who were driving the competency movement wanted to make competencies appear unique and distinctive. So the research was done in a way that gave the appearance of separation between the competencies. Nothing is further from the truth. With such complex, strong links between competencies, it becomes problematic even to give them individual labels. Let us attempt one more metaphor. Imagine a jar of jellybeans, all different colors and flavors. At first glance they look separate. Then you see that tiny wires are connecting them together. You pick up one and 25 more are raised up with it. You can name the white jellybean "Flexibility" and pretend that it is an entity to itself. But the reality is that it cannot be separated from the others. This raises a fascinating question: If the jellybeans are inextricably linked together, then is there such a thing as the one white one? Or would it be more accurate to look at them in handfuls? Would it be better to face the reality that they are stuck together? We think so.

Later in this chapter we present our views of why competencies are linked together. Later chapters present other important findings about the importance of multiple competencies, and insights about how leadership effectiveness increases when competencies are strategically positioned in different clusters of behaviors.

Assumption 3. The more congruence there is between the organization's defined competencies and the individual's, the greater is the likelihood of success.

Fact: This is the only one of the assumptions that our data do not challenge. However, the validity of the assumption hinges on whether the organization has empirically derived its own list of competencies and whether there are good ways to measure an individual's competencies. Our data confirmed that leaders whose profiles were compatible with the high performers in the organization were much more likely to be highly rated than those who were not.

Assumption 4. All competencies have roughly the same importance.

Fact: There are huge differences between competencies' importance. As described earlier, we began by identifying the top tier of all leaders as seen by their peers, subordinates, and bosses, and comparing that group with the lowest-rated group. The question was, "What separates these high and low groups from each other?" The result was the identification of 16 competencies that actually separated the high and low groups. These competencies, selected from a pool of 50 or more, can be grouped into the same categories as the model we introduced in Chapter 1, and are treated more thoroughly later in this chapter.

For example, a common myth in many organizations is that effective executives are prompt and punctual. They arrive at meetings on time and don't keep others waiting. Our data show, however, that the lowest-rated executives were as apt to be punctual for meetings as the best. So, while we are in no way advocating that everyone shows up late to the next staff meeting, we think it is also important to point out that your punctuality will not elevate you above other people. Simply put, ineffective executives are also highly punctual.

If you want to work on improving your leadership capabilities, we advocate focusing on behaviors that truly make a difference. So what are they? We present these later in this chapter.

Assumption 5. Competencies are best developed by a direct focus on that specific competency.

Fact: Our research suggests that one competency is developed in the process of developing another. They appear to be, in many cases, by-products of one another. That means that the direct linear method is not the only way to develop or strengthen a competency. Indeed, there may be better and easier ways that come in from the sides and the back, rather than merely hitting it straight on. Chapter 8 expands on this concept.

3. Unintended Consequences

The largest drawback of the competency movement may have been its unforeseen by-products. We think that the competency movement has sent a series of implicit messages to leaders. These include:

- Competencies are a checklist, and the leader's objective is to check each one of them off. You either have it or you do not.
- Everyone needs to be adequate in any given competency. Chapter 2 emphasized that "adequate" is not the correct target. The target needs to be "great," not adequate.
- The emphasis has been almost exclusively on those competencies on which you are perceived as being deficient. The implication is that the greatest value comes from moving a weakness to a middle range where it no longer stands out.
- No emphasis has been given to taking a relative strength and making it "off-the-chart" strong. Unwittingly, this has contributed to our general pattern of "aiming low."
- It has driven out other powerful and practical techniques for developing people. Management experts ranging from Peter Drucker to Thomas Gilbert have proposed an extremely effective way to improve productivity and performance in an organization. They advocated identifying top performers and then carefully determining what they do differently from everyone else. In every activity in an organization being performed by a number of people, one person figures out extremely efficient

ways to get the job done. That may consist of clever shortcuts or streamlined work processes. Or, it may consist of more efficient ways to work with colleagues in other departments. Research on the productivity of workers shows huge differences between the people doing essentially the same tasks.

To discover what these star performers are doing differently requires careful observation of them, along with interviews about their thought processes and techniques. Then, using these same people (or other trainers), teach everyone in the firm to adopt the best techniques of these top performers.

This extremely obvious and logical method for improving performance has met with great resistance. Few organizations use this obvious means of lifting performance to the rafters. That resistance comes from the "mindset" many managers have that sets major boundaries around what the average person is capable of becoming or producing. Executives just cannot believe that nearly everyone can perform at a high level. Most executives think that peak performance is reserved for just a few. These executives believe that we simply cannot expect or attain high performance from the great majority of our people—including our managers and leaders.

Rigidly defined competencies also may have the unintended consequence of creating cookie-cutter people inside the organization. If the competency system was implemented, would everyone appear to be cut from the same mold? How, then, does the organization attract and retain the maverick who is so valuable in challenging the status quo? Are the wild ducks killed just after they hatch? The concern is that, over time, sameness creates a homogeneity that becomes mind-numbing, and the culture devolves into one of anti-innovation.

4. Poor Execution

The basic premise of competencies was that they would be created from extensive analysis of hard data, not senior executives' personal speculations. However, that has not occurred. Indeed, as one writer observed, "Most of the current activity going on under the banner of competency modeling is really only list making."[3]

What had promised to be extremely rigorous has evolved into a process of compiling the collective beliefs of some senior managers regarding the important attributes of leaders in the firm. Maxine Dalton, of the Center for Creative Leadership, writes, "Seventy percent of the competency models I see are just lists of positive attributes that may or may not have anything to do with management effectiveness. They reflect a half-day, off-site meeting with senior managers in which a list is made with the underlying implication, 'If the CEO says it's a competency, it's a competency.' "[4]

In order to be applicable to the entire firm, the competencies of necessity are quite broad and encompassing. The more general the competencies become, the less accurate they are. However, most large organizations have decided that it is too complicated and expensive to create competencies for each department or section of the organization.

Another execution issue is that competencies are focused on past requirements for effectiveness, and not what the future will require of leaders. This tendency to "look in the rear-view mirror" tends to create leaders who look and act like the current group, which may be exactly what kills the organization in the future. To the extent that competencies are used for developmental purposes, then the competencies should reflect abilities and behaviors required in the future, not the past or present. They should also describe the ability to learn those skills required for future success.

The competencies are not being used for selection and promotion purposes. Many organizations complain that while Human Resources has the list of approved competencies, they are not finding their way into the day-to-day hiring and promotion of people.

- They are expensive to do well and need maintenance over time, as organizations evolve, merge, divest, globalize, and change their activities.
- Development programs have not been tailored around them to any large measure. It is complicated to find developmental activities for many of the competencies. Plus, the competency lists give little help in guiding us to ways in which people might attain these skills.

WHY COMPETENCIES ARE LINKED TOGETHER

We readily confess that we do not completely know the answer to this question. Our current research methods do not give us the visibility or evidence needed to answer this question fully. We are rather confident, however, that there are four plausible explanations. We think all are at work, but it is impossible to define precisely how much of the linkage is attributed to one of these forces versus the others.

The four explanations are the following:

1.   A strength in one competency creates a powerful "halo," so that colleagues, whether subordinates, peers, or bosses, perceive the individual as being effective in a number of other areas because of a strength in one.

2.   In the process of developing any one strength, the individual develops other skills. Getting good at something enables you to be more proficient at several other related activities. We have labeled this the "cross-training" effect.

3.   Self-confidence is increased when any skill is acquired and produces success. People often possess skills but do not use them, because they lack the self-confidence to try them. Success in developing one competency increases confidence, which leads to trying another.

4.   Aspiration level increases when people succeed in any one dimension. It encourages the individual to set his or her sights higher and higher in other realms.

1. The Power of the "Halo Effect"

Solomon Asch in 1946 did experiments on how people form impressions of others.[5] His theory was that perceptions are formed from our view of an entire person rather than by focusing on individual traits and characteristics. In other words, people's perceptions are created from our view of the whole person rather than a rational evaluation of each individual piece. To prove this theory Asch devised an ingenious experiment. He generated lists of attributes that described an individual. The lists were read to two dif-

TABLE 4.1

List A	List B
Intelligent	Intelligent
Skillful	Skillful
Industrious	Industrious
Warm	Cold
Determined	Determined
Practical	Practical
Cautious	Cautious

ferent experimental groups. Table 4.1 shows the characteristics on each list.

As can be readily noted by reading through the two lists, they are identical except for two words. List A has the attribute "Warm," while List B has "Cold." After being provided either List A or List B, each group was then given an additional list of attributes and instructed to indicate other qualities an individual might have. Substantial differences were found between attributes marked by groups who had List A and those from groups that had List B.

Groups given List A would choose additional qualities such as happy, imaginative, good-natured, generous, humorous, wise, humane, popular, altruistic, and sociable. Groups given List B did not select those same attributes. There were, however, some attributes, such as serious, strong, reliable, persistent, honest, and important, that were equally likely to be chosen on either list.

From a brief list of a few attributes, people generalize to a broader set of attributes. Once again, this reinforces the belief that people form an impression of a person as a whole, and therefore they attribute additional characteristics even though they have been given no specific information about the person.

It is intuitive to most people, just based on their experience working with others, that certain traits and behaviors go together. The Asch experiments confirm that, and we suspect that the reader will easily think of many examples of this. People's dress, facial characteristics, country of origin, or manner of speech all trigger stereotypes that we have in our minds. Stereotypes persist because there is just enough truth in them to make them continue to live.

Another researcher tested Asch's basic theory, only this time had subjects actually come in contact with a person. H. H. Kelly, in a follow-up experiment, had students evaluate teachers.[6] Before attending a brief lecture, the students were provided a brief biographical sketch of each teacher. The descriptions were exactly the same except that for some students, one teacher was described as warm and the others were described as cold. The instructor then gave a 20-minute lecture. After the presentation, students rated the instructor. The students who had "warm" as part of the instructor's bio evaluated the instructor more positively than those for whom "cold" had been listed. This showed that the students' perceptions were strongly influenced by the written biographical sketch, and that these perceptions were not altered by subsequent interactions with the person.

The Asch and Kelly research reinforce a powerful conclusion. Some attributes, such as "warm" or "cold," are central traits. When a person is perceived to possess that characteristic, others immediately impute tag-along characteristics. These are glued to the central trait.

We invite the reader to participate in a quick experiment that illustrates this point. In Table 4.2, draw lines between the traits that go together. Match one from the left-hand column with one from the right-hand column. This example comes from research conducted by three psychologists: Rosenberg, Nelson, and Vivekananthan, who conducted a study in which people were asked to indicate the relationships among 64 different traits.[7] The researchers found that various traits cluster together in groups. That

TABLE 4.2

A. Honest	1. Serious
B. Intelligent	2. Wasteful
C. Irresponsible	3. Modest
D. Stern	4. Critical

is, if I have quality A, then people are very likely to believe I have quality B.

From their research, they found that the following traits tended to be clustered together:

A. Honest and 3. Modest
B. Intelligent and 1. Serious
C. Irresponsible and 2. Wasteful
D. Stern and 4. Critical

Their research showed a regular and consistent paring of traits. The powerful finding of this research was the consistency with which people linked one trait with another.

In their research, Rosenberg and his colleagues also measured issues that clustered on four dimensions:[8]

- Bad social (e.g., unpopular, unsociable, boring, cold, moody, dishonest)
- Good social (e.g., honest, happy, popular, reliable, modest, warm)
- Bad intellectual (e.g., foolish, unintelligent, clumsy, wasteful, irresponsible)
- Good intellectual (e.g., scientific, persistent, skillful, imaginative, intelligent)

If people know you have a trait in one dimension, they assume you also have other traits within that dimension. However, people would not assume, for example, that if a person is moody, that person is also clumsy. Moody and clumsy are on different dimensions.

Takeaways from this research include:

1. Perceptions are colored by small pieces of information, which may or may not be correct. (The way the instructor was perceived was colored by whether he had been described as "warm" or "cold.")
2. Initial impressions are used to create an overall view of a person. Knowing a few things, we then fill in the missing pieces in our minds. It is like seeing fragments of a picture and im-

mediately filling in the blank parts of the canvas. (If I find you to be unsociable and boring, that is enough for me to fill in many other blanks. Until you prove otherwise, I assume you are cold, moody, dishonest, clumsy, wasteful, foolish, and irresponsible.)

3. We do not form an overall view of someone by painstakingly assembling all of the pieces.

4. Certain characteristics or attributes are consistently linked together.

5. Attributes are clustered into various dimensions in the minds of most people.

Case Example: John Boyer.   John was a new manager who had agreed to attend a leadership development course. He had been in his new position for approximately six months and was interested in the perceptions of his direct reports. When John had taken over the group, morale was very low. Several direct reports were considering leaving and frustration levels were very high. The previous manager had used his position as manager to benefit his own career. He had a tendency to take personal credit for any accomplishments in the group but was quick to blame any failures on group members. His clever politics had earned him a promotion but left a group in disarray. John's approach to managing the group had been to be fair but firm. It seemed that because people had felt so taken advantage of by the previous manager, they began looking for ways to "get back" at the company. People were frequently late showing up in the morning, assignments were often not completed on time, and the workplace showed an attitude of "We don't care." John started out his tenure as a new manager by interviewing each employee. He took careful notes and was very interested in the career aspirations of each individual. He also asked questions about each person's areas of strength and developmental needs. He quickly found out that this was a highly creative and talented group but they lacked a clear mission and purpose. They had been responding to engineering requests from manufacturing but were not looking at long-term improvements that would take them out of daily fire-fighting activities and allow them more time to work on major innovations.

Two weeks after John took over as manager, he planned a one-day off-site meeting. During the off-site meeting he worked on team building and clarification of the group mission and objectives. The group gave John some challenging assignments. They indicated that they could not accomplish long-term engineering changes unless he could get manufacturing off their backs. The previous manager had simply accommodated all requests from manufacturing, regardless of their priority. John began to realize that the best way to gain the support of his group was to manage the group's priorities and goals with internal customers. His next task was to meet with manufacturing managers in order to gain support for the group's goals and plans. This was much more difficult. The manufacturing organization believed that it should direct the activities of engineering. The problem was that their priorities and problems changed daily, and the result was that concerted effort on solving major problems never occurred. John helped these leaders to see that if engineering could focus their efforts on a few top priorities, everyone's job would be easier. For the next five months John worked on relationships both within his group and with manufacturing. He made a concerted effort to recognize the accomplishments of group members. He started to hold regular staff meetings. He had the group participate in setting priorities and deciding on target goals. Several members of the group with behavior and performance problems were put on notice by John because they continued to show up late for work and miss delivery deadlines.

As John reviewed his leadership assessment results, he was generally pleased. His results were substantially above the norm on all competencies. As John worked through the data with his coach, one of his most positive areas was technical knowledge. The coach, knowing John did not have an engineering background, found that very unusual. "How do you explain this high score in technical knowledge?" the coach asked John. John shook his head. "I can't explain it. I am not an engineer. Everyone in this group knows more than I do. I have worked hard to get up to speed but I still lack detailed knowledge. I can't make a lot of the technical decisions so I review each one with team members who do have the expertise and rely on their knowledge."

Fitting Theory to Our Data.   The previous example provides one strong explanation for the linkage between competencies. Basic links or companionships between traits are well established in people's minds. They are generalized across all people within a culture and are not specific to individuals. Therefore, when a `person observes a leader displaying a specific competency, there is an immediate assumption that this individual possesses a number of other characteristics, despite the lack of any specific evidence to support that.

Many, if not most, impressions others have of our leadership abilities are not totally accurate. People are influenced by their experience, and because of that, they form a general impression (*Gestalt*). Rather than being a totally accurate accounting of each of our competencies and abilities (e.g., Competency a + Competency b + Competency c + Competency d = Overall Leadership Ability), people form their impressions based on an unequal weighing of competencies from bits of knowledge. Even though these impressions are not totally accurate, people cannot be talked out of their impression by a rational, precise accounting of our competencies. People have strong attachments to their impressions.

Many observers react to this and say that it is unfair that others are not accurate in their perceptions. However, this sword definitely cuts two ways. If others have a general impression that a person is a poor leader, then they will probably be negatively biased in their evaluations of specific competencies, and underrate the person's real abilities. On the other hand, if others have a general impression that a person is an extraordinary leader, they will overestimate this person's skills and abilities. While being underrated is unfair, being overrated, while still unfair, is something leaders can use to their advantage. The key is to get the attribution process to work for you rather than against you.

This helps to explain many of our research findings. For example, we found many leaders with extremely high scores on all competencies, and with no perceived weaknesses. The tendency for everyone to attribute positive social behavior and positive intellectual capabilities to someone who possesses one positive attribute sheds light on this phenomenon. The combination of creating an overall picture or *Gestalt* about someone, combined with the strong linkage between traits and attributes, provides insight into this.

It was hard for many people to believe that Richard M. Nixon, who was reared a Quaker, intelligent and well educated, and capable of being elected to high office, would use profanity like a sailor and engage in dishonest acts such as Watergate. Similarly, it was hard for many citizens of the United States to believe that Bill Clinton would engage in sexual misconduct with an intern in the Oval Office. It would have been more understandable if this had happened while he was living in a fraternity house during his junior year of college. Because he was the President of the United States, and a man of obvious intellect and ability, that behavior was inconsistent with people's assumptions.

Why do we present this research and theory about how perceptions are formed? Understanding theory helps in planning a successful strategy. Understanding how others formulate their perceptions helps us to understand why leaders are successful at times and why they fail.

2. Cross Training

The second explanation for the strong linkage between competencies is simply that in the course of becoming good at one thing, you get better at something else.

We see evidence of this in many other areas of life. A musician who plays the saxophone will often switch between the clarinet, alto saxophone, and tenor saxophone. Learning one instrument increases the ease of learning and performing on a different instrument. The athlete who is a runner parlays the endurance and strength gained through running to become a long-distance swimmer and cyclist. Piano players are often extremely fast typists.

Skills Are Transferable.   It is logical to believe that acquiring the skill of conducting effective meetings helps the leader to also be more effective working one-on-one with peers. Developing the skills of communicating powerfully and prolifically provides many of the same skills required to inspire and motivate others to high performance.

The skill of setting stretch goals for your team is related to the skills required to initiate action and focus on results.

3. Success Increases Confidence

When people experience success in one arena of life, it increases their confidence and willingness to try something new.

One of the authors' granddaughters became interested in diving. Going off a board in a typical backyard pool was easy. Then came the 3-meter board, which seemed frightening to an 11-year-old. Finally, the team went to a diving pool that included a 6-meter-high diving board. (That is, jumping roughly from the height of a two-story building into the pool.) As she went to the end of the board, she started to turn back, and the coach said, "You can do it— just jump." She did. Success at previous levels gave her confidence to try. She wanted to be able to dive from the high board, and it was no longer frightening except to her parents and grandparents.

4. Success Increases Aspiration Level

We know that success increases people's aspiration to try and do more. Any growth in one area gives us new skills and the confidence to seek growth in another. Andrall Pearson was a high-visibility executive, having been a senior director of McKinsey and Co., then head of PepsiCo for 14 years, then a teacher at the Harvard Business School who published frequently in the *Harvard Business Review*. In a 1980 *Fortune* magazine article he was listed as one of America's toughest bosses.

Then, at age 76, he became chairman of Tricon Global Restaurants, Inc., and learned an entirely new set of leadership skills. He learned to govern rather than control. He gained an appreciation for the power of human emotion. In earlier years he would display his own intellect and overpower people with his ability to grasp issues quickly. In an earlier leadership role he had told his colleagues, "A room full of monkeys could do better than this."

Today, a new Pearson has desisted from issuing orders to people, and he is asking questions and soliciting ideas. He has become a mentor to many in the firm. Pearson acknowledges that many of his leadership methods are new to him, and that his experience is a capstone of an already remarkable career.[9]

Jacob Bronowski wrote, "We have to understand that the world can only be grasped by action, not by contemplation. . . . The most powerful drive in the ascent of man is his pleasure in his own skills. He loves to do what he does well, and having done it well, he loves to do it better."[10]

As we ponder the ways that competencies are linked together, we have no way of tearing apart the impact of these many forces. Is it a halo effect, or is it the result of cross training? What role does increased confidence play, or escalating aspirations? We may never know the answer, but we are convinced that the answer lies in some combination of the four.

SIXTEEN BEHAVIORS (COMPETENCIES) THAT MAKE A DIFFERENCE IN HOW LEADERS ARE PERCEIVED BY OTHERS

Having presented our concerns about competencies and some suggestions about remedying those concerns, along with an analysis of why they are so intricately linked, we now present our own framework of competencies that make a difference.

How are impressions about leadership effectiveness most powerfully created? Our research shows that raters noticed some competencies much more than others. We believe that emphasizing the differentiating competencies will help leaders create a more favorable impression. Our research confirms that a real impact on employee turnover, customer satisfaction, and profitability occurs only when leadership is perceived as being extremely bad or exceptionally good. Being horrible at a competency gets noticed; being extraordinarily good gets noticed; but being average or good at something does not. Hence, the need for our advice regarding fixing a fatal flaw. If people have a fatal flaw (some behavior or competency that is rated very negatively), this may be the main source of their negative impression. In order to create a change in the *Gestalt* (general impression), people need to make noticeable changes.

We group these behaviors into the same components as the earlier model presented in Chapters 1 and 3. What follows is a more detailed description of these competencies, with further information about how people who score highly on that competency behave, and how people who receive low scores also behave on it.

Character

1. Displaying high integrity and honesty

High performers:

- Avoid saying one thing and doing another (i.e., "walk the talk")
- Act consistently with their words
- Follow through on promises and commitments
- Model the core values
- Lead by example

Poor performers:

- Are threatened by others' success
- Make themselves look good at the expense of other people
- Blame failures on others

Personal Capability

2. Technical and professional expertise

High performers:

- Are sought out by others for advice and counsel
- Use technical knowledge to help team members troubleshoot problems
- Have credibility because of their in-depth knowledge of issues or problems

Poor performers:

- Do not understand the job well
- Are technically or professionally incompetent
- Have become out of date technically
- Fail to understand the technology/profession well

3. Solving problems and analyzing issues

High performers:

- Exercise a high level of professional judgment
- Make good decisions based on a mixture of analysis, wisdom, experience, and judgment
- Encourage alternative approaches and new ideas

Poor performers:

- Fail to anticipate and stay on top of problems
- Do not consider an appropriate range of alternatives before making a decision

4. Innovation

High performers:

- Encourage alternative approaches and new ideas
- Consistently generate creative, resourceful solutions to problems
- Constructively challenge the usual approach of doing things and find new and better ways to do the job
- Create a culture of learning that drives individual development
- Work to improve new ideas rather than discourage them
- Encourage people to find innovative ways to accomplish their goals

Poor performers:

- Have a "one right way" mindset
- Are afraid to challenge existing systems, processes, or approaches
- Feel that new or innovative approaches will cost too much to implement or cause disruption
- Shoot down new ideas or approaches

5. Practicing self-development

High performers:

- Make constructive efforts to change and improve based on feedback from others
- Seek feedback from others to improve and develop themselves

- Constantly look for developmental opportunities (they are excited to learn)

Poor performers:

- Seem unconcerned about any kind of self-improvement
- Are content with their current skills and abilities
- Fear that others might perceive their development of new skills as a sign of incompetence or weakness

Focus on Results

6. Focus on results

High performers:

- Aggressively pursue all assignments and projects until completion
- Do everything possible to meet goals or deadlines

Poor performers:

- Fail to achieve agreed-upon results within the time allotted
- Fail to achieve the goals set for their work

7. Establish stretch goals

High performers:

- Maintain high standards of performance
- Set measurable standards of excellence for themselves and others in the work group
- Promote a spirit of continuous improvement

Poor performers:

- Fail to build high commitment among all employees to team goals and objectives

8. Take responsibility for outcomes/initiative

High performers:

- Take personal responsibility for outcomes
- Can be counted on to follow through on commitment
- Go above and beyond what needs to be done without being told

Poor performers:

- Blame failures on others

- Lose interest before projects are completed and fail to follow through

Interpersonal Skills

9. Communicating powerfully and prolifically

High performers:

- Are skillful at communicating new insights
- Provide the work group with a definite sense of direction and purpose
- Help people understand how their work contributes to broader business objectives

Poor performers:

- Do a poor job of communicating plans to people who help implement them
- Fail to explain the purpose and/or importance of the assignments

10. Inspiring and motivating others to high performance

High performers:

- Energize people to go the extra mile
- Have the ability to get people to stretch and reach goals beyond what they originally thought possible

Poor performers:

- Fail to inspire commitment, high energy, and a winning attitude

11. Building relationships

High performers:

- Are trusted by work group members
- Balance concern for productivity and results with sensitivity for employees' needs/problems
- Are approachable and friendly
- Handle difficult situations constructively and tactfully

Poor performers:

- Are difficult to get along with
- People don't feel free to take their complaints to them

12. Developing others

High performers:

- Are genuinely concerned about the development of others' careers
- Give individuals an appropriate balance of positive and corrective performance feedback
- Give honest feedback
- Take interest in the work of others
- Support others' growth and success

Poor performers:

- Wait too long to give others feedback
- Try to keep good people rather than allowing them to take on developmental opportunities

13. Collaboration and teamwork

High performers:

- Have developed cooperative working relationships with others in the company
- Promote a spirit of cooperation with other members of the work group
- Ensure that the work unit works well with other groups and departments

Poor performers:

- Do not work well with people who have different backgrounds and perspectives
- Promote a spirit of competition with other work groups

Leading Organizational Change

14. Developing strategic perspectives

High performers:

- Know how work relates to the organization's business strategy (line-of-sight connection)
- Translate the organization's vision and objectives into challenging and meaningful goals for others

- Can take the long view; can be trusted to balance short-term and long-term needs of the organization

Poor performers:

- Get caught up in the "day-to-day" and fail to take a longer-term, broader perspective on business decisions

15. Championing change

High performers:

- Become champions for projects or programs, presenting them so that others support them
- Are effective marketers for work groups' projects, programs, or products

Poor performers:

- Tend to follow the lead of others in change efforts

16. Connect internal groups with the outside world

High performers:

- Have demonstrated ability to represent the work group to key groups outside the group/department
- Help people understand how meeting customers' needs is central to the mission and goals of the organization

Poor performers:

- Make day-to-day decisions based on internal needs rather than the needs of customers
- Do not have a broad network outside their own work group

ASSESSING INDIVIDUAL COMPETENCIES

Once the organization has defined the competencies required for success, there is still the task of measuring to what degree any individual possesses that competency. How is that done? In some cases, people at a higher level in the organization make that assessment. With the advent of the extensive use of 360-degree feedback instruments administered to peers, subordinates, and bosses, these have increasingly been used to make that assessment. Finally, we note that the competency movement received a boost from the use of "assessment centers" in the 1970s and 1980s. In this process, participants were assessed by professional staff who had been instructed to look for evidence of certain competencies or behaviors. These characteristics or dimensions by which to measure people had to be defined. This strengthened the resolve of many organizations to finally develop a defensible list of competencies for their leaders.

CHAPTER

LEADERS MUST FIT THEIR ORGANIZATION

Old thieves make good jailers.

German Proverb

B RUCE WORKED IN ADMINISTRATION for a large university, and because of an excellent referral from a university professor he landed a position with a small consulting firm. His role was to start out as the office administrative manager, but he was slated to move quickly into the role of managing director of the firm. At the university Bruce had been a shining star. He was extremely meticulous in his work and paid a great deal of attention to detail. He always made sure to ferret out all the information before making a decision. These were valued traits at the university. As he began his role in the consulting firm he found the environment to be extremely different. In the university the proposals moved slowly through committees. Ample time was allowed for study and debate.

The small consulting firm moved quickly. Partners, all of whom felt they had decision-making authority, controlled the firm as a group. However, one partner would make a decision one way and then a second partner would reverse that decision. The partners would meet occasionally to hammer out the decision and resolve the disagreement. Partner meetings would be hardball discussions where differences were debated openly. The partners, rather than staying in the office to implement decisions, were constantly away on consulting assignments. They assumed that the decisions they made would be implemented.

Bruce approached his new assignment warily and decided that what the firm needed was more deliberate decision making, clear lines of authority, and a committee structure to consider various decisions. He worked for six months to implement these changes. After six months, the only thing Bruce accomplished was convincing every partner that he needed to leave the firm. The partners ultimately recognized that this new role for Bruce was not working, nor was it likely that he would ever succeed. They provided a severance package to Bruce. He quickly landed a job in administration at a hospital. Over the next several years Bruce was promoted in the hospital and enjoyed an excellent reputation with the staff and the physicians.

Was there something wrong with Bruce? Why was he so successful at the university and the hospital but such a failure at the consulting firm? Was there something wrong with the consulting firm? The consulting firm continued to grow and prosper.

What this series of events illustrates is that leadership is specific to the organization. Some combinations of individuals and organizations just do not work out well. While it was certainly true in this episode that neither was without a share of responsibility for the failure, what becomes evident to everyone with a variety of work experiences is that some organizations fit certain individuals better than others. Individuals have unique competencies, beliefs, and experience. Organizations have extremely different cultures and needs. While there can be some accommodation by either the individual or the organization at some point, people are more effective when they are themselves. In his book *Jack Straight from the Gut,* Jack Welch describes his experience in GE shortly after being named chairman:

> At one of my earliest board meetings in San Francisco shortly after being named vice chairman, I showed up in a perfectly pressed blue

suit, with a starched white shirt and a crisp red tie. I chose my words carefully. I wanted to show the board members that I was older and more mature than either my 43 years or my reputation. I guess I wanted to look and act like a typical GE vice chairman.

Paul Austin, a longtime GE director and chairman of the Coca-Cola Company, came up to me at the cocktail party after the meeting.

"Jack," he said, touching my suit, "this isn't you. You looked a lot better when you were just being yourself."

Thank God Austin realized I was playing a role—and cared enough to tell me. Trying to be somebody I wasn't could have been a disaster for me.[1]

In this chapter we will explore the interaction between organizational requirements and individual abilities. We believe that finding the right fit is a key factor of success. At lower organizational levels fit is not as critical, but as people take on broader roles, fit becomes a defining factor in both the success of a leader and of the organization.

TWO POSSIBLE SCENARIOS

Scenario 1

What if research revealed that every leader in the organization needed a high level of competence in five specific behaviors—and everyone needed exactly the same five? Anyone acquiring these five behaviors would become a successful leader as long as they were done extremely well.

Scenario 2

What if research revealed that great leaders need exceptional ability in a few competencies, but the specific behaviors could be different for each effective leader? Great leaders could be unique, widely different, one-of-a-kind versions.

Considering these two scenarios, which would you like to be true? On the one hand, Scenario 1 seems to provide an absolute answer as to what great leaders need to do, the answer that people have searched to find for centuries. By focusing all your attention on developing and improving these five specific behaviors, Scenario 1 would provide a precise formula for success.

On the down side, implicit in this scenario is the assumption that a "cookie-cutter" approach to leadership—that all effective leadership is the same and that individual differences and unique approaches do not work—can be applied.

Scenario 2 provides the opportunity for people to choose the behaviors in which they will excel. The key to Scenario 2 is developing strength in a few competencies that are valued by the organization in which one works.

KEYS TO SUCCESS AND FAILURE

One of the primary focuses early in our research was to discover if there were some competencies that are absolutely essential in order for a leader to be considered great. In other words, "Great leaders always do _____ well." In addition, we looked for competencies that, if done poorly, were a cause for failure. Surely, there must be some behaviors that catapult leaders to success; conversely, there must be others that drag leaders to failure. In the research process, however, it appeared that whenever we found a rule, we always found exceptions to that rule. We found much greater similarity in the causes of failure than we found in the reasons for effectiveness. Rather than identifying a consistent profile or style that always worked for every person, what we found was a tremendous variety in the style, approach, and makeup of extraordinary leaders. What started out as a disappointment in our research soon turned out to be valuable insight on leadership. Extraordinary leaders are unique. Some have one cluster of attributes, while others have a different cluster of attributes.

The only commonality we could find in extraordinary leaders is that they are extremely effective at a few things. While Scenario 1 would make life simpler for those responsible for leadership development, that is not the reality. We suspect most people are glad that Scenario 1 is not the way the world works. It would be mind-numbingly boring.

The good news of our research is that it reinforces the notion of individuality and the power of developing individual talents and gifts. For the authors this comes as a great relief. While both of us hope we possess some strengths, our strengths differ markedly from each other. This fact has been of great benefit in researching and writing this book. The strengths of one author balanced the flat side of the other author. After many years of personal change efforts, being extraordinarily talented at some competencies continues to evade us. It is just not in our bones. (This does not mean we are totally incompetent at these skills, but clearly we are not extraordinary.)

THE LEADERSHIP PARADOX

Leaders are both unique and alike. They are unique in that each one has a different set of competencies that ideally fit the organization in which he or she works. They are alike in that, to be highly effective, they need to have at least one strength in the different sections of the tent. The net effect is that leaders do not appear to be alike, much like different versions of cars all built on the same chassis appear to be different. But the basic components are similar (same drive train, suspension, electrical systems, engine), despite the fact that they look very different from the outside. In the end, leaders are extremely different on the outside, with several fundamental similarities under the surface.

DISCOVERING YOUR GENIUS

A psychologist once observed that the secret to life is discovering what "instrument" you are, and then learning how to play it. Woodwinds are no better than brass, nor are cellos superior to kettledrums. Each does something extremely well, and the musical score will call for that unique contribution. Some people seem to spend their entire lives searching for what that instrument is for them. Others, fortunately, discover their instrument quite early in life.

As individuals we all have competencies and abilities that come to us easier than others. We are drawn to some tasks and resist others. It is difficult to know if our being drawn to some activities results from possessing a unique, inherent skill, or if being good at something causes us to try harder at some skills versus others. Whatever the reason, it is not difficult to observe any group of leaders in any organization and notice marked individual differences. All seem to have both a combination of unique competencies and also other skills where they fare well, but are not necessarily great. A handful have pronounced weaknesses in a few areas.

In an effort to help people discover their genius, one of our colleagues, Kurt Sandholtz, has conducted research with thousands of people.[2] His quest was to determine the method whereby individuals have a "career best" experience, or that constitutes the high point in a person's career. It represents a time when people felt they were making a significant contribution and they were very successful. Understanding these "career best" experiences helps people understand their genius. Gene Dalton and Paul Thompson first developed the core of this idea when they wrote, "If individuals don't understand their unique strengths or interests, they don't have any basis for deciding whether a job or an assignment make sense for them. They are vulnerable to attractive external rewards or organizational pressures. They have little basis on which to form enough conviction to say no to an apparently attractive opportunity. Answers to career questions come from within one's self."[3]

To help people discover what they do best, Sandholtz asks them, "What is the best job you've ever had?" After examining the results of these studies, he discovered that "career bests" have some common characteristics.

First, "career best" taps into a person's talent or competencies. Competencies, as noted in Chapter 4, are skills and behaviors that a person performs well. Second, a "career best" experience tends to highlight what people are passionate about. Passions are things that we love to do, independent of how well we do them. Some love to sing in the shower, despite knowing they do not do it well. Third, a "career best" activity inevitably adds value to the organization. When people describe their job, they don't say, "I was very competent at doing this job, I loved to do it and nobody in the organization gave a hoot."

A basic requirement of a "career best" activity is doing something that is valued and provides benefit to the organization. According to Sandholtz, activities and jobs mentioned were frequently a "product of luck rather than planning." Rather than having planned out each stage in their career, individuals tended to say of their "career best" that they were "just in the right place at the right time."

THE COP MODEL

In an attempt to increase the frequency of career bests and make them more of a planned event rather than a stroke of luck, Sandholtz and Ron Cutadean came up with a model that describes the primary drivers of a "career best" experience.[4] We have adapted that model and call it the COP model, where C = Competencies, O = Organizational needs, and P = Passion. We display the COP model graphically using a Venn diagram with three intersecting sets, as shown in Figure 5.1.

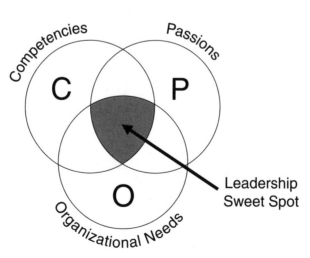

FIGURE 5.1   The COP model.

A leadership sweet spot occurs when there is an intersection of competencies (e.g., skills or behaviors a person performs well), organizational needs (e.g., outcomes that an organization values), and passions (e.g., activities people love to do).

Competencies

Competencies are those skills, behaviors, and abilities that a person does extremely well. Our research on the impact of strengths arbitrarily defines these as behaviors rated at the 90th percentile by other people. A competency can also be an area of knowledge or expertise. As you think about yourself and your abilities, some of these competencies are behaviors that you tend to be naturally good at, while others have been developed over years of steady growth and practice. They may be skills at casual conversation, writing, understanding complex problems, conceptualizing models, listening, giving direction, or staying calm under pressure. To understand your competencies you might ask yourself: When people talk about my strengths, what do they mention first? Where have I been successful in the past? What abilities do I seem to do better than others?

Organizational Needs

The "O" in the COP model stands for organizational needs. In order for leaders to be successful or for an individual to find the "leadership sweet spot," the competencies people have and the passion for what they want to do have to be valued by the organization. Typically, organizations value competencies and passions of individuals that have a fairly direct impact on the success of the organization. Many organizations seem to have a narrow set of competencies and passions that they value. People can argue about whether the organization "ought" to value particular competencies when it does not, but the fact remains that in order for people to find the "leadership sweet spot," there needs to be an intersection of competencies, organizational need, and passion.

Passion

Just because we have competence around a skill does not mean that we will have passion. I might have a great voice but decide that there is no future in singing, or I might detest getting up and performing in front of others. Competence, yes, but passion (I love to do this, I want to do this, doing this gives me a personal high), no. The result is an undeveloped competency. Passion and competence can function independently of each other. People's passions may be in sports but physically they are uncoordinated, slow, and weak. People in general have an interesting attitude about passions. They feel that what they love is naturally given to them. Some people seem to be controlled by their passions and rarely attempt to broaden them. Other people see that the things that we become passionate about can change over time. We can develop passions for things that we did not really like at one point in our lives.

To help understand your passions, Dalton and Thompson[5] suggest you might ask yourself the following questions:

- What do I really enjoy doing?
- What events bring me a great deal of personal satisfaction?
- Which activities energize me in such a way that they hold my interest? When do I lose all sense of time?
- What activities do I daydream about or imagine myself doing?

Research on People in the Sweet Spot

Contrasting people who are experiencing the sweet spot against others in the organization reveals substantial differences in both performance and attitude. Those who are in the sweet spot:

- Add more value than their colleagues
- Are ranked as higher performers
- Generally work more hours per week
- Are not looking for another job
- Are more engaged and motivated
- Are learning and developing new skills
- Are having fun . . . and are fun to work with

Barriers That Get in the Way of Finding Your Sweet Spot

Competency plus Organizational Needs but No Passion

In this situation (Figure 5.2) a person has the competence and the organizational need is present, but there is no passion for the job. This person will often feel bored, stuck, or "pigeon-holed." In this situation a person might have a job he has been working at for a long time; he has great competence, but he has been in his position for so long that he fails to see any challenge or excitement.

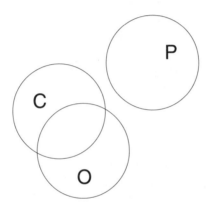

FIGURE 5.2   C + O, no P.

Organizational Needs plus Passion but No Competence

In this situation (Figure 5.3) a leader works in an organization that has a need and where the leader has a great deal of passion, but not a high level of competence. Passion and desire can never make up for competence. This person is sometimes viewed as incompetent, but more frequently he is viewed as average. In this situation the organization needs a particular competency, and the individual has a strong desire to attempt the competency but lacks the ability to do this skill with above average expertise. In our research we found several examples of this. One was an organization that engaged in upstream exploration for oil, and the organization's most prominent need was technical competence. The organization was composed of geophysicists, engineers, and geologists, who had extensive expertise and ability. Leaders who lacked the level of tech-

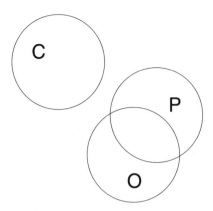

FIGURE 5.3   O + P, no C.

nical knowledge to "keep up" were often viewed as the poorest leaders.

Competence plus Passion but No Organizational Needs
In this situation (Figure 5.4) a leader has the right combination of competence and passion, but all are built around skills and competencies that are not needed in the organization. There is a fascinating philosophy that many people have that an organization ought to accommodate the needs and passions of an individual. Having coached people in this situation, they often respond with something

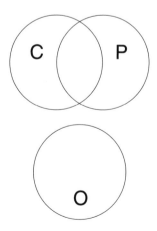

FIGURE 5.4   C + P, no O.

like, "Well, this company needs what I have to offer, but it is just too dense to understand and appreciate how I can contribute." This is a bad fit. Not every person is going to have a satisfying and productive career in every organization. Frequently, individuals get a job in an organization and when they discover that their contribution is not valued, they push back and try to change the organization in an effort to make things work. They assume that their inability to be successful in the organization says something about them. In reality, all it says is that the organization does not value their contribution. They feel like they are a failure rather than a bad fit. So often we see individuals who have struggled and been miserable in one organization move to a different organization, only to find themselves being valued, contributing, and making a real difference.

Using the COP Model
When your competence and passions intersect with organizational needs, the outcome is always positive for the individual and the organization. The individual is doing something he or she is competent at, and has energy or passion about the tasks to be accomplished. The organization is getting good results in return. Our research has helped us understand that some competencies are better at creating leverage and success in an organization. Chapter 4 shows the research on 16 key competencies that have a higher likelihood of leveraging overall leadership effectiveness. These 16 competencies provide a great deal of latitude in terms of selecting competencies that a person can develop into extraordinary strengths.

Organizational Competency Drivers
When there is an intersection of competence and passion with an organizational need, this creates an opportunity for an individual to show extraordinary leadership. Displaying exceptional skill on a competency where there is no organizational need fails to provide much clout in terms of leveraging leadership effectiveness.

Imagine that you are a member of a small team in a high-technology company that has the unpleasant task of downsizing a group of people by half. Each person is discussed. Strengths and areas of needed improvement are reviewed for each person. All of the people are selected for dismissal except one. It is difficult to choose between two employees. There is a fair amount of disagreement in the group about the two people. Finally, the person sitting next to you, who has been a strong advocate for keeping one of them, says, "She is a great pianist." What would be your response? Probably, you would say, "What difference does that make?" While being a great pianist is a very nice skill to have, unless it fills an organizational need it does not benefit you at work.

In this chapter we have avoided being prescriptive about skills that everyone needs to do well in order to be a great leader. Our advice is to build a high level of competence in three to five skill areas, balanced across the major areas of the tent we described in Chapter 3.

In researching the profiles of different companies it is apparent that different organizations have specific profiles that point to key competencies absolutely required in order to be successful. Organization profiles reveal one, two, or three dominant characteristics that tend to define a key competency for that organization. Doing well on this skill or competency places you in good company with most other members of the organization. However, doing exceptionally well on this competency does not tend to leverage overall leadership effectiveness. The reason for this is that everyone does the competency well so it is almost impossible to differentiate yourself from most others. Doing poorly on these competencies, however, would be a certain path to failure. These organizational competency drivers tend to hurt more than help. In order to be successful in an organization, it is critical for people to understand what these competencies are and to possess a reasonable level of skill in them.

What Organizations Value

An implication of the COP model is that in order to be successful in an organization, people need to combine their competencies with their passions and then find an organization that needs what they have to offer. In the same way that people come with different and unique personalities, so do organizations. No two are exactly the same. In the same way that we have courtships with a variety of different people to find the one that best fits our own personality, so should people find a match between themselves and the organization for which they work. Many people try to accommodate their own personal style and desires to the needs of an organization. While this can be done successfully, frequently this leads to frustration, job dissatisfaction, and failure to be promoted and advanced. Finding an organization where there is a good fit often allows people to truly excel.

Different Strokes for Different Folks

In the process of being external consultants, the authors had the opportunity to become acquainted with many different organizations. After years of executing successful projects in a variety of different organizations, our firm was invited to propose doing a project for a large health care supplier. One month earlier we had been asked to propose some work for a telephone company. The presentation was a winner; we received great reviews and were awarded the work. We modified the presentation slightly and presented essentially the same thing to the health care company. We didn't even have to wait for them tell us that we did not get the health care contract. By the end of the presentation it was evident. Evaluating our performance, we did not feel any differently about the quality of our presentation from one company to the next, but it was evident that the telephone company loved us and the health care company did not. After talking with other consultants, we came to realize that the difference was not us, but mostly within them. Again, let us reiterate that there was nothing wrong with the health care company. But the things that they valued, their style, and the way they thought about the project in question were completely different from ours. As a postscript to the story, we were later talking to another consultant who was familiar with the health care company because of other projects he had done with them. He commented, "You're just lucky they didn't hire you; you would have hated the project." It turned out that this consultant had a similar style to ours, and after completing his project he vowed never to work for them again.

After analyzing the results from 22 different organizations, we have identified some common organizational profiles. These profiles highlight the things that organizations emphasize as strengths. Frequently, an organization might have several of the strengths listed below bundled together.

One of the authors recently visited a large bank. Upon looking through their aggregated leadership assessment data it became evident that they were an "avoiding mistakes"/"customer emphasis" organization. Both issues were very strong and positive for 80 percent of the leaders. If you work for an organization that has a profile of being an execution organization, you need to be good at executing (e.g., getting projects done on time and within budget—no excuses). A mismatch hurts a person's chance of success, and everyone needs an environment where he or she has a reasonable chance to succeed.

ORGANIZATIONAL PROFILES OF PRIZED COMPETENCIES

Based on research on 22 different organizations, we found 13 profiles of competencies that may be valued by an organization. In most instances organizations had two or three of the characteristics that described what the organization valued, though one appeared to dominate. In an effort to help readers assess what their own organization values, here are some of the more pronounced organizational characteristics. The opportunity here is to judge the "goodness of fit" between what your organization truly values and your own pattern of competencies.

Technology Emphasis
In the technology organization, leaders need to be highly knowledgeable and viewed as having technical expertise in the core activity of the firm. Although you would imagine that these firms were high-tech companies, we have found this characteristic to be very strong in construction companies and natural resources organizations as well. In a technology organization people thrive on

technical knowledge and expertise. A frequent sign that you are in a technology company is that people often talk in code. New employees frequently need a translator to understand what people are saying. At HP the best technical experts were called "Grey Beards." These sages had spent their lives inside HP, developing new and exciting technical innovations. They were looked on as heroes in the organization.

Working in a pharmaceutical company with a strong research emphasis puts a high premium on understanding chemistry, molecular biology, and pharmaceutical science. Those lacking that technology background were perceived as "second class citizens."

Advantages.   This organization runs on cutting-edge technology. Leaders are expected to learn and stay abreast of the latest developments in their field. For people who enjoy technical challenges, this organization is extremely fulfilling. As a leader, people need to understand the technology and then combine that with other leadership competencies that make a difference.

Disadvantages.   In this organization the inherent belief is that you can solve any problem with technology. Here linear thinking can be carried to an extreme. A colleague worked for an oil company in Canada during the 1980s oil crisis. As the price for crude went up, their plan for exploration grew at the same rate. After reviewing an extremely large expansion plan and the personnel required to staff the project, my friend calculated that they would need to hire every geophysical scientist who graduated from every university in the United States and Canada in order to staff the expansion. His calculation did not faze the planners at all. The only thing that stopped the project was a change in the price of crude oil.

Excellent Execution
In this organization there is a substantial need to drive forward and achieve results, to get things done on time, to stay in budget and always make your numbers. Leaders enjoy challenging results, and they often run on adrenaline. There is constant energy in the air. People inevitably come to work early and stay late. This organiza-

tion attracts or encourages people who aspire to climb the corporate ladder of success. Goals are always aggressive and challenge everyone's abilities. Frequently these organizations have high rewards for the best performers and a process to constantly "weed out" the bottom 10 percent.

Advantages.   This organization moves fast, and change happens quickly. If people enjoy challenges and like to stretch themselves, this organization will fit them well. People who have high career aspirations can be very successful, and typically these organizations offer a great deal of movement and promotional opportunity. Employees from a company that had a strong reputation for being an execution organization would also indicate that their company was a good company to be from. Many employees had a 10-year plan: they would rise to a high-level position, cash in on their stock options, and then take a position with another company where the pace was not as quick but they would receive a competitive salary, and have less risk and less reward.

Disadvantages.   As with any great conquest, there are typically many dead and wounded. The reality is that if you don't keep up, you're out. Individual success is often a function of company viability and economic conditions. In a bull market with a great product, this can be extraordinary fun. But in a bear stock market, with a bad economy, these companies can become extremely harsh environments. People leave because there is often little loyalty.

A consulting firm was asked to do research for a company whose international executives were leaving the organization in high numbers. They were a strong execution company. The world was in the middle of a monetary crisis and the bonuses of the executives were based on profits in U.S. dollars. Every one of the executives was underwater in their stock options and their bonus plan. Their logic was simple: leave and go somewhere else to get a fresh start, rather than trying to dig out from under a compensation plan typical of an execution-focused company. There was no personal loyalty to senior executives. It was all "head" and very little "heart." So when the numbers worked out to make it better to leave, there was not a moment's hesitation.

Avoiding Mistakes

In this organization there is a critical need to do things right. Excellence, quality, and conformance to standards are the organizational bylines. However, the reward for taking on a new project or taking some initiative is not as great as the punishment for making a mistake. So there is an enormous emphasis on checking every written document two and three times. Presentations are rehearsed and re-rehearsed. Every column of figures is added and re-added to make sure there are no mistakes. This is a frequent phenomenon in organizations that have large corporate staffs. Their role often evolves into one of "cop," where the emphasis is on catching mistakes made by an operating company.

One of the authors was reviewing a presentation with a client to be presented before their chairman. After seeing the presentation, she said, "I have some feedback for you." "Great," I commented. Her feedback was, "You need to be a bit more buttoned up." At first I wasn't quite sure what she meant. "What do I need to do less of?" I asked. Her reply, "Don't ask so many questions. Just give the chairman the facts. And keep the presentation short. The more information we give the chairman, the greater the chance for his disagreeing with something you say."

The quality movement has created many organizations in which quality has permeated every aspect of the corporate culture. An additional aspect of some of these organizations is a reluctance to engage in innovation, risk taking, or creative thinking. The organization is run by policies and procedures. There is a great need for order and precision in the way things are done.

Advantages. Leaders take pride in order, deeply analyze every aspect of a project, and do high-quality work. Organizations that emphasize safety or quality standards often have this strength. If you enjoy order and doing things by the book, this organization will fit you well. Typically, people in these companies will be given extra time to polish and completely finish assignments. Getting 80 percent right is not a beneficial approach in these organizations. If a person craves predictability, this is the ideal company for her.

Disadvantages.   Frequently the organization is slowed down by bureaucracy and excessive details, and is frequently risk averse. People who like to operate in a fast and freer model should avoid these companies.

Customer Emphasis

Leaders are totally focused on satisfying customer needs and responding to their requests. Leaders take pride in knowing customers, working personally with them, and solving their problems. Customer interests are often placed before those of the employees or the shareholders. If there is ever a problem between a customer and an employee, the customer is assumed to be right and the employee wrong.

One of the authors thought he knew what it meant to be customer-focused, but then was asked to build an assessment tool for a company that was obsessed with customers. Some of the items that were created to assess the intensity of their desire to understand customers included:

1. Continually seeks information about customers' underlying or future needs?
2. Can describe the customer's business from the customer's viewpoint, not the company's point of view?
3. Spends enough time in the marketplace to understand the underlying, unmet needs of customers?
4. Makes other people get inside the customers' world?

A major part of leaders' evaluations were based on the results to these questions.

Advantages.   This company enjoys absolute clarity about what customers currently want and need. Typically, this organization is successful at generating a high level of customer loyalty and satisfaction. Many people inside truly enjoy serving customers. It gives an empowering feeling to the people inside.

In an analysis for an insurance company it was found that employees who reported success in being able to resolve customer problems were much less likely to quit their jobs. Not being able to fix customer problems made employees frustrated with their jobs. To be effective in a customer-focused company, people need to have a strong orientation toward service. Customers can be difficult and challenging. Exceptional customer service is rarely convenient or done without some additional effort. People who enjoy this work provide the services simply because they enjoy delighting a customer.

Disadvantages.   Leaders are so focused on pleasing the customer that they lose sight of internal operational issues and long-term direction. Some organizations find it impossible to say "no" to a customer, even when the request is unreasonable. And many organizations find it hard to define people or companies as "non-customers," because doing business with them is too expensive or difficult.

To enjoy this organization means that people have to love customers. Not all customers are enjoyable to work with, and to do this job well people have to accept the good with the bad. If you enjoy internal interaction rather than customer interactions, this may not be the ideal organization for you.

The Genteel Organization

Leaders in this organization focus on developing a kind and considerate organization. Confrontation never occurs. Serious issues are usually swept under the carpet. Performance reviews are avoided or couched in extremely gentle terms.

One of the authors recounts, "I was working in a company in Minnesota and asked an internal employee what it was like to work in the company. His response was, 'We are all Minnesota nice.' 'What is Minnesota nice?' I asked. The employee explained that people in the company were extremely polite with each other. They were always pleasant. They never said negative or demeaning things about other employees. After hearing all this I commented, 'Sounds like a great place to work,' to which the employee responded, 'It is, but you never know what people really think of you.'" Some organizations have created a culture that encourages people to play nice.

Advantages.   This organization is a genteel place to work. Employees are "Boy Scouts"—they are trustworthy, loyal, helpful, friendly, courteous, kind, obedient, cheerful, brave, clean, and reverent. Typically employees will stay with the organization for a long time. There is little unforced turnover.

Disadvantages.   Often candor is missing from this kind of an organization. Sometimes it is difficult for people to grow and progress in this organization because they need focused, tough feedback, but never get it. Conflicts rarely occur, and people conform rather than disagree. In a recent meeting of a trade association, a member of the board commented, "Our problem is that we are just like the companies we come from. These are all really nice companies where people are pleasant and considerate of each other. While I enjoy that a great deal, in order to move this association forward we need to confront some difficult issues and give each other some tough feedback. I am not sure we are up to the task." For people who like to play hardball, working in this organization can be a real challenge. Their career progression might be limited because they are too pushy.

The Candor Organization
Leaders in this organization "tell it like it is." Typically there is a strong feedback culture, in which feedback flows rather freely both up and down the organization. Those who thrive in this company need to be good not only at receiving feedback but also to be effective at giving others feedback. While listening to a conversation between two leaders in a candid organization, one author heard a leader comment that a direct report did an ineffective job of presenting her findings. The other leader immediately asked, "Did you give her that feedback?" "No." The other leader replied, "Well, then, you're in more trouble than she is."

Advantages.   You always know where you stand and what you have done right. A feedback-rich company can be a great organization that provides excellent learning and growth opportunities. If people have an open, accepting attitude about feedback, they will enjoy working for an organization such as this.

Disadvantages. Some people are not ready for this kind of honesty, on either the giving or the receiving end. Some people like to figure things out for themselves, and for them this type of organization can feel extremely invasive.

The Learning Organization

In a learning organization, people learn from mistakes rather than hiding them. Development of skills and talents is valued, and people are constantly looking for different or unique learning opportunities. There is typically a strong value for innovation. People are constantly collecting feedback and looking for a better understanding of what happened and why.

Advantages. In this type of organization it is permissible to make mistakes, but not okay if you don't learn from your mistakes. People are strongly focused on self-development and personal improvement. This organization gives people homework and it is important to get your homework done.

Disadvantages. The cost of development can be expensive, and employees typically expect regular and consistent development opportunities. These organizations can be a bit disorderly because people are always reinventing the wheel. If you have difficulty accepting new ideas and changing, this may not be a good organizational choice.

The High-Integrity Organization

Doing the right thing is valued by leaders in high-integrity organizations. There is a very strong emphasis on honesty and ethical behavior. Many voluntary organizations focused on noble causes have this strength. People have strong desires to promote the cause of the organization, and typically there is a high level of congruence among organizational members about what is appropriate and what is not.

Advantages. Integrity is a strong vocal value and is encouraged at all levels of the organization. Success is measured not only by getting results, but also by how you went about getting them.

Disadvantages.   It is tough to practice what you preach. Saying it and doing it are two different things. Some organizations set the bar so high that most leaders are viewed as hypocrites when they withhold information or change direction. Some organizations get too zealous about promoting their version of the "right thing." This organization enforces compliance from people to follow the leader. Make sure before joining an organization that is focused on doing the right thing that their belief about what is right squares closely with your belief.

The Fair Organization

One of the most frequent complaints coming out of organizations is that promotions and advancements are biased. Whether it is a "good old boy" network, a bias toward MBAs from certain schools or toward golfing buddies, this issue is frequently a source of dissatisfaction in many organizations. Organizations that have developed fairness as a key strength have figured out how to create an organization relatively free from bias. Leaders who have a strong desire to treat people with fairness learn to pay careful attention to their biases. Frequently these organizations have fewer levels and greater equity in pay and benefits. There is often a push to treat everyone the same rather than have one tier of benefits for people at one level and different benefits for those at another. These organizations eliminate executive parking and boondoggles along with a propensity to hire people of a certain gender, race, age, or school background.

Advantages.   Employees feel a strong positive feeling toward the company. These organizations are good places to work, with high commitment from employees. Frequently, employees will have long tenure with these organizations.

Disadvantages.   For individuals who enjoy getting ahead, these organizations become frustrating after a short stay. Some people want to be separated and enjoy having the opportunity to get twice the bonus as others. Sometimes the downside of fairness is that things are too fair and big performance differences are not noticed.

The Political Organization

The political organization is often referred to as a "good old boys" club. Politics and connections are among the most critical factors in determining who will be promoted and who will get a raise. For people who work in these kinds of organizations there is a fair amount of predictability. For those who know the rules and how to play the game, this organization can be a reasonably good place to work.

Advantages.   If you are one of the chosen few, this organization offers great opportunities. In order to succeed in this organization a person has to have a keen sense of politics and a willingness to play the political game.

Disadvantages.   If you are not one of the chosen few, this organization will be difficult for anyone trying to get ahead in his or her career. For people who don't enjoy playing politics, this is not a fun place to work.

Celebration Organization

The celebration organization is built on individual efforts and opportunities for rewards. Organizations with this strength find ways to reward people well for strong individual efforts.

Advantages.   For people with strong independent attitudes and a willingness to work hard, this organization offers unlimited opportunities.

Disadvantages.   Many of these organizations are multilayered sales organizations that are dependent on having exceptional products.

The Bureaucratic Organization

The bureaucratic organization has established strong bureaucratic processes and procedures and sticks to them. Many but not all government or utility organizations fit this model.

Advantages.   This organization is very predictable. It is great for people who love order and hate chaos.

Disadvantages.   Can be boring and unchallenging, but it's a job.

The Virtual Organization

The virtual organization is a new type of organization that is emerging. In these organizations, people are combined together to form a group, but work independently. The group may only meet together physically in a rented conference room, and the interconnection might be through a Web site. This organization attempts to leverage the power of the group, but each person acts as an independent entity.

Advantages.   Low overhead. Lots of independence. This provides the ultimate in freedom for the person who is self-disciplined.

Disadvantages.   Trying to get everyone focused can be a bit like herding cats. Working here requires a willingness to take risks. It also requires patience and flexibility. The virtual group needs to develop a high level of trust and a set of cultural values that keep the group working together. It can also be extremely lonely.

IMPLICATIONS

It is critical for leaders to understand their individual areas of competency, the things that bring them passion, and the needs of their organization. The "leadership sweet spot" that is the intersection of these three elements holds great promise for both individual and organizational success. It is rare to find a perfect match between individual competence and passion and organizational needs. We know that individuals can develop new competencies to fit the needs of an organization. We also know that organizations can change their culture, which requires leaders with different leadership competencies. We find the idea of the COP model compelling, but we also find people rationalizing the lack of intersection in their personal situations. Individuals will complain that the organization really ought to value what they do, and organizations are narrow-minded in terms of what they need. These rationalizations do not help the individual or the organization to become more successful. A key to success for leaders is to find their own personal "sweet spot." For each person there is something that he or she can do extremely well. There is a competency with which they can make an enormous contribution. The late Gene Dalton spent most of his career researching how people achieve success in their careers. He found that people who are successful are constantly focused on how they can make a contribution to the organization.[6] It may take time to develop a competency. Organizations need to be patient and assist with that individual development, but ultimately organizations need to be successful or they cease to exist. When an individual can provide an extraordinary competency that an organization needs, the only other component that is required is passion. This is the element that is most underrated and yet potentially the most critical part of the model. Love, desire, motivation, inspiration, and passion are in the final analysis the greatest differences between good leaders and great leaders.

C H A P T E R

GREAT LEADERS POSSESS MULTIPLE STRENGTHS

Most problems cannot be solved. Most problems can only be survived. And one survives problems by making them irrelevant because of success. It's amazing how many minor ills the healthy body can stand without any trouble. One focuses on success, especially on unexpected success, and runs with it.

Peter F. Drucker

One shining quality lends a luster to another, or hides some glaring defect.

William Hazlitt

The awareness of our strength makes us modest.

Paul Cézanne

AN APPROACH TO IMPROVEMENT

Imagine that you were working to improve your leadership effectiveness. To start the process you participate in a 360-degree assessment of your skills and competencies. The assessment is given to your boss, several peers, and direct reports. The results of the assessment are compiled and create the profile shown in Figure 6.1. The profile shows series of leadership competencies based on the assessments of others. For your convenience, each of the leadership competencies is sorted from the most positive competency to the least positive. This gives you a quick overview of your results. If this were your leadership profile, which issues would you select for

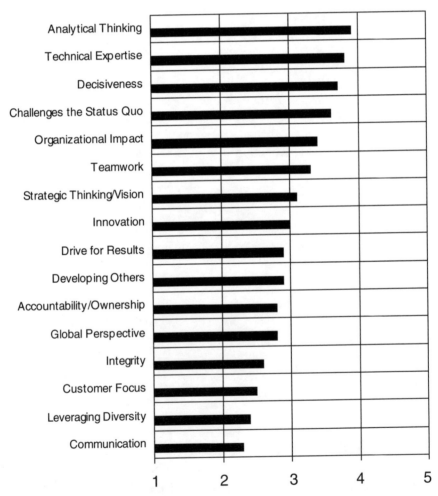

FIGURE 6.1   Sample feedback.

change? Mark the ones that would be your focus of attention for the next six months.

In this profile some of the leadership competencies are more positive than others, but nothing stands out as being extremely positive or negative. No competency stands out as either a profound strength or a terrible weakness. In our experience, when people get feedback like this they always seem compelled to focus their attention on the least positive items. Things that have been said earlier in this book may have prompted you to consider some of your strengths. But that would be an extremely rare event in the absence of receiving this apparently "counterintuitive" or contrarian message. Something in our culture says that you pass over the higher scores, and go directly to the lowest ones. In this example, one of the areas for improvement would likely be communications. Typical plans for change would have the person systematically tackle the lowest scores, get those fixed, and move on to the next lowest scores. That logic assumes that it is the areas of lower effectiveness that hurts this person's performance. People seem more satisfied with a fairly consistent profile, with all competencies at about the same level.

PHILOSOPHIES OF EFFECTIVENESS

Most people, whether consciously or unconsciously, adhere to a philosophy that their effectiveness is substantially hurt by lower performance in any area. The solution is, of course, to fix the weaknesses. This belief seems so dominant because it has to have been reinforced by our previous and current experiences. We are not certain of the genesis of this belief. Possibly it stems from our educational experiences. The recollection many have of school is a focus on what they did wrong. Think back. Can you remember taking a test and having the teacher or professor spend additional time emphasizing the answer that everyone in the class got correct? On the other hand, do you remember reviewing the answers the class got wrong? (You could argue that there is a certain logic to focusing on the problems missed, or the information that no one could recall.)

We argue, however, that time spent emphasizing the success people had would also have been extremely valuable.

Another explanation is that we all seek to be well-rounded, "Renaissance people." The assumption is that we should be good at everything. There is something inherently weak or inferior about acknowledging that there are some things I do well, and there are some things I don't even try to do. We admire the "iron man" who runs a marathon, swims 3 miles, and then rides a bicycle for another 50 miles.

Whatever the source, there is a pervasive belief that I should eliminate my weaknesses, and by so doing I will become a more effective person. In work situations, performance appraisals most often search for some deficiency. The approach of telling people some good news, then focusing on areas where they need development or improvement, and then finishing up with a positive comment or two is standard procedure in many organizations. (Is it any wonder that people begin to wince when they hear the positive comments, knowing that it is often the precursor to the important message of their deficiencies?)

It is perfectly understandable that managers who can give only 4 people out of the 20 in their group a superior rating will focus discussions on deficiencies rather than strengths. This provides the rationale for why some get a raise while others do not. If the manager were to focus only on positive issues and then give a "meets expectations" rating, that might be very confusing to the direct reports. Even those who get an "exceeds expectations" rating will often be provided feedback on areas where their skills are not quite as positive.

YOU'RE THE COACH

To understand this basic belief more objectively, we propose jumping to an entirely different realm. Imagine that you have agreed to be the soccer coach for a competition soccer team of 12-year-olds. You are excited to work with the team. After agreeing to be the coach, you learn that 20 children have signed up to try out for the team, but the team can only field 15 players. Because this is a competition soccer program, it is necessary for some children to be cut from the team. On the first day of practice you explain that you only have 15 slots on the team and that everyone is going to have to try out. Five will be cut.

You proceed to run the children through a series of drills. On each drill you select the two or three children who were superior and two or three who did not perform as well. After an hour of intensive drills, three-on-three "shoot-outs," and races, your roster becomes increasingly clear. Three of the children are clearly not at the same level. They should be moved to a less competitive league. Two additional children were close, but did not perform well on several of the drills.

Now comes the tough part. You make out your team list. You gather all the children together in a huddle and thank them for their effort. You tell them that you are proud of everyone and that it takes a lot of guts to try out for competition soccer. You then read off the names of the children who made the team. Fifteen children are elated. Five of the children look quite dejected, though they keep a "stiff upper lip." Luckily they have kind and supportive parents who bolster their children. As you begin to gather up the equipment and jerseys, one of the children who was cut approaches you with a dejected look. This was one of the two children who were close to making the team. She gets your attention and says in a quivery voice, "Coach, why was I cut? What can I do to play next year?" You desperately want to make this child feel better. You look at your notes. There was one drill where the child's name was jotted down as superior but then two others drills where the child did not perform well. What's the most constructive answer?

If you tell the child about what was done well, that makes her feel good, but starts her wondering even more, "Why was I cut?" The typical recommendation from most people on how best to approach this situation is to start with the positive, but then help the child understand that your decision was justified because of some failing on the child's part. Most coaches would describe the child's performance on the two drills where her performance was low. That will enable the child to understand that your decision was fair. A good way to close the conversation would be to say something like, "You are almost there, if you keep practicing I think that you will be playing competition soccer next year for sure."

As the child walks away and takes that long drive home with her parents, she will probably ask herself the question, "Why was I cut?" To which she will answer, "Because I blew it on two drills." In other words, failures come because of mistakes. But what would have happened if this child had been an extremely accurate kicker, or had been extremely good at playing goalie? Would the mistake on the two drills have been irrelevant?

The reality of this situation is that the child was cut because there were no outstanding strengths, and above that, her performance was poor on two drills. Which of those is more important? We think most coaches would overlook flaws on two drills if they saw tenacious determination and competitive spirit, or if they saw strong kicking ability or skill at playing goalie. The question here is not only what to tell the child about why she was not chosen this year, but more important, what to tell her about how best to prepare for next year.

Our belief is that emphasizing the child's weak performance on two drills is the wrong message. It would be far better to acknowledge that as of now you did not see important strengths, and that is what this child should work on in preparing for next year. What a terrible year it will be for her if her entire focus is on "not messing up on the drill." How much better it will be if her focus is on getting really good at some specific skills that make players valuable to the team. Most coaches are looking for raw talent and believe they can teach children to correct mistakes.

As they think about this short scenario, most people can replay hundreds of real-life situations about themselves from their own history that are very similar. Through this reinforcement and conditioning, people have come to the common belief that it is their mistakes, weaknesses, and poor performance on tasks that keeps them from being successful.

In our research we have found that in fact leaders with very negative ratings on competencies were perceived less positively overall. We call these problem issues fatal flaws. Fatal flaws need to be corrected. There is, however, a significant difference between fatal flaws and areas that are slightly less positive than others. Let us call these rough edges. A person performs at an adequate level. For many leaders we have noted their tendency to focus their efforts for improvement on rough edges, using the same logic as if it were a fatal flaw. Most people believe that lower-scoring competencies tend to hurt more than profound strengths help.

Look at Figure 6.2. Who do you believe would be perceived as being more effective as a leader? Surprisingly, in our research studies of over 8000 leaders, Person B was perceived to be more effective.

Most people are more concerned with eliminating any perceptions of weakness than they are focused on developing strengths. This approach is reinforced by organizational practices that punish people for either weaknesses or rough edges but frequently fail to encourage people to develop strengths.

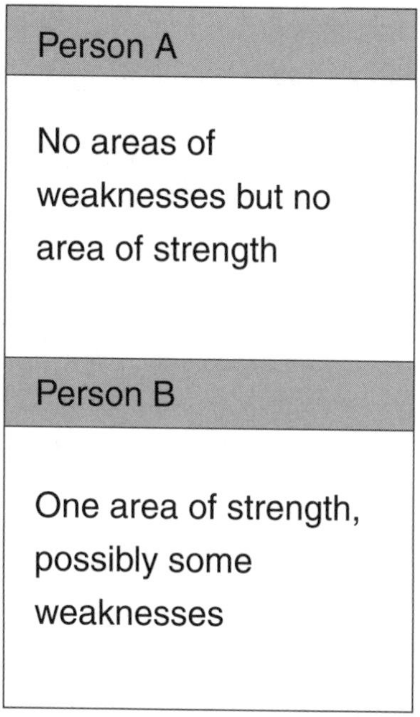

Person A
No areas of weaknesses but no area of strength
Person B
One area of strength, possibly some weaknesses

FIGURE 6.2   Person A versus Person B.

RETHINKING THE PERSONAL DEVELOPMENT PLAN

Look back at Figure 6.1. Let's reconsider the best development plan for this individual. Rather than drilling into the less positive scores and attempting to elevate them to a higher level, we strongly contend that this person would be far better off selecting three of the higher scores and striving to push them to the highest quartile. Doing that will propel this person's career forward far more sure-footedly and rapidly than trying to fix the lower scores.

What Is a Strength?

A strength is something we do well. The question is how well. Many managers seem satisfied when the results of a 360-degree assessment show slightly above-average scores on all competencies. But that same person would be highly disappointed if her child came home from school with all C+'s on his report card.

In our research we found a dramatic effect that strengths could have on the overall perception of a leader's effectiveness. That effect was present only when a competency stood out. Leaders with a variety of competencies that were positive but with none that stood out did not show that same impact on overall leadership effectiveness.

In a relative sense we have defined strengths in most of our studies on leadership as a skill or competency at the 90th percentile. In an absolute sense we define a strength as a 4.5 or higher rating on a 5-point scale. This rating requires at least 50 percent of the responders to mark the most positive response and the others to mark the next most positive response. If any lower evaluations are given, then a majority of the responses on a 5-point scale need to be the most positive response.

Impact of Strengths

To understand the impact of strengths and weaknesses on overall leadership effectiveness, we researched results of assessments from 2000 leaders and followed that with a second study of over 6000 leaders. The results of the two studies were remarkably consistent.

When asked, "What would you guess the overall effectiveness percentile would be for people with no strengths?" most people indicated they thought it would be approximately the 50th percentile. Figure 6.3 shows the results.

In our studies, leaders who had no perceived strengths were, on average, rated at the 34th percentile. Possessing no strengths plunges you to the bottom third in terms of perceived overall leadership effectiveness.

Why were leaders with no area of strength perceived on average to be in the bottom third for overall leadership effectiveness? They lack a redeeming quality, skill, or ability. They may not be ineffective at anything, but they also are not terribly effective at anything.

Figure 6.4 shows the results for leaders with one strength. It is impressive that leaders with one strength move from on average the 34th percentile to the 64th percentile. Imagine, a 30 percent increase just for possessing one strength! This shows the powerful influence of being good at any one competency. Consider a hypothetical situation where you are asked to choose between hiring two employee candidates. Candidate A has no areas of weakness but nothing stands out as a strength. Candidate B has a few minor weaknesses but a

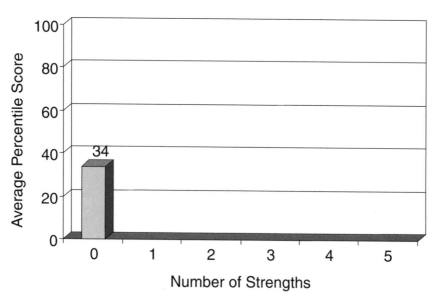

FIGURE 6.3   **Average percentile score 1.**

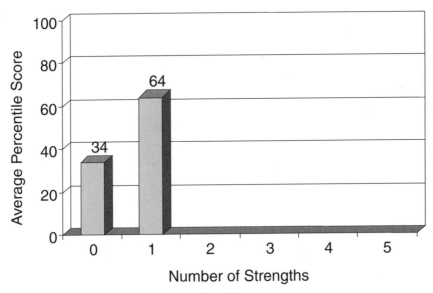

FIGURE 6.4   Average percentile score 2.

profound strength in an area critical to accomplishing the job. Whom do you hire? Most people admit that the candidate with the strength would most likely be more successful. The data in our studies clearly demonstrate the profound influence of having one thing that you do extraordinarily well. This is also consistent with the research about leaders presented in Figure 6.2.

Figure 6.5 shows the influence of having multiple strengths. Note that the results in Figure 6.5 show that leaders with three strengths are at the 81st percentile on average.

Leaders with five strengths are at the 91st percentile. When we have challenged leaders to move from the 50th percentile to the 90th percentile, their response was most often that it seemed impossible. Their perception was that they needed to be perfect in almost every competency in order to be at the 90th percentile. That clearly is not so, but it is a hard concept for many to absorb. To be at the 90th percentile simply required a leader to be highly skilled at five competencies! This seems achievable to most aspiring leaders.

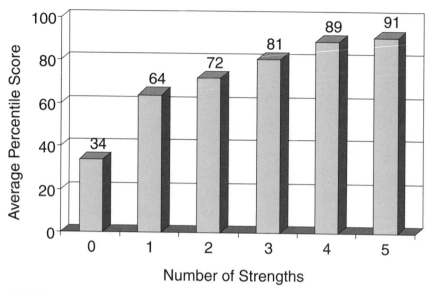

FIGURE 6.5   **Average percentile score all.**

After presenting this research at a conference with participants from a variety of companies, one of the conference participants asked one of the authors the following question: "What is the most significant finding from your research?" The answer given was a bit academic, carefully including many of the various insights covered in this book. The participant's response was, "No, that stuff is all important, but the thing that is most impressive is your research on the impact of strengths on overall effectiveness." The participant went on to explain his answer: "When I saw the research that showed the impact leaders can have on bottom-line results I was both impressed and depressed—impressed that the impact occurs and depressed because I thought there was no way to develop those kinds of leaders. Those leaders are born, not made. Then you showed me the strength research. When you understand the key to being at the 80th percentile is having three strengths, it seems possible. Developing four strengths also seems possible for a large number of our people. It also seems clear to me that our managers have invested all their energy in trying to fix a nit here and there rather than concentrating on developing three strengths."

How Much Should I Bite Off?

If a person has a strategy for personal improvement that relies on incremental improvement of weak areas and moving all competencies to higher and higher levels, this seems like an overwhelming, maybe impossible task. Our research indicates that people can only be successful at change if they focus efforts on change in a few areas. We recommend a maximum of three areas of improvement at any one time.

The Wrong Change Strategy

When you adopt a personal change strategy that focuses efforts for change on three competencies this year (which are incrementally improved), three next year, and so on, the strategy for change would take 15 to 20 years to slowly move each competency to more positive levels. If one believes that it is weak areas that will inevitably hurt you and that a strength pushed to an extreme becomes a weakness, then this change strategy makes sense. But the reality is that this strategy will not help leaders move from good to great. The process takes too long and the effort required is too high for this strategy ever to pay off.

Can Strengths Be Pushed Too Far?

We examined our data to see if we could confirm the assumption held by many, that strengths pushed to an extreme become a weakness. Nothing in our data confirmed this commonly held belief. We do know from our analysis that building some strengths requires balancing some competencies against others.

For example, managers who have a very strong results focus but a very low people focus will never achieve the maximum results because they will not capture the trust and respect of those they lead. However, to advise people to back off their focus on results and focus only on people is not the solution to better leadership. The key is to do both behaviors extremely well. Doing one behavior well does not inhibit doing the other well, but the two competencies do require different skills. Our research bore out that having strengths in "Focus on Results" and "Interpersonal Skills" created an extremely powerful combination of competencies. Both were then viewed as strengths. These competencies utilized simultaneously catapulted people to even higher levels of overall effectiveness. Finally, none of our research hinted that backing off from any strength ever led to increased overall effectiveness.

POWERFUL COMBINATIONS

Brett Savage, a long-time colleague and senior consultant with BT.Novations, told the secret of his success playing high school football. Brett was 6 feet 4 inches tall, fairly slender, and a strong runner. Brett's physical appearance was more like that of a basketball player than a football player. But Brett had another talent: he could catch anything thrown anywhere close to him. At 6 feet 4 inches, Brett towered over the defensive backs who attempted to cover him. His success in football came from a simple play. Brett played the end position. He would sprint out for a pass, get to his predetermined destination, and the quarterback would throw the pass high. Brett would jump to catch the pass, but no defender could come close to the ball, because the defenders could not touch him while the pass was being thrown without drawing a penalty. There was little they could do but wait for him to catch the ball, and then they would tackle him. The strategy was flawless, and as Brett explained his success he said, "The combination of height and good hands was powerful."

When considering strengths and the impact of combinations of strengths on leadership, we were interested to see if the most effective leaders had consistent combinations of competencies. To research this (see Figure 6.6), we examined leaders who had excellent interpersonal skills (e.g., this competency in the top quartile) but were not rated as excellent in terms of focus on results. We then looked at the leaders who were at the 90th percentile in terms of their overall leadership effectiveness. Only 9 percent were at the 90th percentile. We then looked at leaders who were in the top quartile for focus on results but were not exceptional on interpersonal skills. In this case 13 percent of these leaders were at the 90th percentile in terms of their overall leadership effectiveness. We then studied

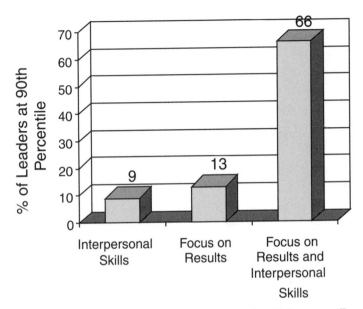

FIGURE 6.6   Percentage of leaders at the 90th percentile.

those leaders who were in the top quartile for both focus on results and interpersonal skills. In this case, 66 percent were at the 90th percentile in terms of their overall leadership effectiveness. Clearly, this is a powerful combination. Both skills are valuable and lead to success, but the combination of being excellent at both skills together substantially increased the probability of overall effectiveness.

This research led us to the conclusion that it is not strengths that hurt a person's effectiveness, but strengths standing alone without counterbalance. That is what creates the perception of a strength pushed too far becoming a weakness.

Powerful combinations do not require that people back off one competency in order to do another well. The secret to building success as a leader is to be excellent at powerful combinations of skills. We have found that there are many such powerful combinations. The more differentiated the combination, the more potentially powerful is the combination.

The effect of powerful combinations is to erect and lengthen the tent poles that lift the overall leadership tent to new heights.

Ten Powerful Combinations

1. The first powerful combination is giving others performance feedback and building trust. Having the ability to give people straightforward and candid feedback is a wonderful skill. Feedback, however, is not always accepted. A powerful combination is having the ability to provide feedback and also being trusted by others. If others have trust, then their assumption is typically that the feedback is given to help them. Without trust, feedback is often perceived as self-serving on the part of the giver of the feedback.

   Another closely related powerful combination involves trust and the ability to persuade others. Persuasion without trust is shameless selling. It is preaching in hope of gathering converts. When people are trusted, their ability to persuade others to accept their position increases substantially.

2. A second example is a combination of the competencies of interpersonal skills and listening. In our research on behaviors that differentiated high- and low-performing leaders we found that listening was not a behavior that was an effective differentiator. High performers were not much better at listening than poor performers. Listening, however, can be a very beneficial skill when combined with other interpersonal skills. We found a powerful combination between a person's listening behavior and the perception by others that the leader had good interpersonal skills. Typically, people with good people skills have the ability to be considerate of others, to be friendly and show concern for others' situations. Many people, when trying to act with consideration or be friendly, are only seen as being fake. A key to consideration is having the ability to really listen to others and carefully understand others' issues and situations.

3. The third example combines the competency of inspiring and motivating others with technical knowledge. Many people have a strong desire to influence others. This is a critical skill that leaders need. We found that a powerful combination was the "ability to influence" combined with being "well informed." Many people attempt to influence others without having done

their homework. They don't understand the issues well enough to articulate their position. Many people feel that they will be able to influence based on their charm and good looks. Unfortunately, this rarely works. What works is intelligently explaining the issues and providing rationale for others to follow your position.

4. A fourth pair combines competency in connecting with the outside world and inspiring and motivating others. Another problem with influencing others comes when people have been too insular in terms of their focus. They understand the position or the commonly held view of insiders, but lack insight outside the company or organization. Frequently there is arrogance about knowing more about what customers want than customers know themselves. Those with a clear understanding of the outside world and a knowledge of what customers want can combine that knowledge with the ability to influence others and thus leverage their leadership ability.

5. Another powerful pair is a combination of technical expertise and innovation. In many organizations, having strong technical expertise is a valued competency. Innovation is also an important skill. A powerful combination is innovation combined with strong technical expertise. Technical expertise and knowledge are not of much use unless they are put to work. Those who can come up with innovative ideas and solutions to problems show the ultimate application of their technical knowledge.

6. The next pair combines developing strategic perspective with innovation. Another power combination with innovation is the combination with strategic perspective. Those who combine a clear strategic perspective with innovative ideas create better strategies. The combination is powerful because without it a person's perspectives might be strategic, but neither new nor innovative.

7. Our research showed another powerful combination of two competencies: teamwork/collaboration and developing others. A key skill for leaders is their ability to develop others. One of the problems that can occur in developing others is that leaders can appear to pay more attention to one person's develop-

ment than to another's. Then the leader is perceived as playing favorites. Combining the ability to develop others with the ability to build a strong and unified team solves this problem and creates a developmental environment for everyone. This creates a positive organizational climate.

8. This combination links focus on results with communicating powerfully and prolifically. The ability to get others to achieve excellent results is always a valued skill. A powerful combination involves the ability to communicate powerfully and prolifically combined with the ability to focus on results. A key issue in achieving extraordinary results is helping people know where, how, and when, and having that message delivered in multiple formats and time frames. Great leaders typically need to learn to communicate.

9. The ninth combination links teamwork/collaboration with establishing stretch goals. Many people think that the way to have a positive experience as a team is to create a pleasant and calm work environment. Yet as people think about teams that they have valued, they most often select a team that accomplished a significant goal: a team that won a championship, accomplished an impossible goal, or did something that was above and beyond the call of duty. A powerful combination is teamwork combined with high standards and stretch goals. The combination creates a team on a noble mission. Missions bring people close together and help form friendships. A team with a calm and pleasant work environment may be only a country club.

10. The last combination combines the strategic perspective competency with problem-solving/analytical skills. Having strategic perspectives is an important leadership competency. A powerful combination is combining strategic perspective with problem-solving ability. Without problem-solving ability a leader with strategic perspective may have the ability to understand the strategy, but with a strong problem-solving ability this evolves into the skill to create new strategies. Strategies are in essence only solutions to problems about how companies compete and win.

THE HALO EFFECT

As we noted in Chapter 4, a halo effect occurs when our perceptions of others are distorted either positively or negatively. After studying results from thousands of leaders, it became evident that strong positive and negative halo effects occur. Results for the best leaders showed that the perceptions of others rated almost all competencies at the 90th percentile (they can do no wrong). Results for the worst performers showed that the perceptions of others rated almost all competencies at the 10th percentile (they can do no right). We have come to believe that both are a distortion. When leaders perform extraordinarily well on a few behaviors, they begin to be viewed in a very positive light, and others' impressions of them on other competencies tend to be distorted in a positive direction. The opposite effect seems to occur for those with a few profound weaknesses. Consider our day-to-day experience with people who have achieved some measure of fame. How many times have you been disappointed to hear a speech by a star athlete? Why did you believe that he would have something insightful or even interesting to say? Just because a person performs an athletic feat well does not mean that he has the ability to speak, write, or communicate well. The notion of product endorsement by famous people provides validation for the impact of the halo effect. Having a famous person endorse a product creates more sales of that product. This is the direct impact of the halo effect. We see the effect on the negative side when we demonize people who have made serious mistakes.

The halo effect is very real, and everyone has experienced its impact. The important issue for leaders is to get this effect to work for you rather than against you. We believe the key to getting the halo effect to work for you is to build up a few profound strengths. L. A. Festinger wrote a book called *The Theory of Cognitive Dissonance*.[1] In the book he describes the idea that people have a different set of beliefs or knowledge elements to which they hold. A belief might be as simple a thought as "I like ice cream," or "My manager is a terrible leader." Dissonance is created when there is psychological conflict between different beliefs (i.e., "My manager is a terrible leader" and "My manager is very good at solving complex and difficult problems"). Through hundreds of experiments, Festinger and other researchers have demonstrated that when dissonance occurs people will do whatever is necessary to reduce the dissonance. When leaders improve their abilities on a few competencies, this can create dissonance in the minds of others. Other people ask themselves, "How can this leader be so effective on some things but less effective on others?" The tendency is for others to close the gap on the dissonance, and typically this involves a positive halo effect for leaders who develop extraordinary strengths.

The implication of the halo effect is that when strengths are pushed to higher levels, the halo effect tends to push up competencies that are not as positive. This creates a fairly level profile. For those who worry that they need to improve on their weaknesses because that is what their manager will focus on in performance discussions, the halo effect can help them. Rather than trying to incrementally improve a few less positive issues, focusing efforts on substantial improvement in a few key strengths will create a positive halo effect in the way a person's manager perceives him. A few less positive issues fail to show up because of the presence of a few profound strengths. Most managers focus on less positive issues when they fail to see any real strengths that draw their attention. The extraordinary strengths are the keys to guaranteeing promotions, bonuses, stock options, and high performance appraisals for two reasons. First, those strengths help to produce tangible results. Second, they create a powerful "halo" that settles in around the person.

Fatal Flaws Must Be Fixed

The bearded lady at the circus said, "Everybody's got something wrong with them. With me, you can tell what it is."

Richard Needham

Maturity is coming to terms with that other part of yourself.

Ruth Tiffany Barnhouse

MAGNIFYING STRENGTHS TO THE FULLEST has been one of the main messages so far. In doing so, we may have implied that weaknesses should never be the focus of a personal development plan. If that is the case, it should be corrected. In many cases, focus on a weakness is absolutely the correct thing to do.

A NATURAL PLACE TO BEGIN

As we have already observed, people challenged to improve their leadership effectiveness or, for that matter, effectiveness at almost anything, have an amazingly similar plan for improvement.

- Step 1: Assess areas of strength and weakness. Being really good or even moderately good at something means you don't have to worry about it, so immediately look at your low scores.
- Step 2: Decide which weakness is most significant, usually because it has the lowest score.
- Step 3: Develop some plan of action to fix the weakness.

In fact, in some cases, working on a weakness is the best approach to improving. Those cases involve a category of attributes that we will call fatal flaws.

FATAL FLAW PROFILE

Suppose that the profile in Figure 7.1 was an assessment of your leadership effectiveness as reported by your subordinates. The profile shows their perceptions of your effectiveness on a variety of leadership competencies, A through P. The longer the bar, the greater your perceived effectiveness.

Competency J is perceived by others as an area of significant weakness, and for the sake of illustration, suppose item J is "Capable of learning from mistakes." An extremely low score on this dimension is a fatal flaw. In our research we found that people with this profile, if they improve their behavior on item J, will experience a dramatic improvement overall in the way their subordinates perceive them. That improvement lifts everything with it. If the fatal flaw is not corrected, it will act as a drag on the overall perception of leadership effectiveness. It is impossible to prove, of course, but we believe that even one extremely low score has a negative halo effect. The extremely poor performance in the one competency drags down the perceptions on all other competencies.

Frederick was the director of research for an international pharmaceutical company. A brilliant chemist, he towered over others in his grasp of the technical aspects of the research process. But his personal manner was curt and abrupt. He cut people off in meetings. He rejected suggestions or ideas for procedures that were not his own.

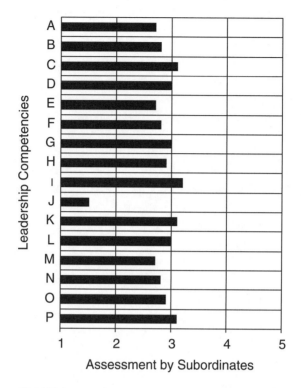

FIGURE 7.1   Sample assessment of your leadership effectiveness.

The other disciplines of molecular biology, pharmaceutical science, and clinical medicine felt that he failed to listen to their input. After extensive feedback from other people and through surveys, Frederick began to change the way he treated others. Making changes in this one specific arena caused his overall ratings to escalate to much higher levels. Conclusion: If you have a fatal flaw—fix it.

The Puzzling Evidence about Fatal Flaws

An analysis of our data reveals five patterns of behavior that consistently lead to a failure in leadership. Possessing one or more of these virtually makes it impossible for a person to be perceived as an effective leader.

The conventional wisdom is that a lack of integrity or honesty is the classic fatal flaw. Indeed, we still believe that to be true. When people talk of the qualities they most admire, the most frequently noted characteristics are honesty, integrity, being a "straight shooter," saying what you really think, and never fudging the truth to please the group you are with.

What was surprising in our study of hard data regarding business and public-sector leaders was the virtual absence of leaders perceived as lacking honesty and integrity. In fact, there were so few cases of that, we have no objective way to analyze and discuss it. We can only assume that dishonest leaders who survive over time are a decided rarity, and are hopefully moving to complete extinction. Nevertheless, it is obvious from cases like Enron and Arthur Andersen that dishonesty exists and sometimes infects senior executives and other managers.

Five Fatal Flaws That Consistently Lead to Failure in Leadership

1. Inability to Learn from Mistakes

There is an extremely interesting body of research on derailed executives. Morgan McCall, Jr., and Michael Lombardo have written extensively regarding executives who were expected to go all the way to the top of their organizations, but who got derailed. These researchers compared those who were derailed to those whose careers took them to senior positions in their firms. Their findings contain some extremely valuable lessons. Derailed executives made about the same number of mistakes as those whose careers continued onward and upward, but derailed executives did not use setbacks or failure in an assignment as a learning experience. They hid their mistakes from others, not alerting colleagues to the consequences of how their mistake would affect the colleagues' activities. They did not take immediate steps to rectify what they had done. Finally, they tended to brood about the mistake, constantly reliving it for years afterward.[1]

Those whose careers continued to soar did exactly the opposite. They readily acknowledged what happened to those about them, alerted colleagues to the potential consequences, did their best to fix it, and then proceeded to forget about it and move on in their career. Our research confirms that the inability to learn from mistakes is the single biggest cause of failure.

We can only speculate about the reasons for this. Is failure to learn from mistakes a symptom of not being willing or able to face reality, because it is painful? Or is it symptomatic of arrogance and unwillingness to move across the emotional hurdle to accept the fact that "I" did something wrong? Or do these people genuinely not recognize the serious consequences of what they have done? ("That problem I had was no big deal. It doesn't really matter.") Or is it because they have never learned the skill of objectively analyzing their own behavior?

We know the reasons differ among people, but little research has been done on why some people learn from past experience, while others seem destined to repeat the same mistake over and over.

An executive with a brilliant mind and many accomplishments had one fatal flaw. He made quick decisions about people, dismissing some as being incompetent after a 20-minute interview. Others were tagged as his "A" team because of one thing they had done or said. No amount of subsequent disconfirming information would change his mind. He selected one executive as his VP of Finance. Countless people in the organization warned the CEO of this person's reputation for backstabbing and sinister political behavior. Worse yet, this behavior was exactly opposite from the culture the CEO was espousing that he wanted to create—a culture of openness, innovation, and trust. The pattern of hasty promotion decisions continued to other key appointments, with one mistake after another. Finally the VP of Finance was successful in ousting the CEO, through an end run to the board. Several people commented, "We tried to tell him, but he would not listen."

2. Lack of Core Interpersonal Skills and Competencies
This failure comes from two sources—sins of commission and sins of omission.

Sins of Commission.   When leaders are abrasive, insensitive, browbeating, cold, arrogant, and bullying, this is a sure pattern that leads to failure in today's world. That behavior was tolerated 50 years ago, but seldom today. This cluster of behaviors, which could be called interpersonal ineptness, is a major factor in the downfall of leaders. In the Human Resources profession there has been the saying, "We hire people for their technical competence and fire them for their interpersonal incompetence."

No amount of other talent and ability is capable of surmounting this deficiency. No combination of intelligence, hard work, business acumen, and administrative skills covers over this lack of interpersonal skills. Being interpersonally inept inevitably sinks leaders.

Sins of Omission. We are often stunned to see the number of people in middle management positions in organizations who lack the most rudimentary of social skills. These basic human skills include:

- When you talk to people, look them in the eye.
- Learn and use people's names.
- When talking with people, say or do things that let the other person know you are listening and understanding.
- Do not dominate the conversation and take all the "air time."
- Sincerely inquire about others' ideas and activities.
- Laugh at others' jokes and attempts at humor.
- Praise others' hard work and efforts in furthering a good cause.
- Smile when meeting and greeting other people.

Many aspiring leaders fail to use these extremely fundamental interpersonal skills. Furthermore, these skills become the basic platform for the skills of leading group discussions designed to identify and resolve problems, giving and receiving feedback, coaching, making powerful presentations, and running effective work-team meetings.

3. Lack of Openness to New or Different Ideas

The third cause of failure is rejecting suggestions from subordinates or peers, insisting on doing things the same old way, and being generally closed to new thinking. This is a major turnoff for subordinates. It produces two negative consequences.

One is the impact on subordinates. People feel ignored, their ideas unappreciated and their contribution undervalued. This unwillingness to consider new ideas also creates a stultifying climate of stagnation. People's development is seriously curtailed. Morale degenerates, and turnover under such leaders escalates.

A second consequence is that good ideas and solutions fail to get implemented. The organization becomes stuck. Because good ideas are squelched, people stop thinking about better ways to do things. The organization misses out on improvements that come from accepting new ideas from multiple sources. The total quality movement verified that the best ideas for process improvements came from the people who were working directly in that arena, not from experts from the outside.

Many consulting firms have developed a successful practice by interviewing employees and seeking their opinions about the serious issues the organization faces, and what they would recommend as solutions. These ideas are then combined, bound into an expensive leather-bound report, presented to upper management, and the consulting firm then presents a hefty bill to the company for their services. The fact of the matter is that the employees would have been willing to tell the executives exactly the same things, had they been asked. In fact, according to many we talk with, they have usually tried to pass on those messages, but no one was listening. Companies could improve the level of commitment of their workforce, get excellent ideas for improvement, and save a good deal of money if they would seek answers from their own people. Not doing so is a fatal flaw of leadership.

Many of us have worked for leaders whose automatic response to every idea or suggestion was a negative one. One company describes these people as their "abominable 'no' men." It is impossible to calculate the damage such a person does inside an organization, measured either in the number of good ideas that get permanently squelched, or by the number of talented people who permanently exit the organization, completely turned off by this leader's behavior.

The one thing worse than a leader who constantly says "No" is the leader who pretends to listen, and then does nothing about it. Pretending to listen raises the hopes of the employee, and these hopes are dashed when no action is taken.

Leaders are often beset by twin demons—arrogance and complacency. The belief that your ideas are superior to everyone else's is an ultimate expression of arrogance. Unwillingness to listen to others' ideas and experiment with them is a further expression of arrogance. These leaders feel threatened by good ideas coming from others. Maybe they grew up with the mistaken assumption that because you have a formal title or role as the manager or director, that means you should have answers to all problems and that ideas for changes should all emanate from you.

Ralph was a senior executive in the research division of a semiconductor company. When anyone had an idea that was revolutionary or outside the normal way of doing things, they would go see Ralph. We asked why he thought that was the case, and he was exceedingly clear about the reasons. "I don't ever discourage a new idea. Ideas are tender and need to be nourished. So I ask lots of questions and give the person encouragement to pursue it, unless I'm positive it won't work. If I have the slightest belief it could succeed, I am enthusiastic about it. Over the years, that's paid off in some remarkable advancements."

4. Lack of Accountability

The leader who does not assume complete responsibility for the performance of a work group is bound to fail. One of the key qualities that sets a leader apart from others is mindset. The leader moves beyond feeling responsible only for his or her own performance and productivity and is concerned about the performance of the work group. This is one of the key elements separating a Stage II "individual contributor" from a Stage III leader. Stage II people feel responsible for their personal productivity and performance, but Stage III leaders expand that to the entire group. Should they fail to assume that sense of accountability for the entire group, they fail as leaders.

Accountability or feelings of responsibility can be defined in four major categories:[2]

1. Behavior with subordinates
2. Behavior with upper management

3. Behavior with other groups

4. Personal attitudes and values

Following is an analysis of each of the four categories.

1. Behavior with Subordinates

- The leader takes complete charge of the group, never shirking decisions by wishing to remain "one of the group." The effective manager defines performance goals, and does not relieve individuals of their own responsibility.

- The responsible leader passes praise and credit along to subordinates. The leader neither takes personal credit for things that were produced by others, nor takes credit for things produced by the team.

- The leader is willing to terminate poor performers when necessary, understanding that the performance of the group is more important than salving the feelings of one person.

2. Behavior toward Upper Management

- Accepts criticism for mistakes, and buffers the group from excessive criticism.

- Ensures that the group meets expectations of upper management. The responsible leader discovers exactly what is expected, and tenaciously makes sure that the unit produces to those expectations.

3. Behavior with Other Groups

- Responsible leaders do not let anything fall in the cracks between their group and another, whether inside the firm or an external supplier. Instead of shrugging their shoulders and saying, "It is not my responsibility," the responsible leader says, "If it is not someone else's clear responsibility, then we'll do it."

4. Attitude of the Responsible Leader

- The accountable leader strongly identifies with the group, so that the group's success is his or her success. This means putting organizational goals ahead of personal ambitions, and putting the welfare of the total organization ahead of their own department or unit. The accountable leader does things for which there may be no immediate reward, but does them because they are the right thing to do and will help the organization in the long run. The irresponsible leader does only those things for which there is an immediate reward. Finally, the responsible leader uses the organization's resources as it they were his or her own.

- The accountable leader places more emphasis on acting responsibly than on their desires for power and authority. In *Management: Tasks, Responsibilities, Practices*, Peter Drucker states, "Management has no power. Management has only responsibility." It has authority only as long as it performs and even then only enough to discharge its responsibilities.[3]

One point deserves special emphasis. Being accountable describes the appropriate behavior when the performance of the work group is going well and when it goes badly. We have all seen the leader who accepts the credit when things go well, but should the group's performance falter, points the finger to subordinates who have not performed their duties properly.

That is exactly the opposite of what effective leaders do. When things are going well, the effective leader ensures that the praise is given directly to the people on the firing line. The leader brings them into meetings and has them interact directly with the senior members of the organization. These leaders invite subordinates to make presentations on the team's success to other departments or to senior executives. And if things are not going well, they accept complete responsibility and never pass the blame to subordinates. The buck stops there.

Accepting responsibility also means pushing the people senior to them in the organization to make needed, timely decisions. One of the hallmarks of responsible behavior is when the workgroup is being held up by the lack of approvals or decisions from people above. In that circumstance, acting accountably and responsibly means taking what some might see as a risk, and pressing for decisions to get made.

5. Lack of Initiative
The fifth "fatal flaw" is the failure to make things happen. It is the lack of producing results, driven by the fact that the leader does not

initiate action. Not making a significant dent in the overall performance of the group drives a huge nail in the aspiring leader's coffin. Leaders must make things happen. Lack of initiative is totally the opposite of what the organization needs and expects.

One measure of a leader's effectiveness is the number of initiatives he or she personally champions. What projects has this leader started? What outcomes have this leader's fingerprints all over them? What has happened that would not have occurred, had this leader not been present?

The leader with initiative stops to consider the current reality and asks questions such as:

- What is missing that would make a big difference?
- What needs to be done that only I can do?
- What could I do that would make a significant difference to the performance of this work team?
- What are others expecting me to do?
- What one thing could occur that would make a significant difference to the performance of this group?

Then the leader with initiative takes steps to make those things happen. His is a totally different mindset from the leader who waits and responds to events after they happen. The image that best describes it may be that of a surfer. If the surfer gets positioned in front of the wave, the consequence is a wonderful ride into shore. But if the surfer is a fraction of a second too slow and behind the wave, he simply bobs up and down in the ocean and waits for the next wave. Getting out in front requires real effort and initiative.

What the Five Fatal Flaws Have in Common

As we study these five patterns of behavior, three things stand out. First, each is extremely obvious. They are observable by anyone with even the most casual of connections to the leader in question. Everyone close to these leadership behaviors feels their impact (or in this case, their lack of impact). No one is immune. They have a huge influence on the organization, because the leader has an enormous "ripple" effect in the organization.

Second, these five fatal flaws tend to be mostly "sins of omission." Each case is marked primarily by an inability to do something. It is defined by failure to initiate activities, not discovering the causes of failure, ignoring obvious needs, not reaching out, not taking initiative, not seeking out new ideas, not connecting with people, and not exerting energy to make things happen. It could be summed up as complacency and general apathy. The 360-degree profile of these people is right down the middle. These are the people who are perceived as lukewarm and "blah," because they are not effective in making things happen.

Third, the five fatal flaws are not intellectual deficiencies, but much more on the "emotional intelligence" side of the equation. These flaws arise from emotional and behavioral dimensions, and seldom because of knowledge or technical incompetence. The person with these fatal flaws basically lacks the ability or discipline to initiate or get things going. In nearly every case, a serious effort to remedy that deficiency would result in some significant changes for the better.

One of the authors worked with a vice president of administration who had been responsible for all maintenance, new construction, personnel, public relations, and purchasing. He was a tyrannical leader and lacked effective interpersonal skills. His were the only "good ideas," and no one made suggestions for improvements because they were certain they would be "shot down." People inside his areas often talked about "Don't rock the boat." The result was the lack of any new initiatives.

One fascinating but tragic consequence was the devastating impact this person had on each of five subordinates. None was ever promoted. They had been so smothered by his leadership that they became incapable of taking initiative or embracing new ideas from other sources.

Following the termination of the vice president and despite a new leader with a totally different approach, over the next two years each of the directors who reported to him ultimately resigned under some pressure or was terminated. They never recovered from their experience of working under this tyrant. This is the impact of leaders with fatal flaws, and this example illustrates how fatal flaws often go together and amplify each other.

Fixing Fatal Flaws

If a leader possesses one or more of these characteristics, action should obviously be taken to remedy that deficiency, make that weakness irrelevant, or to move that person back into a role of being an individual contributor where that behavior is less necessary. (In fact, however, those five fatal flaws will also stand in the way of the "professional, individual contributor" being highly effective in the long run.) People can overcome these characteristics. First, the organization can ensure that the person knows he possesses one of these "fatal flaws" and the serious consequences this will have on his career. If the person is willing to change, he can often make significant contributions to the organization.

The organization usually has a sizable investment in this individual, and this now tests several fundamental convictions of the organization's leadership. These include:

- Can people really change?
- Are people truly valuable?
- Does the organization have a responsibility to help the person who is willing to change?
- Do people possess latent talents and abilities?
- Is it worth the organization's investment to help an individual fix a fatal flaw in his or her leadership skills?

We contend that the organization owes it to the leader to provide developmental experiences that will provide a positive path to remedy dysfunctional behavior. These may include external or internal programs, or a coaching/mentoring relationship that provides ongoing feedback to help change the leader. Chapter 10 provides several avenues that could prove helpful to the individual wanting to change, and Chapter 11 provides suggestions for the organization and its efforts to help such leaders.

Prescription: Massive Doses of Feedback.   This is a perfect use of the 360-degree feedback process. Once it has been established that a leader has a major deficiency in one of the areas described above, it should be made clear to the leader that change is expected.

One powerful strategy is to indicate that nine months from now we will do a follow-up round of 360-degree feedback instruments with the subordinates, and the expectation is that these areas will be remedied. The setting of a clear expectation for change, and the creation of a powerful sense of urgency about it, is the most likely way to erase fatal flaws.

Why Feedback Works.   Inside everyone's head is a picture of how they see themselves. It describes what sort of person they are, what values they possess, their overall pattern of behavior, and sums up the image they have of themselves. In most cases, the leader with a fatal flaw is totally unaware of it. For example, the leader who immediately rejects others' ideas would in great likelihood describe herself as being full of confidence and having such extensive experience that she knows what ideas will succeed and which will fail. Such individuals are usually unaware of the perception that they reject everyone else's ideas. How can that be changed?

Feedback in the form of coaching, team discussions, or 360-degree surveys (if honest and direct) provides "disconfirming information." The messages conveyed would be contrary to this leader's self-perceptions. This creates a dilemma and forces some action. The leader now has one of several choices to make.

First, she can deny the information. But if it comes from multiple sources that are clearly reliable and have no personal axe to grind, it becomes extremely difficult to deny this consistent pattern of feedback.

Second, the leader can choose to change her self-concept. She could say to herself, "Well, OK, I guess I am arrogant and think my ideas are the only good ones that exist." For the person possessing some general health of character and personality, this is unacceptable and illogical.

Third, she can change her behavior. For most people faced with a barrage of disconfirming information, the easiest course of action is to change the behavior. That is the power of feedback.

Clearly, some fatal flaws will be specific to the position the person occupies. For example, the director of research and development will not usually survive unless he is perceived as being highly technically competent. The head of sales will not survive if she is perceived as lacking important interpersonal skills. A partner in a CPA firm will not survive, regardless of how good an auditor he is, if he takes the initiative to generate revenue and develop customer relationships. In these cases, the person does not always need to transform the weakness into a strength, but the behavior needs to be taken from the liability column and made into a neutral characteristic at worst.

Different Responses to Feedback.   People respond differently to feedback. That is something we have all observed. The work of one researcher may shed light on those differences. Tory Higgins, chairman of the Department of Psychology at Columbia University, has been honored for his distinguished contributions to the field of social psychology. His research concludes that people fall into one of two camps in their fundamental orientation on how they regulate their behavior. The first orientation is toward achieving positive outcomes. He labeled this a "promotion" orientation. This group of people wants to make positive things happen. Their focus is on achievement.[4]

Promotion Orientation
Higgins concludes from his research that this group is highly motivated by positive feedback. It reinforces that they have accomplished what they set out to do. Positive feedback means that others have noticed what they did. Their intention to produce something or complete a project met with success. Positive feedback is the reward for doing that. In the parlance of investing, this group sees success as achieving big gains. Yes, there might be periodic losses, but so long as the gains are there in the long run, the short-term losses are quite acceptable.

These people are devastated by negative feedback. It wounds their self-esteem. Their intention to do something worthwhile has not been recognized, or their efforts were a failure. Negative feedback is exactly what they did not want to hear, and thus it becomes highly demotivating to them. They pull back and become deflated by criticism.

Prevention Orientation

The second group of people has a "prevention orientation." Their objective in life is to avoid negative outcomes. Averting failure is what life is about. The way to avoid failure is constantly to monitor what you do, and instantly head off any impending mistake or omission. Thus, someone mentioning to you that there is an error in your draft of a report to upper management is greatly appreciated. That enables you to avoid looking bad to those receiving the report.

As investors, this group is in the camp of "Don't lose anything." Success means never having a stock go down. It is perfectly all right not to have spectacular gains, or even gains that mirror the performance of the overall market, so long as nothing is lost.

Feedback for people with a prevention orientation.   Any information that alerts this person to an impending problem or difficulty would be sought after and greatly appreciated. This group welcomes what others might see as "negative feedback."

In contrast, this group is not enthralled with positive feedback. For them, it comes across as hollow praise and not genuine; or it is seen as fairly useless. Positive feedback does not help this individual steer clear of failures, so it has little value.

The takeaway here is that one kind of feedback may be extremely helpful to some people, whereas it may be irritating to others. Much of that has to do with their orientation to life. Be aware that two people may respond very differently to exactly the same feedback, based on their life-orientation.

Fatal flaws in the "prevention" camp.   Those people we described earlier with fatal flaws may be in either the prevention or promotion camp. For those in the "prevention" camp, their behavior is almost always characterized by a lack of openness to new ideas, because new ideas are risky. There is a much greater possibility of mistakes happening when you try something new, so they are thinking, "Reject new processes or approaches as long and hard as you can."

This "prevention orientation" group would also like to be divorced from any accountability, because that way they can avoid the negative outcomes attendant with poor performance. Their position: "Never have your fingerprints on a project that might fail." "Always get someone in between you and a risky program, so that if it does not work out, you can blame them." Much of life is spent in following the maxim: "It doesn't matter whether you win or lose, it's how you place the blame." They want someone to be the scapegoat in case of failure.

Finally, this group does not initiate new projects or programs. Why? The less you do, the less likelihood there is for error. The more things you get underway, the greater the chances are for something to go wrong. So, the key is to do as little as possible and survive. Keep your head down. Don't draw attention. Don't rock the boat. That is success. If someone gives me information that helps to avoid failure, then I am forever grateful.

Higgins' research sheds light on why people respond so differently to feedback, and helps all leaders to be clearer about the right type of feedback to give to others, depending on their basic orientation to life.

Another social psychologist at Columbia University, Carol Dweck, conducted extensive research with school children and developed a framework similar to Higgins'. Her research on feedback sheds further, but consistent, light on this fascinating topic.

Dweck's research showed that people fell into two categories that she called "improving" and "proving." The first category, "improving," views the world as an opportunity to learn and grow. Problems they encounter that are hard or highly time consuming are welcomed because that means they can "improve" themselves. Mistakes are viewed as useful feedback.[5]

The "proving" group of people view life as a process of justifying or proving themselves to others, particularly those in authority. Therefore, problems that are hard or time consuming become a threat, because they show that the person was not as capable as others had thought. These people, therefore, tended to shrink away from difficult tasks and revert to tasks that were easily accomplished. They developed a helpless and dependent behavior.

We find much consistency between these two research endeavors. The "improving" and "promotion" orientations seem quite analogous. Likewise, the "proving" and the "prevention" orientations seem similar. Dweck's research focused on the right and wrong kinds of feedback to give to anyone. It did not distinguish the feedback that would be more appropriate for one group than another.

Dweck concluded that the wrong feedback to give was anything that was global, general, or that could be construed simply as praise. If a well-meaning parent tells a child, "You are really smart," or "You are a gifted student," what is that child to think when a week later he is in agony in a class in which the teacher has given him a problem he cannot solve? Or, what is the employee to think after a manager has told her what an intelligent and talented employee she is, and now she has been given a report to write and she simply is not making any progress on it?

On the other hand, think of the positive outcomes from the parent who tells the child, "I really admire how hard you've worked on learning the multiplication tables," or "You have really been creative about looking for different ways to get the information for your term paper. When you combine that with how tenacious you have been, I know you will come up with a good paper."[6]

Or, consider the leader who tells a subordinate, "I want to compliment you on how hard you have been working, and at your ability to overcome the obstacles in your path on this project. The progress you have made is a reflection on your focused effort."

The difference in these two approaches may seem subtle to some, but they are extreme opposites. The first is focused on the person and his or her innate abilities. The second approach is focused on the process he or she has used to tackle a project or a problem. That focus may be on the intensity of the effort, or on the innovative approaches to it, or on the ability to overcome obstacles, or it could be on the ability not to be distracted by other things. The benefit of the second approach is that anytime later, if this person is feeling a challenge in solving a problem or completing a project, his or her thought processes will be different. The question will not be, "Did my parent (or my boss) lie to me about being so capable?" "Did I used to be smart, and have I lost it?"

Instead, the thought process after the second pattern of feedback will be, "Maybe I'm not working hard enough." "Perhaps I haven't been innovative in looking for other ways to solve this problem." "I need to work harder to overcome some of the barriers that exist in our systems here." In short, the focus is now on the process that is being used, not on his or her fundamental intelligence or worth as a person.

These two bodies of research on feedback have given us better ways to understand the different reactions to the same feedback, and also provide a good template for a better approach to giving feedback. First, examine the nature of the individual and whether positive or negative feedback will be of most value. Second, whatever the person is like, keep feedback focused on the behavior or process the person is using, and not on him or her as a person. These two powerful ideas greatly enhance our understanding of the feedback process and how it can help leaders overcome fatal flaws.

C H A P T E R

New Insights into Leadership Development

I dreamed a thousand new paths. I woke and walked my old one.

Chinese Proverb

There are always many choices, many paths to take. One is easy. And its only reward is that it's easy.

Anonymous

WARFARE THROUGH THE 1700s to the middle of the nineteenth century was characterized by rows of soldiers marching straight toward their enemy. The opposing forces would do the same. Despite the fact that cannons and rifles being fired straight at them would kill thousands, it was not until the American Revolution that this pattern was challenged. When American revolutionary soldiers fought the British, they hid behind trees, lay prone on the ground to avoid being easy targets, and fought an entirely different type of war. In this chapter, we propose a similarly radical approach to developing leadership skills. Rather than continuing the "frontal assault" approach that has been popular for so long, we propose a different way to attack the problem.

Suppose that in an effort to improve your leadership effectiveness you wanted to improve your professional or technical expertise. Think about an action plan that you might formulate to accomplish the goal of improved technical/professional expertise. Write down the actions that you would take to improve. Then, thinking about your own plan, look at Table 8.1 to see how your plan compares with ones we have seen from many others facing this challenge.

Table 8.1 is a classical, linear plan. We define that as a plan that plots a straight-line development path from the current performance to a desired future state. It is a classic frontal assault. It is also extremely logical and characteristic of many people's propensity to identify a problem or challenge, put their heads down, and run straight at it with full force.

Figure 8.1 is a graphical depiction of a linear development plan. This plan works especially well in circumstances where a person's performance is poor and the need for substantial improvement is clear.

In a recent conference with professionals in employee development from several different companies, we asked representatives what percentage of the action plans made by individuals were linear. Their answer was that virtually all action plans are based on a

TABLE 8.1   Sample Action Plan

One Person's Plan of Action

Action Number	Action to Improve Technical and Professional Expertise
1	Sign up for a night class at the local university
2	Attend more professional conferences and workshops
3	Read technical and professional journals
4	Broaden network with other professionals and ask for coaching and mentoring on specific topics
5	Read latest books in the technical and professional fields
6	Get on a task force that will stretch current knowledge and expertise
7	Find some training courses that will increase depth of knowledge

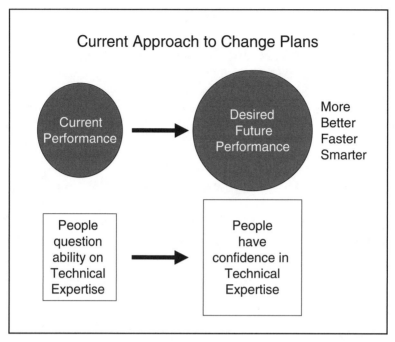

FIGURE 8.1   Current approach to change plans (linear development model).

linear logic. We then asked when the linear plans worked best. Again, a consistent answer from all participants: "Linear plans work best for people who are moving from poor performance to good performance." We want to emphasize that linear plans work well especially when people can identify a problem to be solved or poor performance on a competency. But what about the situation where a person's performance is good and the individual is trying to move to a higher level of performance? Will the approach that helps people move from bad to good be as effective in moving from good to great?

Case Study.   Jane Larson was a project leader in an exploration department of a major oil company. Her career had progressed nicely, but for the last two years she felt her career had stalled. Six months ago she participated in a 360-feedback process that provided her with an assessment on a series of competencies. To her surprise, she was rated lower than the average of her colleagues on technical expertise. In this organization, the one quality that is highly valued is technical expertise. To Jane, these results were a blatant wake-up call, and so she decided to make a significant change. Even though she felt fairly current, she decided to rededicate herself and broaden her understanding of related fields. She attended a technical conference, read every journal from cover to cover, and started an independent research project with a university. To get a sense of how all this work was helping, she asked her manager to have a career discussion with her. In the discussion she described all of her efforts to hone her skills and build a broader knowledge base. Her manager was pleased with all her efforts, but then she asked the critical question: "Do you think that all this work will help others see that I have a great deal of technical knowledge and expertise?" Her manager sat back in his seat, and paused to prepare his answer carefully. "Well, Jane, I don't know if any of this is ever going to make any difference until you have the guts to speak up in a meeting and share your knowledge with people. The problem isn't how much you know, it's what you do with what you know!"

Jane Larson is a good example of a linear action plan not being helpful. In reality, Jane did not need to take additional classes, read journals better, or do more research. Her problem was that she failed to share her knowledge and expertise with others. The perceptions of others were based on the behavior she demonstrated to them rather than the knowledge that she had packed in her head. In reality, others cannot tell how much she knows if she does not share the information.

NONLINEAR DEVELOPMENT PATHS

Since almost all development plans are linear (because that is the prevailing logic), we looked for a technique to help people understand alternative development paths. In our approach, we took each of the 16 differentiating behaviors and analyzed the relationship between that specific behavior and the other 15, plus a number of other behaviors. When an individual showed a high level of competence on a specific behavior, we looked at other behaviors that were also highly rated. Then we analyzed leaders who were rated poorly on that differentiating behavior and observed that the same companion behaviors were also rated poorly.

We call these related behaviors "competency companions." They are companions because they seem to be permanently glued together. In the spirit of Sherlock Holmes, we believe that these competency companions provide excellent clues about an alternative way to develop important leadership skills—and to improve the likelihood that you will be perceived by those about you as possessing an important, differentiating competency.

Figure 8.2 provides two examples of competency companions associated with technical expertise. Leaders perceived as having the best technical expertise were also perceived as having high competence in interpersonal skills and standards of excellence. Also, those

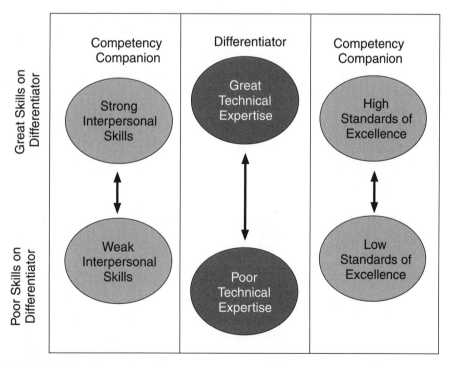

FIGURE 8.2   Examples of competency companions associated with technical expertise.

perceived as having the worst technical expertise typically had poor interpersonal skills and low standards of excellence.

If you conclude from this analysis that having excellent interpersonal skills causes a person to have technical expertise, you are probably wrong. Because two events consistently happen together does not prove that one causes the other. But much of science has to rely on the fact that when two phenomena are consistently linked together, you make the presumption that one of them causes the other, or that each has some impact on the other.

In a college course on descriptive statistics, the professor was attempting to explain the purpose of descriptive statistics, particularly correlation coefficients. He chose as an example a phenomenon in nature. He said, "There is an extremely high correlation between the frequency of crickets chirping and the temperature." There was a pause. A student raised his hand and said, "Professor Peterson, are you saying that as the temperature rises, crickets chirp more frequently?" With a totally deadpan expression on his face, Professor Peterson replied, "No, I have always assumed that when crickets chirp more frequently, it causes the outdoor temperature to rise."

Most people would have an explanation for the relationship of temperature and crickets chirping, and this could easily be proven by simple experiments. However, in many situations, when two things happen together, the mechanisms that link them together are not entirely clear. All you can say is that they occur together, and you can make some educated guess about the cause-and-effect relationship that links them together.

The Link between Interpersonal Relationships and Technical Competence

To return to our example of technical expertise and interpersonal skills being tied together, we could offer some explanations. This result is strongly supported by groundbreaking research done by Robert Kelley at Bell Labs. The research looked at the productivity of scientists. After studying hundreds of scientists, all of whom were experts in their field, the researchers found that the engineers who were most successful (they dubbed them their "stars") were not those with the highest IQs or those who were the most knowledgeable. Kelley wrote, "Our data showed no appreciable cognitive, personal, psychological, social or environmental differences between stars and average performers."[1] What they found was that these stars performed their work differently. They developed strong networks within the organization and worked with others in a totally different manner than the "non-stars."

To elaborate, some of the interpersonal skills identified in the Bell Labs research were behaviors such as:

- Helping colleagues solve a problem
- Helping others to complete a task
- Giving others credit for any success
- Expressing a desire to hear others' ideas
- Not imposing their ideas on others
- Being concerned with coworkers' personal needs
- Utilizing the skills of coworkers
- Working quietly, without fanfare
- Putting the objectives of the team before their own[2]

For those who have worked in technical organizations, there is another reason why it comes as no surprise to find that there is a relationship between technical expertise and interpersonal skills. It relates to the "stars'" way of communicating about technical issues. We have observed that the most able technical people have sufficient confidence to express complex ideas in lay terms, and not hide behind jargon. Insecure scientists are afraid to expose the fact that their discipline is not as precise as others are led to believe. To be perceived as being highly technically competent demands a person who can communicate effectively about their discipline to many groups.

What Happens When Interpersonal Skills and Technical Competence Are Not Connected?   Recently, one of the authors was having dinner with a friend who is currently a university president. A question was asked about what kind of interesting activities filled his day. He commented, "Well, today I had to fire a professor." Someone at the table asked, "Why? What rules did he break? Was he incompetent?" "No he was not incompetent!" replied the president. "He was very current in his field. The problem was that no one in his department could remember a staff meeting that he attended that did not end in an argument. He was absolutely impossible to get along with and created so much friction in the department that nothing was getting done." In this case, the professor's lack of interpersonal skills made the professor's technical competence irrelevant. It ceased to matter. People no longer paid attention to his technical competence.

In another situation, we were working with the management of a chemical company research laboratory. Their work was highly specialized work and they had recruited absolutely the brightest and best scientists in the world. The productivity of the lab had come under considerable scrutiny. In order to understand better what some of the problems were with this group, many of the scientists were interviewed. In an interview with one of the leading scientists, the interviewer asked him to describe a typical technical review. Each of the scientists was asked to present new research studies before all the scientists for their review. The interviewer asked, "Are the technical reviews helpful?"

The scientist replied, "Not at all."

"Why?" the interviewer asked.

"Because when new scientists present their ideas for a new area of study they aren't asking for input, they are just showing off how much they know. Several times I have listened to scientists talk about research that we have already determined is never going to work. We have tried the same experiments before. They always fail. But rather than help this idiot out, we just sit back and inwardly grin because we know that they will fail. By letting them work on this research it just helps my work to look even better and gives me a lot better chance of getting a big bonus." The scientists in the lab saw themselves as competing against each other for recognition, rewards, and promotions.

Here again, the lack of effective interpersonal skills seriously erodes the perceived technical competence of this laboratory. We estimate that this culture, with high scientific and low interpersonal effectiveness, was costing the company a minimum of millions of dollars each year. The number could be in the billions if the comparison is made to what that group of scientists could have created, had they created a high-performance work environment.

Having strong interpersonal skills does not help people become any smarter, but it does help them to share the knowledge that they have, influence others effectively, communicate the things that they know, and build collaborative, trusting relationships with others.

The Link between Having High Standards and Technical Competence

Similarly, having high standards of excellence does not make people smarter, but if you apply the logic of the Rosenberg et al. research presented in Chapter 4, a good explanation emerges. Recall that the research showed that the following adjectives were clustered together in people's minds:

- Scientific
- Persistent
- Skillful
- Imaginative
- Intelligent

We submit, then, that in most people's perceptions, the qualities of technical competence (scientific and intelligent) and high standards of excellence (persistence and skillful) are also linked together. If I see you display one, I assume you have the other.

Therefore, by championing extremely high standards for every activity, I have subtly caused others to have an elevated view of my technical competence. Certainly, on the flip side, a person with minimal technical competence would never impose lofty standards of excellence on a team or on colleagues. Similarly, the leader who remarks, "Oh, I don't care if we finish on time," or "Let's not bust our tails on this project," is not a person we assume has great technical credentials or ability.

WHAT ARE COMPETENCY COMPANIONS?

Competency companions (or behavioral buddies) are simply best friends. They tend to go everywhere together. When people are effective at one of the 16 key differentiating behaviors, they tend to do the companion behaviors equally well. Conversely, when people are ineffective at a differentiating behavior, they tend to perform the companion behaviors poorly. Again, we are not implying that one behavior causes the other. Later in this chapter we provide our analysis of various reasons for why the linkage occurs.

Competency companions provide excellent clues for making significant improvements on a differentiating behavior. People need to examine their level of competence on a differentiating behavior and then review each competency companion. They can examine situations from their own experience when poor performance on a competency companion affected the perception of their ability in the differentiating behavior. The question to ask is: "If I were to improve my performance on competency companion A, would it improve my performance on the differentiating competency B, or at least would it enhance the perceptions of others regarding my ability on differentiating competency B?" Looking for situations or past experiences where two behaviors might have been linked will help people to identify a competency companion that may be the key to developing extraordinary talent on a differentiating behavior.

Mechanisms of Competency Companions
Why do competency companions leverage improvement in certain behaviors? We believe that there are a variety of reasons for the impact that is evident when both the competency and the competency companion are rated positively. We are clear that there are different mechanisms creating the impact. The following is a list of six mechanisms that best explain the competency companion phenomena.

1. The competency and the competency companion fit together in people's perceptional systems. The Rosenberg, et al. research found that certain characteristics fit together in most people's minds. If you have attribute A, people assume you have attribute B. If they know you don't have attribute B, they question if you could possibly have attribute A. Therefore, the first explanation of why competency companions create impact is that perceptually people believe these characteristics fit together, and

improving one helps create the perception that the other is more positive.

2. Competency companions facilitate the expression of another competency. Consider the linkage between interpersonal skills and technical skills. What appears to be happening is that having strong interpersonal skills facilitates the sharing of knowledge, the persuasion of others to a new position, and positive interactions in terms of solving problems. We do not believe that improving interpersonal skills makes technical knowledge grow or makes a person smarter. It is possible that because of good interpersonal skills, a person may choose to coach and mentor colleagues. This may improve actual technical ability. For the most part, however, the impact of interpersonal skills on technical ability seems to be that it facilitates the communication of technical knowledge and enhances the appreciation other people have of a person's technical skills. When Mary speaks up in meetings, others start to see how smart and capable she is, and their perception of her technical ability goes up.

3. Achieving a high level of skill in one behavior helps develop a related behavior. For example, one of the strongest competency companions for "developing other people" is being skilled and interested in developing yourself. If leaders do not have a good career plan for themselves, it is most difficult to assist their direct reports in creating career plans. If people feel stuck in their careers with no place to go, it is harder for them to be of much assistance to others. However, if leaders learn to develop their own careers, that will be an invaluable start to assisting others with the same process.

4. One competency is a building block or a core element of the other competency. One of the most interesting competency companionships that we found related to integrity. A strong companion behavior to integrity is concern and consideration for other people. Simply put, those perceived with high integrity have a high level of concern and consideration for others, and those perceived with low integrity lacked consideration for others. Consideration for others is a vital component of the

broader competency labeled "integrity." A person who has no problems taking advantage of another person lacks integrity.

5. Competency companions change the context in which we operate. We found a strong relationship between a person's ability to communicate and the extent to which a person is trusted. Typically, when people attempt to improve their ability to communicate, they focus on the message and the delivery (e.g., what they say and how they say it). This research indicates that if people trust a leader, then the leader does not need to give a world-class speech. The fact that people have a great deal of trust in the leader will cause the message to be accepted. Without trust, however, no amount of great oration can make people accept the message.

6. Developing a competency companion changes the person. Most people have had the experience of dramatically changing a skill and then finding interesting side effects. Learning to play golf well gives a person increased confidence. A regular exercise program makes a person less stressed. Focusing effort on accomplishing a stretch goal causes depression to go away. Strengthening a competency has the capacity to change a person's perspective, attitudes, and outlook on life.

Examples of Competency Companions
We have found that for each competency there are six to eight competency companions. It is beyond the scope of this book to provide an exhaustive list of every competency companion, but we provide here one example for each of the 16 differentiating behaviors. We have organized these into the five elements in our leadership model. We are in the process of compiling a complete list of competency companions. For further information on competency companions, contact the authors by going to www.extraordinaryleader.net.

Character—The Center Pole of the Leadership Tent

Improving Integrity
When characterizing people with low integrity, we visualize a person who purposely tries to take advantage of other people. How-

ever, many people who experience integrity problems don't always fit that mold.

Sean was a bright and very honest young man from a foreign country. He was very religious and was in his final year of school in the United States. In his home country, his family was well known. He was approached by a group of investors and offered a very good salary to go back to his home country and sell his fellow citizens on an investment opportunity. The men who approached Sean were regular churchgoers, and so he assumed that they would be able to deliver on this investment. He trusted these men, so he did not ask many questions or check out the viability of the investment. Because of the reputation of his family, Sean was very successful in signing up millions in investments. After a short time an initial payment was made to investors. That money was distributed to each investor. A short time later Sean learned that the investment scheme had failed. He was left holding the bag.

Many other people report an experience similar to Sean's. They do not intentionally attempt to deceive other people, but in the end their integrity is compromised. They trust another person but fail to aggressively ensure that promises made by others will be kept. When we looked at the competency companions to integrity, we found that those rated high in integrity were also rated high on assertiveness. Those rated low in integrity, on the other hand, were rated low on assertiveness. Those with high integrity were very effective at stepping forward and addressing difficult issues, confronting conflict, being direct, and facing up to difficult situations.

Having high integrity will never be easy. It requires that people be assertive in checking out the facts, ensuring that commitments are met, and demanding that whatever is sold is also delivered.

Personal Capability—The Second Pole Lifting the Leadership Tent

Becoming a Better Problem Solver

What if a person wanted to improve in problem-solving skills? Obviously, that improvement could be in the way they are perceived, or in actually improving those skills—and hopefully both. We examined the competency companions for effective problem solving and analytical skills. We found that one of the highest correlates was initiative. People perceived as being good problem solvers and highly analytical were also perceived as taking a great deal of initiative. Those perceived as poor problem solvers were perceived as having low initiative.

Robert Kelley describes initiative as the most important work strategy in separating the "stars" from the rest of the pack at Bell Labs. He illustrates his point by describing two new hires, both with similar credentials: 3.8 GPAs from respected universities, strong summer internships at computer companies, and lustrous recommendations from professors.

Henry holed himself up in his office as if he were writing his dissertation or studying for a bar exam. He collected volumes of technical documents to acquaint himself with the latest ideas. He began learning how to use exotic software programs he thought might be helpful in his work. He would surface only for a bathroom break or a mandatory staff meeting. "What's going to count," he remembers thinking at the time, "is whether I can prove to my co-workers how smart I am."

Lai set aside three hours each afternoon to work on her assignment. In whatever time was left of her workday, she introduced herself to co-workers and asked questions about their projects. If one of them needed a hand, or faced schedule pressures, she volunteered to help. And even though Lai was new to the workplace culture, her colleagues appreciated her willingness to help them out, especially given that their problems were not hers.

Kelley continues describing Lai's actions:

- She found a colleague who could not get a software program to work, and Lai recalled a new programming tool she had picked up in an advanced course in college and offered that solution to the colleague. She offered to work on the software problem while the colleague finished the larger project.

- When new software tools needed to be installed on everyone's computers, the assumption was that everyone would use the traditional approach of installing it themselves, largely by trial and error. Lai had installed the software during her internship and thought it made more sense for one person to move up the learning curve and do it for everyone. She volunteered. It ended up taking two weeks, instead of the four days she had estimated, but she stuck it out and completed all of the installations.

- A colleague who had been scheduled for an all-night lab testing session was suddenly called away to a funeral for a family member. When the manager convened a meeting to see how this absence could be covered, there was much looking at the floor and "covering your face" behavior. As the supervisor was about to make an arbitrary assignment to some unwilling person, Lai volunteered. She later recalls, "I figured that it was most important to get accepted into the team, and what better way than to help them out."

Lai was on her way to becoming a "star" in the Bell Labs vernacular. It had little to do with being technically competent, but everything to do with taking initiative. Kelley writes, "Average performers—who constitute 60 to 80 percent of the workforce—don't get it. That group is most likely to view initiative taking as activity for activity's sake, getting stuck doing someone else's work, or taking on work that is not part of their job description. Cynical average performers see it as kissing up to the boss or colleagues."

It might surprise readers to know that Henry, the loner Bell Labs hire, believed he was taking initiative. "I gathered up the latest technical information and learned about the latest software tools so that I could do a bang-up job on my assignment. Nobody told me to do any of that," he told the researchers.. What Lai understood and Henry did not is that only certain actions earn the initiative label.[3]

How Do I Improve My Effectiveness in Developing Myself?
A key skill for all successful leaders is the ability to continuously improve themselves. Too often, leaders achieve some office or position and then come to believe that the learning phase of their career is over. They assume that, like graduation from school, there is a time of learning and a time of execution. Our research pointed out the importance of continuous self-improvement in order for

leaders to become exceptional. Looking at those who showed great ability to practice self-development, we found a strong relationship with integrity. That is, people who were viewed as highly competent in terms of developing themselves were also viewed as being extremely honest and straightforward. At first glance the two behaviors seem unrelated. What does self-development have to do with integrity and honesty?

Consider, however, the research done in helping people overcome alcoholism and drug addiction. One of the major hurdles in getting help for people to deal successfully with addiction is getting them to acknowledge that they have a problem. Alcoholics in the early stages are inevitably in denial. An alcoholic who showed up for addiction counseling was asked, "Why are you here?" He answered, "Because my spouse thinks I have a drinking problem." To which the counselor replied, "Go home and keep drinking. I can't help you until you think that you have a problem." In most cases of drug and alcohol addiction it becomes evident to everyone else that the person has a problem before it becomes evident to the person himself or herself. Frequently you hear the stories about people who have to hit rock bottom before they finally wake up and say to themselves, "I have a drinking problem." In many addiction treatment programs, people use the practice of introducing themselves by saying, "My name is John, and I am an alcoholic."

Honesty is a striking feature of the relationship between self-development and integrity. People who are good at self-development have the ability to evaluate their strengths and weaknesses honestly and to acknowledge their strengths in behavior A and that they are less effective in behavior B. Keep in mind that for some people their problem is their lack of faith in their strengths. They discount their own abilities. People who are poor at self-development might be rationalizing their performance in less than objective ways. They tell themselves that they did a good job when they did a poor job. They ignore feedback from others. They debate the reactions of others, saying, "They are only saying that because they are out to get my job, or they are jealous of my abilities." There are levels of self-honesty. Some people come to accept the feedback others give them but still resist being perfectly honest with themselves about what they do well and problems that need to be improved. Being absolutely honest with one's self and refusing the opportunity for self-deceit is a key skill for extraordinary leaders.

How Can I Become More Innovative?
An examination of the competency companions for innovation found that innovative leaders were also good at learning from both their successes and failures. At first blush, this again seems like an unlikely combination. Most think of innovation as the ability to produce creative ideas and to get those ideas implemented. Learning, on the other hand is the ability to absorb new information, to recognize patterns, to see cause-and-effect relationships—all ultimately culminating in new behavior.

We think it is probable that those who are not innovative have lost some ability to learn. They aren't paying attention to what is transpiring in their environment. They rationalize rather than change their behavior. Good learners carefully observe their environment, they study how things happen, and they are inquisitive about cause-and-effect relationships. A key to being innovative is increasing one's ability to learn.

Focus on Results—Another Pole Lifting the Tent

Helping Others Achieve Exceptional Results
The ability to set stretch goals is a critical piece of motivating people to achieve exceptional results. We found in our research that setting stretch goals was one of the 16 differentiating behaviors. Setting stretch goals is a behavior that is easy to talk about but harder to do. Some propose a simple path: develop what you think is a reasonable goal, then multiply by two. In the end, many leaders back off because they are uncomfortable asking others to take on a task that they themselves view as unreasonable or impossible. The first step in setting stretch goals is for you to believe in the stretch capacity of people. Jack Welch speaks often of the enormous capacity of the workforce to do more. He said, "There is an unlimited amount of juice in that lemon."[4]

Two independent consultants were discussing how to establish their appropriate daily rate. The older consultant said, "It's easy, you look in the mirror and start saying incremental numbers as if you are talking to prospective client. When you hit a number that makes you smile, back up one number and that's your rate. The important thing about getting your consulting rate is that you be able to convince a client that you're worth your fee. When you smile at a fee, then you know you're not worth it and so it's impossible to convince any client of that."

We found that leaders who were effective at setting stretch goals were also effective at risk taking. It appears that leaders who are willing to challenge the status quo and take risks also have the ability to convince their work group that they can achieve an almost impossible goal. People who play it safe, carefully analyze what is possible, and take reasonable steps forward will never be very effective at setting stretch goals.

How Do You Get Others to Feel Responsible?

Frequently, parents struggle with children in school who forget assignments, fail to study for tests, and seem unmotivated to improve their performance. Parents often comment, "Why can't my children just be more responsible?" The implicit theory is that if people have responsible attitudes, they will act responsibly.

Recently, a daughter was struggling in school. I had a fatherly discussion with her and asked her to describe the problem. "I'm depressed," she said. "And I can't concentrate on my homework if I am depressed," was her excuse. She was obviously discouraged. In my opinion, most of her discouragement came from failing some exams in school. I challenged her to go to work and study in spite of feeling discouraged. Knowing she would probably need more than a pep talk to succeed, I arranged a tutor to meet with her several times a week. The tutor provided both knowledgeable advice and friendly support. Soon the daughter's grades started to improve. As her grades improved, her depression went away. Once her study habits had changed and she felt more confident that she could be successful, she started to act substantially more responsibly. Rather than go out with friends, she would say, "Sorry, I have homework."

Sometime attitudes do precede actions, but frequently actions need to precede attitudes. An important differentiating competency is taking responsibility for outcomes. Oftentimes people approach improvement by concentrating on improving the attitude. People feel that a person needs to feel more responsible before he or she can act more responsibly. One of the key competency companions to taking responsibility for outcomes is taking action toward achieving results. This research indicates that those people who are perceived as acting in a responsible manner for outcomes also are seen as taking action toward achieving results. If people begin to act, it conveys to others a great deal about their attitude. The best way to convince others that we are responsible people is by our actions.

One of our frequent consulting activities is conducting employee surveys to assess the attitudes of employees on key issues that drive the success of a business. One of the frequent problems with survey efforts is that senior leaders can view the survey efforts as a nice activity but not essential for the success of their business. It is critical to the success of such projects to get senior leaders' commitment to the project. In our usual approach, we enlist senior leaders' involvement at the beginning of the process. We interview them and ask them for their opinions on what issues are critical for the organization to be successful. Frequently, a leader will find an item on the survey that is almost a direct quote from his or her interview. Using the survey to assess their specific issue can take leaders from sideline spectators to quarterbacks in the survey rollout. The survey moves from being described as "the consultant's survey" to "our survey."

How Do You Get More Productivity Out of Other People?
One of the most frequently used competencies is "focus on results." The underlying theme is always the same: keeping others focused on the task, aggressively pursuing assignments, driving hard to make things happen, and being totally dedicated to the accomplishment of the task. When leaders attempt to improve their focus on results, they often put a great deal of emphasis on the drive or push to emphasize results. When done to excess, such leaders become grownup bullies who constantly prod, check, demand, and annoy others. These behaviors can be effective in the short run, but in the long run, nobody wants to work for a bully.

We again found an unlikely companionship. Our analysis found that leaders who were effective at focusing on results were also effective at giving others feedback and providing coaching. Leaders who only push people to perform better typically focus on the outcome but don't help people much with the journey.

Giving people feedback is time consuming and difficult, and frequently is not done well in most organizations. One employee, commenting on his lack of feedback, said, "I don't know if I am in line to be the janitor or the chairman of the board. Please give me some feedback." Why is it that most poor performers are surprised to hear that they are receiving an unsatisfactory performance review? The reason is that leaders don't like to give feedback. They assume that employees will figure it out on their own. They assume that because they didn't give a reassuring smile, employees will figure out that they are doing something wrong. Sitting down with employees and providing straight, candid feedback can be time consuming and emotionally difficult for leaders, but leaders who do this well achieve better results.

One leader had an effective approach to giving feedback. Whenever she saw a problem, she would schedule a meeting with the person and say, "Our performance review is scheduled four months from now. I want to give you a positive appraisal at that time, but if it were to happen right now I could not do that. Let me explain why, and let's figure out a way to fix it before then." She would then explain her concerns about this person's performance and proceed with a joint problem-solving discussion of how to fix the issue.

Feedback needs to be timely and in close approximation to when the problem behavior occurred. Good coaches provide loads of feedback. They stand on the sidelines and yell, give halftime talks, or call time-outs and give people clear, specific feedback. Leaders need to learn to give feedback.

Interpersonal Skills—Another Pole That Raises the Tent

What Could Be More Powerful Than a Good Speech?
When thinking about how a person communicates powerfully, most people concentrate on how a message is delivered. It was interest-

ing to learn that one of the strongest competency companions for communicating powerfully is involving others. In other words, those who were viewed as powerful communicators asked people for their input, encouraged alternative approaches and new ideas from others, and made sure that others were in agreement. Leaders rated low in their ability to communicate tended to concentrate on getting their message delivered. Those rated low would give their speech from their prepared presentation but failed to ask for input from the audience on whether they agreed and how they might view the issue differently.

What Is the Key to Getting Managers to Develop Their Direct Reports?

In a recent conference of employee development experts from several different companies, we asked the question, "What is the key to getting managers to develop their direct reports?" There was no lack of input from the audience. Some of the recommended actions were

- Teach managers how to coach others.
- Do behavioral modeling skills training on how to have a developmental discussion.
- Publish clear development pathways.
- Make the performance improvement process more developmental and less judgmental.
- Provide people with a model to help them understand how career development works.
- Reward managers for employee development.

We then asked how many of the companies were doing most of the activities on the list. Most companies indicated that their managers had been taught, coached, provided a model, and rewarded; but that their organization needed more. Based on our research, we found that leaders who were effective at developing others tended to be interested in their own self-development, while those who were ineffective at developing others had little interest in developing themselves. We then suggested, based on this research, that one of the best ways to get managers interested in developing others was to make sure these managers had a good development plan themselves. A large food company provided a training program in which managers and individual contributors were taught how to create an individual development plan. In evaluating the effectiveness of the individual development plans, it was found that those managers who were interested in their individual development were the ones most likely to facilitate the creation of effective development plans with their direct reports.

Imagine a manager who feels that she is at a dead end in her career. She does not have a sense of what she might be doing in the future. What kind of career discussions would this person have with her direct reports? She might be trying hard to say the right words, but inside she would say to herself, "Why should I give you career advice? If you get promoted, you will be at the same dead end as me. There is no future in this company." Or she may say to herself, "I have no future in this company, so why should I give you hope? They will probably make you my boss."

A good solution for making an organization more developmental is to make sure that managers and leaders feel they have a clear career plan and developmental opportunities in their future. Leaders will act developmentally if they are being developed.

How Do You Build a Great Team?

Our analysis on the competency companions to teamwork revealed that having trusting relationships is strongly associated with good teamwork. That makes sense. Most relationships depend on trust as a basis for the relationship. Teams without trust suffer from conflicts and competition between team members. It is easy to talk about trust, but it tends to be an elusive quality for many leaders. To understand better the real meaning of trust, we did an analysis to determine its competency companions. Those leaders who were trusted also had the following characteristics:

1. *Consideration for others.* A key behavior to leveraging trust is having a high level of concern for how one's behavior affects others. Often, lack of consideration is demonstrated when dead-

lines or problems occur in the group. It is easy to be considerate when everything is running smoothly. Balancing the need to get the job done with sensitivity for others' needs and problems demonstrates true consideration.

2. *An open, friendly style.*   Trust is made much easier when leaders are open and friendly rather than abrupt and dismissive. Those who are viewed as easy to get along with are also viewed as trustworthy. Leaders who work hard to win people over to their position rather than demanding that people accept their position also build trust.

3. *Noncompetitive.*   As people go through school and finish college, they often feel they are in constant competition with others. Grading on the curve makes students view others as competitors who could hurt their grade. As new employees begin work, entry-level jobs provide the same context. Consulting firms hire hundreds of MBAs and inform them that half will be weeded out in one or two years. Only one in ten will make it to partner. A key transition for leaders is moving from viewing others as competitors to viewing others as team members. Behaviors that kill trust are behaviors such as taking personal credit for the accomplishments of others or being threatened by the success of other members of the work group. Leaders show support for other team members by backing them up when they make an honest mistake and accepting blame for failures of the group rather than criticizing the performance of individual team members.

4. *Others have confidence in the leader's abilities and knowledge.* Expertise builds trust. Having confidence in a leader's ability to achieve difficult goals is a key aspect of trust. In addition to being friendly and considerate, being reliable and right is a critical aspect of building trust with others.

5. *Careful listening.*   It is interesting to note that there is a strong relationship between listening and trust. Some people might believe that you talk other people into trust. This finding suggests that listening to others in a way that shows a person is interested in what they have to say builds trust.

6. *Candor.*   A key ingredient of trust is honesty. Being frank and
   honest in dealing with other people is critical to building trusting relationships. Telling people what they want to hear in an
   attempt to be nice or protect them from the truth only erodes
   trust in relationships. Sometimes information is confidential and
   cannot be shared with others. Leaders with candor can be
   straightforward about the fact that they cannot share specific information.

How Do You Inspire Others?
When people think about inspiring others to high performance, they
often visualize giving people a locker-room-style pep talk, or wav-
ing a flag while leading others into battle. What might the competency companions to "inspiring others" be? Again, we did not find
the obvious. Leaders who were rated as highly inspirational were
also rated as having positive expectations of others. It appears that
inspirational leaders have faith in the people with whom they work.
They believe that others are capable of great accomplishments. They
believe others will work hard, follow through on assignments, and
do whatever is needed to accomplish goals. Having positive expectations of others predisposes leaders to expect more, check less, and
encourage people to give their best. Having lofty expectations of
others is closely related to inspiring them.

   Another competency companion of inspiring others is getting
people the resources they need to do the job. This seems rather mundane and not very inspirational. We are reminded of a former dean
of the Stanford Graduate School of Business who was asked what
his major accomplishment as dean had been to that point. His reply was, "Getting an adequate supply of chalk and erasers into the
classrooms." Leaders often create a compelling vision of what needs
to be done and the gains that will be created from successful accomplishment. However, as employees start to do the real work, they
look for the resources to support them, only to find that systems
don't work, equipment is on order, or added personnel can't be hired.
The military version of this is advancing troops faster than their
supply lines. The troops may gain a great deal of ground but run

out of food and ammunition. Leaders who inspire provide needed resources at the same time.

Leading Organizational Change—The Final Tent Pole

What Is a Powerful Way to Get Others to Change?
In our analysis of competency companions for championing change, we found that leaders who were good at creating change also were perceived as excellent role models. It becomes much easier to get people in an organization to behave in a particular way when the leaders act as role models of the desired behavior. In fact, some change agents argue that it is virtually impossible for an organization to change its culture until its leaders' behavior is consistent with the values of the culture. One explanation for this strong link is found in the power of role models. The old saying, "What you do thunders so loudly in my ears that I cannot hear what you say," is true.

When David Kearns was attempting to introduce a company-wide quality initiative, two vice presidents remained carping critics of the program. Both had been good performers in their roles, but Kearns constantly admonished them to get on board. By not doing anything about these two dissidents, Kearns would have become an extremely negative role model for what he sought to accomplish. He terminated them both and let the organization know that it was because of their nonsupport of the quality initiative.

How Do You Get Leaders to Be the Antenna to the Outside World?
One key differentiating behavior that distinguished extraordinary leaders was their ability to connect their organization to the outside world. As technology and innovation affect every aspect of an organization, having a vision for what is going on outside one's own organization is critical for every successful leader. Our analysis of competency companions for connecting to the outside world found that a strong companion behavior was having a broad focus and perspective.

One of the fascinating aspects of graduate education is that most graduate programs continually narrow the focus of one's study. An early indication that a person has succeeded in life is that he has mastered a specific field. Individual contributors learn quickly that a key to success is oftentimes to narrow one's focus and become an expert in something. Many early experiences in a person's career reinforce that idea. What was helpful at one point in a career, however, frequently becomes an obstacle as people are promoted to leadership positions that require broader responsibility and perspective. With a narrow perspective, attempting to connect to the outside world is like looking at the world through long tubes that only allow you to see a limited part of the world. A broader perspective helps leaders to recognize the interrelationships among various events and their impacts on technology, society, and government.

How Do I Get Others to Accept a New Strategic Course for My Organization?

Good strategists believe in logic and careful analysis. Many believe they can win almost any argument and solve any problem with enough analysis and good logic. They also typically believe that as long as a strategy is logical, others will embrace the strategy. That is how they came to embrace the strategy, so others ought to do the same.

We found an interesting relationship between strategic perspective and self-confidence. Leaders who were viewed as having excellent strategic perspective were also rated as having high self-confidence. The relationship here seems to be that in order to get others to believe in you, you have to exhibit strong belief in yourself. Self-doubt, hesitation, changing your mind, or introversion can take a well-analyzed, logical strategic plan and turn it into a dead issue. Two critical issues are relevant here in considering self-confidence.

First, while self-confidence is an attitude, it is communicated to others in terms of behavior. A person may have a great deal of self-confidence, but his behavior communicates to others that he lacks confidence.

Second, self-confidence without competence is a very dangerous combination. In one analysis we found that leaders with high self-confidence but low competence were among the worst managers evaluated. Inevitably their operations lost money, and inevitably they never believed their feedback. They were sure they were right and nobody was going to prove them wrong. Self-confidence is a trait that ought to be displayed only when a person is absolutely sure that he or she has the right answer.

A New Approach to Development

Our competency companion research provides a unique perspective on how leaders can change. Current approaches toward development encourage people to develop linear development plans. Linear plans can be effective especially if a person's current level of performance is poor. Most linear plans help leaders make the transition from poor to good. However, the major focus of this book is helping leaders transition from good to great. The competency companion research provides leaders with a new map on how to reach their ultimate destination. This map provides alternate routes, which, for the most part, are unintuitive.

These new routes come out of research. The statistical analysis indicated that two behaviors were highly interrelated. We then looked for the rationale of why the one behavior impacted the other. Often, when leaders try to build exceptional effectiveness on specific competencies, it becomes difficult to find an effective way to improve. When performance on a competency is good, using a linear mindset is useless because leaders already perform the competency reasonably well. However, the nonlinear approach suggests that in order to be highly effective at competency A, I also need to be highly effective at B and C.

Our experience in helping leaders develop strengths by looking through a complete set of competency companions is that, typically, leaders will find one or two of the companion behaviors in which their effectiveness is inadequate. One leader commented: "The companion behaviors I needed to work on stood out like a sore thumb. It was so obvious what was holding me back." Leaders can usually arrive at their own rationale for why performing poorly on the companion behavior impacts the competency on which they are working to develop exceptional strength. The added insight provided by the competency companions is very powerful. Our analogy of the tent is useful in understanding how companion behaviors impact overall perceptions of leadership effectiveness.

Again, effective leaders have a great deal of tent in the air. The companion behaviors represent poles that are either nonexistent or short. By building the effectiveness of the companion behavior, more of the tent is lifted into the air and the overall perception of leadership effectiveness is increased. Leaders who have experienced this approach have found it to be a valuable tool in their efforts to make the transition from good managers to great leaders.

9

A CASE STUDY IN LEADERSHIP DEVELOPMENT—THE U.S. MARINE CORPS

> Leadership is a potent combination of strategy and character. But if you must be without one, be without strategy.
>
> *General Norman Schwarzkopf*

A QUESTION THAT CONTINUES TO LINGER on most people's minds is, "Can you really develop leaders?" "Aren't they born that way?" The general population continues to wonder whether the thing called "leadership" is something implanted at birth, or if it can be developed. If it could be shown that even one organization successfully transforms "regular" people into effective leaders, that question could begin to disappear. One key reason for this chapter describing the work of the U.S. Marine Corps is our attempt to put that question to bed, once and for all, by describing an organization that successfully develops leaders.

WHY THE MARINES?

Our specific interest in the Marine Corps as an example of success in developing leaders came from several sources. In the mid-1980s, one of the authors came to know Pat Townsend, a retired Marine officer, a writer, and a leadership development practitioner. Townsend frequently noted that the Marines excelled in their ability to develop leadership, and that no organization on earth had more experience in developing leadership than the military. He urged that serious attention be paid to what the Marines did. In hindsight, we fear that message fell on deaf ears. It was not a time when the military was held in high esteem. Time passed, however, and in 1998 articles about the Marines began to appear in national publications.

Then one of the most useful pieces of original research to be produced on the topic of leadership was conducted by a partnership of McKinsey and Company, Inc., and The Conference Board. The objective of the research was to understand the genesis of energized workforces, which they defined as "any group of employees whose emotional commitment enables them to make or deliver products or services that constitute a sustainable competitive advantage for their employer."[1] This became a three-year effort involving a large research team. Organizations studied included Avon Products, First USA, Inc., The Home Depot, Johnson Controls, KFC, Marriott International, McKinsey and Company, Inc., Perot Systems, Southwest Airlines, Texas Instruments, 3M, the U.S. Marines, and the Vail Resorts, to name a few.

Our interest in that research stems largely from the insights it provides about leadership, as a key factor in producing an energized workforce. If leadership is ultimately measured by results, then an important intervening variable is the energized or mobilized workforce.

When asked about the merits of all the leadership development processes that he had observed, Jon Katzenbach, the research team's leader, unhesitatingly replied, "In my opinion, the best leadership development process in the world is at the U.S. Marine Corps." Many of his insights regarding that process have been published.[2] Earlier, David Freedman wrote an extensive review of the Marines' approach to leadership development in an article in *Inc.* magazine.[3]

Tom Clancy wrote a book, *Marine*, that gave a detailed and inside view of a Marine Expeditionary Unit.[4] We now seek to link the insights of their research with our own.

It is our conclusion that the Marines have come to utilize some extremely powerful leadership development practices. They arrived at this through their long experience and seeing what worked, rather than coming at it primarily from any scientific research study. We feel that our findings, primarily from an empirical research perspective, are solidly confirmed by the Marines' experience. And in addition to the fundamental principles, the Marines have developed practical methods through which to make these things happen. The confirmation of the underlying truths may not be half as important as their practical experience in making all of this happen.

TWO LEADERSHIP GROUPS

There are two distinct groups of Marine leaders to be considered. The Marines recruit young men and women to join the Corps, and their development path generally takes them to becoming noncommissioned officers. A small percentage is later sent to college, often to the Naval Academy, to become officer candidates, but they are the exceptions. Most officer candidates are recruited from colleges, and the Corps recruits the brightest and most qualified people they can obtain.

The Talent Base for Noncommissioned Officers
The Marines do a good job of recruiting, maybe the best of all the military services. They assign some of their best people to staff local recruiting offices. Nine out of ten applicants are rejected, and they will not accept high school dropouts or someone with a GED certificate. The recruiters contact over 250 young people to find one qualified candidate.

However, the Marines make no pretense of getting the best and brightest young people coming out of our finest high schools and colleges as recruits. The reality is that their recruits, for whatever reason, have usually decided not to go on to college. Seldom was the recruit the student body president or the class valedictorian. Only in rare cases have the recruits distinguished themselves through some remarkable achievement in their schooling or extracurricular activities. Many recruits have had minor convictions (most often traffic violations), and casual use of alcohol and drugs is common. A large percentage comes from troubled homes. Female recruits have often been subjected to some form of abuse in their homes. Approximately 50 percent of the women ultimately describe having had an abusive upbringing. All the usual predictors of success are not generally present in this group of recruits. Yet many of them are transformed into effective leaders after a two- to three-year period of time, and go on to display remarkable leadership skills as their careers continue. It is for that reason we felt it important to include this description of this organization's success in leadership development. In short, it can be done. Leaders can be made.

The Talent Base for Commissioned Officers

The commissioned officers of the U.S. Marines are college graduates. A few officers come out of the U.S. Naval Academy at Annapolis, but the number is usually less than one-tenth of their need. Most officers have been recruited from a variety of colleges in the United States.

These officer candidate recruits go to Officer Candidate School at Quantico, Virginia. Their course roughly parallels that of the general recruits, but with more emphasis on leadership development and other operational skills required of an officer. Their training is equally as physically demanding, and the hours per day are just as long. They must learn to use a rifle just like any other Marine, and they must also pass an annual physical fitness test like every other Marine. This group is also transformed into effective leaders. The percentage of success and the short time involved far eclipse that of any private-sector organization. We can learn a number of important lessons from the Marines' approach.

LESSONS FROM THE MARINES' APPROACH

Development Begins with Understanding the Unique Leadership Tasks Required. Leadership is a team effort rather than a solo performance. The Marines' emphasis on teams cascades through their leadership development. They pair a highly seasoned noncommissioned officer with a newly appointed lieutenant and allow the two of them to work together for several months. This eliminates many mistakes. The new officer has a sounding board with whom to think about strategies or tactics.

Jason Santamaria recounts his own experience of being put in charge of a 125-man combat unit.[5] He gave orders to have the troops issued gas masks and clean rifles in the same afternoon. That caused all of the Marines to miss dinner. An experienced first sergeant gave Santamaria useful feedback. He explained that his mistake had occurred from his failure to consult with the experienced leaders (noncommissioned officers) of the unit. From then on, Santamaria noted that he faithfully consulted with these seasoned leaders. That is a lesson in leadership that does not often get mentioned in a conventional MBA program.

Tom Clancy wrote about the development process for noncommissioned officers. He said, "As a Staff Sergeant you will probably be assigned that most dreaded of duties, a new 2nd Lieutenant to watch over and hopefully make into a useful officer."[6] The commissioned officers learn to rely heavily on their staff of noncommissioned officers.

Everyone Is on the Team. Daniel Freedman described the Marines' culture in these terms, as he told of a complex mission being planned by a Colonel Moore. "Moore will make the final decision among the three [alternatives being proposed], though he not only allows disagreement but practically demands it. This is standard Marine thinking; enlisted men and women and officers alike are expected to express concern about questionable decisions and orders, and one of the biggest mistakes an officer can make is to ignore or squelch such questioning."[7]

In fact, one of the common myths of leadership is that they go off by themselves, devise a clever strategy, and then come back to the organization and announce it to the eagerly awaiting masses. Leaders have often been reluctant to seek others' opinions about organization structure or long-range strategy, feeling that these were things they alone should be doing. Their belief is that to involve others would be a sign of weakness. Fortunately, that idea has undergone major change. Today, the most sophisticated leaders recognize that they are not expected to have all of the answers or to define the strategy of the organization by themselves.

Leaders Must Be Able to Cope with Rapidly Changing Leadership Patterns.   The Marines are clear about the oscillation that occurs in organizations between highly collaborative, team-based organizations in contrast to situations that call for a strong, single leader. Effective leaders must be able to recognize the difference, and to function comfortably in either situation. Katzenbach and Santamaria argue that "clarity creates trust."[8]

Private-sector executives are fond of talking about their management team, when in reality it has few functions of a true team. Good leaders know the difference, can function well in either environment, and can act as a follower in another single-leader work group. Part of their training involves planning a complex mission, and then shortly before executing it, having the roles and responsibilities of the group changed. For example, the patrol leader becomes the medic, and a new patrol leader comes into the group. Circumstances change rapidly, and everyone must be prepared to deal with rapid change.

Leadership Requires the Use of Peer Discipline and Pressure. The high level of commitment and loyalty in the Marines comes from not wanting to let your peers down, as much or more than from the pressure of not disappointing an officer. In private-sector corporations the emphasis is more often on pleasing a boss.

"Proving" behavior is pervasive in the business world, and it involves the individual having a strong need to look good in the eyes of a boss. Because of that, the discipline from the organization comes largely from the person who can hire and fire you.

The Marines, in contrast, emphasize group discipline. It has long been recognized that their primary motivation is to protect their comrades. Discipline ensures a deep commitment to the organization, to the unit, and to comrades. Thus, the strongest motivational forces come from within each person, and from colleagues.

Leadership Involves Planning and Performing Under Intense Time Pressure. The Marines train people to plan a mission down to the smallest detail, but the planning process is often compressed into a few hours. David Freedman describes one exercise he witnessed at Camp Pendleton in these words: "The Marines don't know what awaits them on shore, but they are confident that six hours of planning and preparing have left them better equipped to face it than most military units would be after six months." He goes on to note, "The art of a hard strike drawn up and delivered at lightning speed may once have seemed as far removed from the domain of a business as a moon shot. But with month-long high-tech-product life cycles, just-in-time manufacturing operations and overnight global currency crashes, the business world might just be coming around to the Marines' point of view."[9]

Speed is of the essence in the Marine's world. They prefer the benefits of a 70 percent solution that, while imperfect, can be reached immediately. Their position is that rapidly executed, mediocre decisions at least stand some chance of success. Those who are on the scene of the battle can often correct any flaws. The 70 percent decision implemented now is always better than a 100 percent decision implemented late.

Leadership Demands Reducing Complexity to Manageable Simplicity. The Marines are dedicated to a "rule of three." They organize using this principle, so that a corporal has a three-person firing team, a sergeant has three firing teams reporting to him, a lieutenant and a sergeant have a platoon that consists of three squads, and so it continues upward.

The same principle is applied to strategy and tactics. When confronted by a situation with seemingly infinite alternatives, the leader is taught to narrow them down to three plausible alternatives. (The Corps experimented once with changing the number to four, and noted that people's effectiveness sank dramatically.) Having defined three reasonable scenarios, the task is then to analyze these and select the best one.

When receiving an assignment, the Marines are taught to take time to define an order's "essence." They work hard to put the order in its simplest form, relevant to all who participate, and yet to keep the statement brief. In some ways this is analogous to a vision or mission statement in a company, though it is more operational.

Then the Marines are taught to pause, to determine the team's strengths and potential weaknesses in carrying out the mission, to state clearly the assumptions that are being made (for example, that the enemy will not use nuclear or biological warfare), and to define the actions they must not take (killing civilians, destroying historic buildings, or alienating the local population) and the information they need to execute the mission.

CONTRAST WITH LEADERSHIP TASKS IN BUSINESS AND INDUSTRY

The Marines have some leadership tasks that may differ in emphasis from those in business. The point is that they have successfully designed their leadership development around those unique requirements.

In the private sector, there may be more emphasis on the need for the leader to perform a wide variety of tasks, such as:

- Create a vision for the group
- Affirm values
- Define a strategy
- Inspire and motivate people
- Step back to see the big picture, see large realities
- Anticipate the future, think long term
- Resolve interdepartmental conflicts
- Allocate resources
- Connect the group with the outside world
- Influence people in wide circles
- Explain to stakeholder groups the reasons for various actions
- Serve as a symbol/perform symbolic acts

Obviously, many of the leadership functions in the Marines are exactly the same. Inspiring and motivating people are necessary in both situations. Focusing on results is required in both. The leadership development content and processes must address the needed tasks or processes, but these are no more complex in the private sector than those faced by the Marines.

Leadership Attributes
Are the fundamental attributes required of a leader in the Marine Corps the same as those required in a private-sector firm or in a government agency? In earlier chapters we described our research on necessary attributes. We now compare them with those the Marine Corps leaders need to develop.

Character. Much of the entire induction and training process in the Marines is designed to inculcate a new set of core values. These emphasize a strict code of honor and honesty. The process begins as recruits are inducted and then sent to the Parris Island training center. Each new recruit is asked if there is anything in his or her background that would keep him or her from serving effectively as a Marine. The recruits are told that any lies detected after this point will be grounds for immediate dismissal. However, an admission of some past mistake will generally be worked out in a way that will not damage their career.

If an officer suggests that an enlisted person fudge the truth, he can be called to task by the enlisted person. One visitor was about to board a helicopter, and as he was being escorted aboard, a message came that the necessary paperwork for this visitor had not been completed. Getting it done would delay the flight. An officer said to the messenger, "We could just act is if the order came too late." The messenger looked the officer squarely in the eye and said, "But that would not be correct, sir." The officer smiled, and said, "You are absolutely right, we'll wait for the proper paperwork to be completed." This emphasis on character produces leaders who are trusted. Leaders ask nothing that they are not willing to do themselves. The entire training process emphasizes tenacity and persistence in the face of tough obstacles. Marines practice self-development. Their overall development process creates enthusiasm and pride, and generates a philosophy of continual improvement. The emphasis on absolute honesty and candor is so strong that it caused at least one observer to wonder if the values of the Marines are not deviating significantly from those of our society at large.

The personal character dimension of leadership is defined by a set of principles that guide Marines' conduct. The Marines created a book of leadership principles, and new recruits are expected to memorize 11 leadership principles. These are the touchstone for all discussions on proper leadership behavior.

Personal Capability.   The development process builds the necessary knowledge about the overall organization, as well as required technical knowledge about several functional areas. It teaches a rigor in problem solving and analyzing thorny issues and does that via countless specific examples presented by senior officers. These sessions consume 50 hours a month for six months. Through planning multiple missions in short time spans, leaders learn to sharpen their problem-solving techniques. Being in a feedback-rich environment ensures that people will learn ways to improve their own effectiveness. Innovation is encouraged through a culture that does not punish failure or tell people exactly how to do things, but that emphasizes desired end states.

On a more mundane yet important level, Marine officers learn to dress the part. Whether acting as a recruiter, when dress uniforms are often worn in public gatherings, or as a drill instructor wearing an immaculate uniform and the "Smokey Bear" hat, how the leader is dressed is important. Along with dress, one personal capability that officers develop is a command voice. Clancy writes, "Like the famous 'rebel yell' of the Civil War, it is impossible to describe, but you know it when you hear it." Clancy notes that every drill instructor and Series Commander has developed this voice, and that it makes every statement, comment, or order given to the new recruit "sound like the voice of God himself. The first time you experience a drill instructor in full regalia and command voice is something you never forget."[10]

Over time, the Marines seek to broaden the horizons of their people. They encourage further education, including going to college. The Marines often pay for attendance at a university. Some are encouraged to seek a commission as an officer by attending the U.S. Naval Academy at Annapolis.

Focus on Results.   The objective of every method of leadership development is to provide the tools for accomplishing strategic goals. This begins with the process of carefully defining the essence of the mission, creating three meaningful alternatives, selecting one of those for implementation, defining the desired end state, analyzing the strengths and weaknesses of the team that will execute the mission, defining what must not occur, preparing a detailed plan of implementation, and it ends with executing the plan. All of this is designed to give the aspiring officer the tools with which to produce better results.

Interpersonal Skills.   One Marine officer who was visiting a private-sector company was stunned to observe that the manager did not know the employees' names. The Marine remarked that he was expected not only to know the names of his people, but also to know the names of all their family members. We describe elsewhere the emphasis on courageous and frank dialogue. Marines treat each other like family. During training they are taught always to be alert to ways to prevent accidents, always to help a fellow Marine, and they often refer to each other as "sister" or "brother." Relationships are characterized by trust and mutual respect. Honest but civil dialogue is encouraged. There is also a strong emphasis on team activities and extensive communication within the team.

Leading Organizational Change.   At lower levels in the organization, the Marines' development process puts leaders in an operating role, but does not emphasize the processes for bringing about organizational change. Executing missions effectively is what we have earlier described as Stage III behavior, but is not the visionary, statesman role, nor the role of transforming the culture. The reality of most organizations is that they need a limited number of such people. Senior officers in the Corps are trained to think and act on a larger scale and a longer-term basis.

THE PROCESSES AND TOOLS OF LEADERSHIP DEVELOPMENT

The Marine Corps techniques for developing leaders provide several valuable lessons.

People Development Requires a Significant Commitment of Time from Many in the Organization. The Marines invest enormous amounts of time and organizational resource in their leadership development process. The private sector, if it becomes serious about developing stronger leadership, must begin by greatly increasing the emphasis placed on the training of new people. Every future leader must be inculcated with the mission and values of the organization. Research has shown that thoughtfully conducted new employee orientation not only improves immediate productivity, it also increases the length of time people stay with the organization. Plus, better-trained employees in turn create more satisfied clients, which in turn produce greater profitability for a business.

The Marines' time commitment to develop first-level managers provides a similar contrast to prevailing practices in the private sector. Years ago, companies provided one- to two-week programs for people who had been individual contributors to prepare them to take on a new role as supervisors or first-level managers. Today there is an enormous push to reduce time off the job. Organizations are striving to have development days cut to hours, and hours cut to 20-minute snippets of learning. A large number of organizations provide no formal development to newly appointed supervisors or managers.

In contrast, the Marines send officer candidates to Quantico, Virginia, for a 10-week stint of development. There they are exposed to both theoretical as well as practical information about leadership, and a variety of skill-building activities.

Leaders Need to Find Their Natural Strengths, and Not Be Forced into an Unnatural Mold Created by the Organization. The Marines' approach to leadership development is quite different from the stereotypes that exist about how the military develops officers. Rather than being rigid and insisting that everyone perform in a similar style or process, the Marines understand that there are many effective leadership patterns. The Marines have discovered that some of their leaders succeed because of their technical expertise. Others are powerful team builders. Still others excel in their organizational skills. Some are extraordinary in their ability to see the potential in people and their ability to bring it out. Rather than force-fit their leaders into any one mold, those responsible for leadership development observe the natural strengths and encourage the leader to magnify that quality. By placing officer candidates in demanding situations, seasoned observers can spot leadership strengths and weaknesses. Their process is exactly opposite of what many would assume. Their emphasis is on helping potential officers find their own voice and magnify their natural tendencies.

Leadership Is Best Developed with Highly Engaging Learning Methods. Nearly everything the Marines do in their leadership development process is highly involving, not merely academic. Leaders make plans under severe time pressure, and then execute them. Some methods are physical. For example, aspiring leaders are given the challenge of getting a wounded comrade across a small river, reported to be mined, with only a few boards and some rope.

Other assignments are more cerebral. A challenging mission is defined for them and they must come up with three detailed alternative courses of action in the next six hours, and then choose the best alternative from the three.

At the conclusion of a project the group engages in an "after action review" that focuses on what went well and how it could have been improved. This is one of the most powerful learning devices the Marines and other military services use. It is a perfect example of team-based leadership. In this process, everyone involved in a mission comes together and psychologically takes off their stripes, and then conducts a totally open, candid discussion of what went well and what could have been improved. These detailed reviews provide an extremely valuable learning process, and emphasize the democratic nature of the organization. The format for this review involves a detailed discussion of questions such as:

- What was our intent?
- What actually happened?
- Why did that happen?
- What can we learn from those events?
- What actions should we take now in preparation for future, similar events?

Action Learning Projects
The bulk of the entire development process includes a variety of extremely engaging activities, and their power comes from the fact that they are highly practical, relevant to the job the Marines will actually be performing, and require a physical or visceral involvement that replicates the actual missions they will later perform. During a 10-week-long development program, learning teams carry out a mind-boggling 27 missions, ranging from setting up a humanitarian aid station to a more traditional assault.

Contrast that with the pattern of many executive development programs, in which the participants listen to lectures, are given extensive lists of books and articles to read, see videotapes, and discuss cases presented by the faculty. The level of action required, and the emotional engagement with the activities, is extremely different from the Marines' approach.

More sophisticated programs in industry are moving toward higher levels of involvement, including simulations, task forces dedicated to important company issues, and action learning projects that are extremely engaging to the participants.

Teaching Leadership with Personally Related Stories
The Marines have senior officers tell stories to aspiring second lieutenants of how they personally handled a challenging situation. One officer related how he was given the assignment to secure a mer-

chant ship at sea, after the fall of Saigon. The ship was full of refugees, and the assignment was to secure the ship from the deserting South Vietnamese soldiers who were seizing ships and killing the crews. The officer had never had such an assignment before, but he applied the principles he had been taught about securing buildings. In general, start at the top floor, so that you can drop down on opponents, and move faster downward than they can climb upward to you. Further, hand grenades do not bounce back down on to you.

This riveting story of a challenging assignment provided a powerful teaching device to implant the principle of shifting decision making to the people who are closest to the action.

And recounting "stories" of how they accomplished a challenging mission, such as overtaking an enemy boat on the sea in stormy weather, provides opportunity to explain the thought processes that went into planning the mission as well as the details of its execution. At the Marines' basic school, nearly 300 hours over a six-month period are dedicated to having instructors relate their stories to the aspiring leaders. It is their belief that by digesting this extraordinary number of case examples, the young lieutenants begin to inductively develop guiding principles of behavior regarding the best approach to challenging assignments.

Leadership Development Requires Information and Knowledge about Leadership.   The Marines have approximately 100 books on a recommended reading list. The aspiring leaders are required to read them, and these books are discussed in a serious manner in more academic sessions. These texts are taken seriously, and officer candidates are expected to have read and understood them. There is also an official Marine Corps' manual with which people are expected to be highly conversant. It is the one book from which everyone must be able to quote chapter and verse.

Leadership Versatility Is Developed by Cross Training in Areas Outside One's Area of Expertise.   Lawyers are assigned infantry units to command, while an infantry commander is transferred to head up a supply unit. While there is clearly some sacrifice of short-term productivity, there is an enormous long-term gain in having a cadre of leaders exposed to other areas, and who can move from one venue to another with no serious lapse in performance.

WHO IS RESPONSIBLE FOR LEADERSHIP DEVELOPMENT?

Everyone Assumes Responsibility for Leadership Development. As noted earlier, the noncommissioned officers feel responsible for developing new lieutenants. The gunnery sergeants feel responsible for developing the leadership skills of the sergeants under them. This is not an afterthought. It is a significant part of everyone's responsibility. The Marines believe that everyone must be taught to lead, because one never knows when the appointed leader may be wounded or killed, and the mission must go on.

Leadership Development Is Most Successful When Conducted by the Most Effective Senior Members of Management. We observe that in most corporations, trainers are junior people, hired specifically for that role. More often than not, they have had little or no line experience. There are occasional exceptions. Some organizations enlist line managers to serve as trainers, and the research on that practice has consistently shown that such trainers produce superior results to those whose role is just training.

A new supervisory training system was being implemented in a group of health care institutions. The organization was agreeable to measuring the results of this new program. Measures included the change in behavior displayed by the supervisors, as seen by the subordinates over a six-month period following the training. This was measured through questionnaires completed by the subordinates. Measurements were taken within three large institutions involving hundreds of supervisors.

In one hospital, the results were a quantum leap above the other two. Yet exactly the same program was delivered in each, with exactly the same amount of time being dedicated to it.

Those conducting the research could find only one difference between the organization with such strong results and the other two.

The person who conducted nearly all of the sessions in the organization with the strongest results was the hospital administrator. It appeared that having his personal interest in the process, and the emphasis that his presence gave the program, made an important difference.

No one pretends that these senior leaders are more effective in the classroom, if judged by presentation skills, facilitation skills, or knowledge of the theory. However, they bring credibility and practical know-how. They can tell powerful stories of their personal experiences.

The Marines choose their drill instructors from the top 25 percent of noncommissioned officers. To become a noncommissioned officer (staff sergeant) takes between 8 and 12 years, and then an additional 4 to 6 years to become a "gunny" (gunnery sergeant). It is from this group that the drill instructors are chosen. And of this group, only 80 percent get through the demanding development process. However, the impact they have on impressionable recruits is incalculable.

Tom Clancy wrote in his book, *Marine,* about the graduation ceremony from the final phase of recruit training. He descried how the new Marines rushed to introduce their family and friends to their drill instructor. "Thanks for getting me through Boot Camp" was a frequently expressed sentiment. He then noted watching parents express profound thanks to the drill instructors for the change they saw in their sons and daughters. Clancy writes, "I defy you to watch this moment and not shed a tear or two. I did."[11]

Over a year's time, senior "trainers" can have an indelible impact on 100–500 people. They do it in different ways. Roger Enrico of PepsiCo spent one week with groups of younger executives, both sharing his ideas and seeking their views about how to develop the business. He attributed that process with producing many of the best ideas for developing PepsiCo's success. He testifies that this was some of the best time he spent as CEO.

For many years Andy Grove, CEO of Intel, participated in the company's supervisory development program. When asked how he could take time to engage in that activity, he told the inquirer, "Where else could I spend time that would have that much lasting impact on the people who make our organization succeed?" It is a powerful message when the senior-most person in a firm takes people development seriously.

Unfortunately, those are more the exception than the rule. In general, we observe that while the chairman and CEO of large organizations are the ones who seem most worried about the development of their people, the amount of time they spend doing that is miniscule. Worse yet, the rest of the senior leadership group seems generally uninvolved in any organizational leadership development process. In most private-sector organizations, development is most often viewed as someone else's job, usually someone in Human Resources.

LEADERSHIP DEVELOPMENT BOTH SHAPES AND REFLECTS THE CULTURE OF THE ORGANIZATION

Leadership Development Begins with the Policies and Values of the Organization.   For starters, does the organization believe in promoting from within, or does it normally go outside to fill key positions? This fundamental practice becomes the foundation for the need for leadership development activities and affects the level of seriousness with which it is taken.

The Marines take great pride in recruiting a larger percentage of their officers from the enlisted ranks than any of the other services. They have adopted a "Grow Our Own" program that expresses their emphasis on promotions from within.

Leadership Development Must Be Taken Seriously by the Entire Organization, Not Just a Few People in a Development Function.   While nearly every corporate leader would pronounce that people are the firm's most important asset, most observers do not see actions that reflect that. In many firms, earnings come first, while in others customer satisfaction leads out. We seldom encounter organizations in which people believe they come first.

Marine leaders go to great length to practice people development. They give personal attention to every officer candidate and to every aspiring noncommissioned officer. They consider it a failure when one drops out. They strive to enhance people's self-esteem. Setbacks and challenges are seen merely as feedback and not as grounds for eliminating someone.

Leadership Development Includes Everyone, Not Just a Few Elite, So-Called High-Potential People.   In contrast to most businesses, which go to much expense to test and assess people in an attempt to identify future executives, the Marines train everyone to lead. They don't build a gulf between followers and leaders, but assume instead that everyone should be trained to lead.

The high level of commitment to people development takes the form of doing as much for the people in the bottom half of the bell-shaped curve as for those in the top half of the curve. We think this practice can go a long way toward creating commitment and loyalty in any organization. Rather than waiting for people to fail and then gleefully seeing them depart, the Marines work hard to keep anyone from failing, and measure success by the high portion of people making it successfully through their training process.

The contrast between this policy and that of many private-sector companies could not be more stark.

Continual Improvement in the Quality of the Workforce Occurs through Development, Not Elimination.   Many corporations proudly announce their policy of evaluating everyone on a regular basis, and then each year systematically eliminating the bottom 10 to 20 percent. That has been one of the favorite human resource policies of some of the legendary "tough" executives.

This policy contains a number of serious drawbacks, terrible negative consequences to the organization, and is inherently unfair. This "rank and spank" philosophy deserves serious questioning.

First, it assumes that managers are accurate in their appraisal of subordinates' performance, despite a large body of evidence to the contrary. The consistency of performance appraisals is notoriously low. In some situations good data exist, but those are more the exception than the rule.

Second, it penalizes employees working for an executive who has recruited an exceptionally talented group of people. The first person to be terminated in Group A may be more productive and capable than the person in Group B who is at the midpoint of that group, simply because Group A consisted of an exceptionally talented group of people to start with.

Third, it assumes that people are static and incapable of development. Yet most of us have seen people make significant changes in their performance over time.

Fourth, it assumes that the nature of the job people have been given, the influence of the group around them, and relationships with the immediate manager are all of no consequence. It defines the individual as the only variable in the equation.

Fifth, it pits people in the organization against each other, rather than establishing a performance standard to be reached. It is management's admission that they are not able to set up an accurate performance standard by which to judge people, so the surrogate for doing that is to create a list and arbitrarily cut off the bottom 10 percent.

Sixth, this "proving" orientation has been shown to diminish risk taking and encourages people to be cautious and tentative in their work. People working in such environments are more prone to do just what they are told and not seek to learn from their work.

Such a policy works when there is an unlimited supply of people seeking to work for an organization, because of its prestige, its high compensation, or some other factor. Elite universities practice this with junior faculty.

However, the time has come to seriously challenge the wisdom of this policy. Turnover is costly. Good people are hard to find and expensive to develop. The impact of this policy has never been fully measured. As Jacques Nassar was ousted and Bill Ford took over at Ford, one of the key issues that Chairman Ford was most irate over was the Darwinian HR policy of forcing 10 percent of the workers to get a C grade, which in turn could lead to their termination. That policy triggered numerous lawsuits and put employee morale in the tank. One of Bill Ford's first acts was to change the policy and attempt to heal the organization. In 1980 *Fortune* magazine published an article about America's 10 toughest bosses. Andrall Pearson was one of them. During the time he ran PepsiCo, his practice was to fire the bottom 10–20 percent each year. Colleagues described him as "brutally abrasive." In a recent article describing the new Pearson ("Andy Pearson Finds Love"), now chairman of Tricon Global Restaurants, Inc., Pearson is quoted saying, "Ultimately, it's all about having more genuine concern for the other person. There's a big difference between being tough and being tough-minded. There's an important aspect that has to do with humility." Pearson has come to recognize that a company's success cannot be imposed from the top down, but is the outgrowth of the emotional connection employees feel for the firm. That comes from "attention, awareness, recognition, and reward."

Terminating poor performers who refuse to work hard and tenaciously is clearly the right thing to do, but arbitrarily terminating the bottom 10 to 20 percent of the workforce each year is not the most enlightened policy. Harsh treatment of people is no longer acceptable. As Pearson notes, "People have so many more options than they used to. They can leave—and you can't find more talent just by turning over the next log. Second, that kind of treatment demoralizes people."[12]

The Marines, and other organizations, have demonstrated that you can work hard to have everyone succeed. Weeding out the bottom 10 percent is not the only way to achieve a highly productive workforce.

Diversity Should Be Encouraged, Not Discouraged.   Large corporations develop criteria for selecting future executives. This usually involves an analysis of the competencies displayed by the current executive group, so new people are chosen exactly in their image. This process screens out the maverick, innovative person who does not fit the mold, but who may be exactly what the organization needs. Indeed, Clayton Christensen, in his highly applauded book, *The Innovator's Dilemma,* has noted that the decline of so many large organizations may be attributed to the inbred nature of their leadership, and the formulaic approach they took to running the institution. "Good management was the most powerful reason [these leading firms] failed to stay atop their industries. Precisely because these firms listened to their customers, invested aggressively in technologies that would provide their customers more and better products of the sort they wanted, and because they carefully studied market trends and systematically allocated investment capital to innovations that promised the best returns, they lost positions of leadership."[13]

Everyone Should Be Trained to Be an Effective Leader.   Social scientists and management experts have long argued that seldom was one person the leader and everyone else a follower. Indeed, leadership is a function or set of behaviors that often gets passed around in a group. The person with the loftiest title and supposed power is no longer the one with all the answers and is seldom the one to define the strategy as a solo performance. Given the knowledge that leadership indeed gets passed around, the Marines' approach to training everyone to be an effective leader is the most logical one.

Brigadier General Douglas O'Dell was describing the new Marine Expeditionary Brigade antiterrorist battalion, created in the aftermath of the September 11, 2001, terrorist attacks. He remarked, "This is, in my view, not a general's war, a colonel's war, or a captain's war. This is a corporal's war. It will be fought in back alleys and on rooftops around the world by small units and individual units of Marines."[14]

Let's enumerate some of the benefits of the broad-scale development of leadership.

- Employee commitment soars. Imagine the effect on the level of commitment of everyone in the organization if they realize that the organization really cares about them and is willing to invest in their development. Retention research consistently shows a high level of correlation between people staying with an organization and opportunities for development.

- Bench strength increases. Calculate the value of the bench strength this process produces. The organization can now reach everywhere and find people trained on the basics of leadership behavior. No longer is the organization held hostage by a few high potentials whose threat to leave become grounds for enormous concessions or exceptions.

- Overlooked talent is discovered. We contend that some extremely successful leaders would have been overlooked under the usual processes of selection. This way, everyone has an opportunity to be grounded in good leadership principles, and because of hard work and tenacity some "late bloomers" will show up as great leaders in the future.

- The culture is reinforced. The exposure of everyone to senior officers of the company most certainly builds the leadership skills of the junior people, but also reinforces the culture. Nothing is as powerful as models of behavior, but often the officials of an organization remain very removed and distant from the frontline people. The influence that comes from close contact over many hours is orders of magnitude greater than listening to a prepared speech from an executive in the company cafeteria.

- The organization can be flatter. The Marine's have 8.7 enlisted personnel per officer, in contrast to the Air Force's 4 per officer or the Army's 5 to each officer.

Leaders Should Be Held Accountable for the Level of Commitment and Morale of Their People.   In the private sector we have had the strange notion that while the corporation owned all of the hard assets, money, and intellectual property, managers could do whatever they chose with their people. Some have been reluctant to conduct company-wide employee attitude surveys, lest they be seen as intruding on the leaders' domains. We contend that the company needs to know of declining morale, and managers should be held accountable for any degeneration in commitment and loyalty to the firm. And leaders need to be accountable for developing leaders in their sphere of responsibility.

Leadership Development Requires a Feedback-Rich Environment That Emphasizes Learning from Failure, Rather Than Punishment for Mistakes.   One of the keys to the Marines' leadership experience is an environment that creates receptivity to, and provides an ample supply of, feedback. The culture is extremely tolerant of failure, realizing that failure is the most powerful teacher.

Leadership Development Occurs Best in an Egalitarian Culture. The Marines emphasize the need for open, frank debate on all decisions. That dialogue occurs only when the culture reinforces an attitude in which authority can be challenged with no negative consequences. It also requires a culture in which leaders specify end results, but refrain from telling people the means by which tasks are to be accomplished. This develops initiative and creativity, along with a high sense of ownership.

CONCLUSION

It is obvious that over the 226 years of the Marine Corps' existence, the Corps has learned a great deal about developing leaders. Their experience has shaped their views as to the real requirements of leadership, as well as the optimum ways to select and develop their leaders. Their experience in developing leaders appears to have shaped their culture, just as their strong culture has molded their practices of leadership development. Because of their extraordinary skills and resourcefulness, they transport the president and guard embassies around the world, in addition to being called on for the most challenging special assignments. Their success serves as an extremely valuable model for corporations to study. While it may be premature to advise anyone to adopt their ways "lock, stock, and barrel," it appears that any organization that is serious about developing people can learn a great deal from the U.S. Marines. They prove leaders can be developed.

WHAT INDIVIDUALS DO TO BECOME GREAT LEADERS

All over this country, in corporations and government agencies, there are millions of executives who imagine that their place on the organization chart has given them a body of followers. And of course it hasn't. It has given them subordinates. Whether the subordinates become followers depends on whether the executives act like leaders.

John Gardner

The most dangerous leadership myth is that leaders are born—that there is a genetic factor to leadership. Myth asserts that people simply either have certain charismatic qualities or not. That's nonsense; in fact, the opposite is true. Leaders are made rather than born.

Warren G. Bennis

THE AGE-OLD QUESTIONS

When the subject turns to leadership, someone inevitably asks the questions, "Well, aren't leaders born that way?" Then comes, "Can I really make myself a better leader?" The questions arise so frequently from savvy and well-intentioned people, we feel the need to address them yet one more time.

On the One Hand

We begin by acknowledging that there is a legitimate point of view in arguing that leaders are born that way. The revered guru of management, Peter Drucker, wrote in *The Practice of Management* that "leadership cannot be taught or learned."[1] Added to that is a long series of studies on the personality dimensions of leadership, and the strong evidence that personality does not change a great deal over a person's lifetime. Other researchers have analyzed the profound influence of parents and their role in shaping the values of a child's willingness to take on responsibility, and the role that has in the child's developing leadership abilities. Those characteristics appear to change little over a lifetime.

Harrison Gough, the eminent University of California at Berkeley psychologist, has noted that the "dominance" scale of his California Psychological Inventory is a strong predictor of being selected as a leader. Other psychological tests have been used successfully to select leaders. Leadership abilities are often first exhibited in junior high school, high school, and college. Longitudinal studies of leaders in industry and the military show that key characteristics in leaders show up very early in life and remain quite fixed.

The most powerful psychometric instruments are biographical inventory tests, in which people are asked a series of questions about what they have done in their earlier life. (Were you the captain of any team, the president of any school group, or did you start your own business as a young child?) Because the past is the best predictor of the future, a probing analysis of people's past does strongly predict their future, and leadership patterns are often established early in life.

Add to that the evidence on leadership having some correlation with physical stature (taller people are more apt to be perceived as strong leaders) or body chemistry (higher levels of testosterone in men are correlated with leadership positions), and you can understand why the question is repeatedly asked.

On the Other Hand

While there may be some predictive power of psychological tests and early childhood experience, it is clear that they fail to explain why a good number of leaders succeed. There is clearly no one factor that anyone has identified that consistently predicts who will succeed as a leader. Notable cases of "late bloomers" suggest that people with fairly undistinguished early portions in their careers turn out to be strong leaders. That could be said of both Abraham Lincoln and Harry S Truman.

It is also clear that with such wide variation in organization cultures, if the right match is created, many more people could succeed in leadership. The "dot-com" craze enabled many to succeed temporarily who would never have succeeded in traditional organizations.

In longitudinal studies of leadership, more than a third of the college graduates who were predicted not to move into higher ranks of the firm actually did so, thus proving that hard work, perseverance, and tenacity (and possibly luck) enabled these people to succeed.

Our Conclusion on This Debate

We share the conclusion with others that the right answer is between these two extremes. James Kouzes and Barry Posner wrote, "We would be intellectually dishonest if we did not say that some individuals clearly have a higher probability of succeeding at leadership than others. But this does not mean that ordinary managers cannot become extraordinary leaders."[2]

"A good executive is born when someone with some natural endowments (intelligence, vigor, and some capacity for interacting with his fellow men) by dint of practice, learning, and experience, develops that endowment into a mature skill."[3]

Our view mirrors those above. There is no question that some people come into the world endowed with self-confidence and a keen intellect. That is clearly an advantage. But of that group, only a small number move on to remarkable achievements as leaders. The difference appears to be hard work, thoughtful and tenacious effort, zeal for learning, and a willingness to extend beyond one's normal comfort zone.

So a great deal of what we see great leaders doing is a result of personal effort. If you subscribe to the belief that leadership is not a person, but a series of behaviors that are displayed by a great many in an organization, then it becomes easy to argue that everyone can get better at leadership. So our slightly compromising statements on this subject are

- Some people start with clear advantages, but
- Nearly all people are made better leaders from specific developmental activities.
- Leaders are a lot more "made" than they are "born."

HOW INDIVIDUALS IMPROVE THEMSELVES

In the book *Results-Based Leadership,* 14 suggestions are made regarding the way people can improve their leadership outcomes or results.[4] In this book we are focused on developing the attributes and skills of the leader. Following are 25 suggestions for ways in which leaders can improve the attributes or behavior that are vital in producing those results. The key thing to remember is that improvement that you make on any one dimension spills over to many others. There is no such thing as working on only one leadership quality or attribute. When you improve one, you will invariably be improving several others.

1. Decide to become a great leader.   This is actually two decisions. First, most people do not think of "leadership" in the same terms as other roles in life. At a young age a person may aspire to become a physician, a lawyer, a molecular biologist, an astronaut, or a rock star, but chances are you have never heard of someone saying, "I want to grow up to be a leader." We think of leadership as an adjunct or frosting on some other role. Someday that may change. For people inside organizations, however, the first decision is to see that being a leader in an organization is important and worthy of your continued effort.

The second decision is to be great, rather than just mediocre at this role of leadership. This is the decision to go way beyond the ordinary or average, and make a huge difference in the organization.

One positive element of this decision is the fact that it is not a zero-sum game. Becoming a great leader is something everyone can aspire to, and one person's effectiveness in no way detracts from others' success. In this game, everyone can win and one person's winning actually helps others to win.

When Lleyton Hewitt, the young Australian tennis player, was interviewed after having defeated Pete Sampras for the U.S. Open Championship in 2001, he said, "I dreamed about this moment ever since I was a young boy." Truly excelling at something involves a strong commitment wrapped around a dream.

To become a highly effective leader requires a real dedication to that task and a willingness to act with the intensity and focus that characterizes great athletes.

2. Develop and display high personal character.   The leader walks a difficult line between two seemingly opposing forces. First, the leader must be willing to take the role of leader. That means calling the meeting to order, pushing the agenda along, drawing some people out and toning others down. It means saying "no" to a budget request that can't be funded. It also means having to terminate a long-time friend who is not performing effectively. Being a leader means being willing to take charge and make certain that the group performs well.

We have observed a newly appointed dean in a university who wanted to maintain close ties with former colleagues on the faculty and, in fact, did not want anything to change. So the new dean continued to act exactly like a faculty member and talk like a faculty member (including the inevitable complaints about the university administration). In a few weeks it became obvious that this person would not succeed in his new role, because he was unwilling to take on the requirements of the new office to which he had been appointed.

That same scenario plays out in government organizations and in industry. A leader must be willing to take that role, including all of the activities that a person occupying that role is expected to engage in or perform.

The counterforce to taking the "role" of leader is that people at lower levels in the organization resent arrogance from those in authority. They do not like the leader who conveys an attitude of superiority, condescension, or disrespect. The line between those two forces is a very fine one.

So, the counsel to all leaders is to maintain an attitude of humility. Be willing to laugh at yourself. Do not flaunt the authority you have. Humility will make you approachable. It opens the door to building relationships. The leader needs to find some mirror from which can be learned the way others perceive your character. That mirror may be a good internal mentor. It could be a trusted colleague or subordinate. It could be an effective 360-degree feedback process. Whatever it is, leaders need to have some sense about how people perceive their character. They need to know if they are trusted. Without that, it is not possible to exert strong influence on a work group.

Also, be cautious in the commitments you make, and then always deliver. Be careful not to overstate or overpromise. We are sure that some are saying, "But can people just improve their character?" "What's the best way to make changes in my fundamental personality or character?" The answer to that question might be surprising to some. There has been a belief that the following chain exists:

$$\text{Character} \rightarrow \text{Attitudes} \rightarrow \text{Behavior}$$

The fact of the matter, however, is that people make their attitudes and ultimately their character conform to their behavior. The place to begin is with behavior. Thus, participating in powerful skill-building programs designed to improve interpersonal skills will have a decided effect on attitudes of the participants. When people learn and practice new behavior, there is a remarkable transformation of their attitudes and ultimately their character.

$$\text{Behavior} \rightarrow \text{Attitudes} \rightarrow \text{Character}$$

3. Develop new skills. Enroll in developmental experiences.
There are numerous developmental experiences available to most

leaders. These may be available from within their organization, paid for and sponsored by them. Or they may be available from a local university or college. Others may be available from various suppliers of learning and development materials. The key is for leaders to move outside their comfort zone to do something that will provide some real development. Leaders must be willing to invest in themselves, and many activities require time off the job.

One of the authors has an acquaintance who is a legendary example of self-development. Once a year a group gets together to meet, and the first question people ask is, "Okay, Dick, what have you done this year? Every year Dick embarks on some new adventure into personal learning. These range from sessions with "healing shamans" to seminars on corporate reengineering. Each adds a new dimension to Dick's character and understanding. While everyone would not choose the precise development experiences he chooses, the point is his disciplined approach to taking time every year for his own personal growth.

Attend any development program your organization provides, or those offered by local universities and private organizations. Constantly develop yourself, whether in the ability to deliver compelling presentations before a large group or the ability to write a concise memo on an important business topic. We reiterate that every new skill learned and used lifts that specific skill and numerous others along with it.

4. Find a coach. Many organizations are hiring professional coaches to work with their key executives. They find the investment in someone who is capable of providing objective, constructive feedback to be well worth the investment. The higher people move in the organization, the less apt they are to hear the truth from people about them, so the value of coaches may increase as people move to higher levels in the organization.

It is instructive to note that world-class athletes pay for coaches to work with them. The great tennis players and golfers usually employ personal coaches. Athletes playing on the best professional teams receive constant coaching from people hired specifically to do that. In professional football, there are specific coaches for the defense, the offense, and the "special teams." There may even be a specific "quarterback" coach.

Some executives have created their personal board of directors whose function is to give them feedback on the way they are managing their career and on their current performance in their job.

We see the movement toward coaching as one that will continue to grow. It is driven in part by the fact that most executives are not comfortable with, or good at, providing constructive feedback to people around them. What is especially effective is the coach who calls on a regular basis and discusses the leader's success in taking some agreed-upon action steps. This process builds strong accountability and produces remarkable behavioral outcomes.

5. Identify your strengths.   Peter Drucker argues, "Self-development is making oneself better at what one is already good at. It also means not worrying about the things one cannot be good at."[5] To accomplish this, Drucker advises:

- List your major contributions over the past two or three years.
- Specify precisely the things the organization expects from you, and for which you are held accountable.
- Be clear about what you cannot do, as well as what you can do.
- Look for demanding assignments that make a difference.[6]

With characteristic wisdom and insight, Drucker gives useful advice to all leaders. Taking time to inventory the major contributions you have made in the past few years is a step that few leaders take. But what better place is there to start to understand your strengths? It also reveals where you are likely to make significant contributions in the future. Listing accomplishments also is a good barometer of your focus on results behavior. Everyone who is a leader, or aspires to serious leadership, should be able to itemize a list of contributions to the organization. If you are unable to do that, then consider seriously whether you suffer from the fatal flaw of inaction.

Repeated studies in organizations reveal that people are relatively unclear about what is expected of them, and especially what they are personally being held accountable to perform by their colleagues and bosses. We have argued strenuously that an emphasis on expanding strengths is far more valuable and productive than slogging away at trying to remedy weaknesses.

We begin by appealing to every reader's own experience. Think back to high school and college experiences. Let's assume for a moment that you were extremely adept at mathematics and anything quantitative. Your grades in algebra, trigonometry, and calculus were excellent. On the other hand, grammar and composition came really hard to you. You neither enjoyed language study much nor did you do well at it. To continue, you have decided to embark on a path that would have you recognized as an excellent student. Which path should you choose? Do you work hard at becoming better at English? Or do you decide to leverage your head start in mathematics and excel in that arena?

First, where will your motivation be highest? We think your passion to excel will come in the quantitative arena. You like the fundamental activities involved. Your thought processes immediately gravitate toward quantitative analysis.

Second, where are you likely to feel some constant reward? Again, we argue that you are far more likely to continually receive positive feedback when you are engaged in quantitative activities than in anything having to do with language. It is less likely that people will praise your having gotten to "average" in grammar and composition skills.

Third, where are you apt to make the greatest amount of progress? You could make the theoretical argument that people could improve more in those areas in which they are weak. There is just a lot more room to move up. However, the ceilings are so high in every discipline that no matter how good a student you are now, there is huge room to grow.

Fourth, what is the best path by which to develop credibility? Becoming good at something creates a halo effect of overall competence. It sometimes goes to ludicrous extremes, as when a movie actress is asked for her opinions on the wisdom of building a missile defense system or a Nobel Prize winner in physics suddenly gets quoted for his views on the role of genetics in human intelligence. Why? Because he is extraordinarily knowledgeable and creative in one arena, we assume those gifts spill over into other areas. Whether warranted or not, being good at one thing creates a perception that a person is good at many things, or everything.

Confidence and Competence

Why Working on Strengths Is More Likely to Happen
It is impossible to overestimate the role of confidence in people developing competence. We frequently witness people who at one level would be deemed to be competent. In a safe, sanitary situation, they are able to make an effective presentation. However, they refuse to make a presentation in front of senior managers or customers. Their lack is not of knowing what to do, or even being able to do it. Their lack is confidence to be willing to try in a more challenging circumstance.

We contend that strengths build confidence, and that this confidence spreads like yeast in a lump of bread dough and everything then rises. Hence, working on strengths will be far more likely to occur.

Why Developing Strengths Will Be More Successful
Several forces are at work to make the process of working on strengths more successful than working on deficiencies.

- We have noted that people are more prone to do things they like and are good at. So, an initial willingness to even attempt a behavior is more likely with a strength than a weakness.
- The behavior will come more naturally, whereas something else may feel awkward and uncomfortable.
- Expanding strengths is far more likely to call forth the positive rewards and praise of others than remedying a deficiency.
- The application of a new skill sets into motion a number of forces that often create even further reward. For example, the leader sharpens listening skills, and learns that listening is not sufficient, but that the key is listening and doing something about it. So the manager does. Now, this sets into motion several other forces:
  - The leader's connection with other team members improves.
  - They take on more challenging assignments, partially stemming from the greater respect and attention being paid to them.

- The leader's belief in the team and the leader's focus on helping people to learn suddenly causes people to perform at a higher level.
- They become more insistent that others improve their level of performance.
- Customer satisfaction scores rise, as key customers experience an entirely new level of personal attentiveness from the organization's key people.

6. Identify your weaknesses, and then find ways to make them irrelevant.   This is a Peter Drucker concept and philosophy. No one can do everything. Through delegation, the use of outside resources, or reallocation of work assignments, ways can be found to make weaknesses irrelevant.

The discipline of defining what things you can do and those you cannot perform (or do not like to do) is of great value. The obvious outcome is to structure your role in the organization to play to your strengths, and to find ways to have others fill in the gaps.

7. Fix fatal flaws.   If you believe you are the possessor or any one (or more) of the fatal flaws identified in Chapter 7, then begin immediately to find ways to repair them. Specifically reflect on your experience.

What lessons have you learned from your experience? Specifically, what did you learn from things that did not go well? What have you done differently as a consequence? What will prevent that from happening again?

8. Increase the scope of your assignment.   In one of the best studies of the powerful developmental experiences that leaders experience, Anna Valerio concluded that the first and most impactful experience on the job was to be given a broader scope in your current assignment. That could come via promotion, but could also come as you are given broader assignments that include more functions, greater budget, or more people. The key is that the new assignment is broader and different from those previously held, and above all, an increase in responsibility.[7]

Increased scope may be granted to you from senior people in the organization, or it can be self-generated. Applying for a transfer may be one way to increase scope and breadth. The implementation of a new procedure, or the initiation of new project, can also increase scope.

This increased scope provides a good vehicle for the "Focus on Results" cluster of behaviors. To display this even further, leaders willingly accept special projects, in which working alone or with a small team, they work on an important project to a department or the corporation. From this leaders can learn more about the total organization and achieve greater visibility.

9. Connect with good role models.   Through careful observation, leaders gain business acumen and hone important interpersonal skills. On occasion the people being used as role models give voluntary coaching. They are most often willing to give counsel when asked. However, a great deal can be learned from merely watching and listening. Observe how children learn. They watch an adult eat with a spoon or fork and they imitate them. They watch adults tie their shoelaces and learn by imitating the adults' actions. This concept, known as social learning theory, may be especially powerful in our younger years, but we never lose the ability to learn by watching someone else do something well. In fact, much learning is informal and not obvious to the learner. We just find ourselves adopting some of the effective behavior of another person.

Sometimes the lessons are "what not to do," but lessons are most helpful when they are good examples of the right things to do. That is why it is important to look for strong role models and to pay close attention to how they handle difficult situations.

In interviews with leaders, we nearly always are told about some senior people for whom they worked, who made an indelible impression upon them. Very often, a senior person went out of his or her way to express interest and encouragement. The senior person often took a risk and gave out challenging assignments for which, in retrospect, the person knew he or she was not totally prepared. In some cases the senior person invited the person to visit an important client or to attend a significant industry meeting. Unmistakable in these conversations is the intense fondness felt for this senior leader who had become a role model.

10. Learn from mistakes and negative experiences. We have earlier noted that one of the "fatal flaws" that causes people to have their careers hit a brick wall is the inability to learn from mistakes. The research is clear that learning from mistakes is a very productive tool for self-development. One category of negative experience may be a difficult boss. Another negative experience may be receiving some tough feedback from subordinates. For a person who is willing to learn, however, these experiences can be powerful developmental tools. A healthy attitude toward mistakes and negative experiences is crucial to growth and improved performance. Mistakes are part of the learning process. While some would argue with the following statement, the legendary basketball coach, John Wooden, wrote, "The team that makes the most mistakes wins."

11. Seek ways to give and receive productive feedback and learn to absorb it in an emotionally healthy way. Most organizations are not good at providing feedback to anyone—regardless of level or function. For people to receive useful feedback usually requires a sincere request for it.

The learning and development process relies heavily on feedback to sustain it. There is often a huge gap between how leaders see themselves and how subordinates perceive them. The best way to close that gap is with feedback. Enormous barriers to feedback exist inside organizations. The good news is that when I am presented with disconfirming information about myself, I will more often change how I act rather than change how I see myself. That is the great power of feedback.

Subordinates are in the best position to provide feedback, and when asked for it, the process creates a more wholesome working relationship. Accept feedback as the valid perceptions of others, and first seek to understand the meaning. Assume the givers have pure, positive intent. Keep asking for feedback. It is the golden path to continual improvement.

12. Learn from work experiences. As leaders embark on every project, it is useful to make notes of what is expected to be achieved and in what time frame. Then, the leader can periodically see how the actual results are tracking with the original expectations. That way, every activity and project becomes a learning experience. The leader can then seek to find the answer about why it is going much better than had been expected, or why it is costing more, or why it ran into roadblocks with other departments. An important part of self-development is simply finding the mechanism by which you can learn from every experience.

We turn again to an example from the world of sports. Most football games are played on the weekend, so there is the classic Monday review of the game films. Why? Coaches want the players to learn from their experience. They are fortunate to have films that record the game from several perspectives. Leaders have to create that powerful, compelling feedback process, because it is no less valuable as a way to improve performance in every arena.

13. Study the current reality the organization faces. Good development encompasses improving one's character, one's knowledge, and one's behavior. This topic focuses on knowledge. One important leadership development exercise is to step away from your organization and look at it through the eyes of a security analyst. Then look at it as if you were a competitor. Then stand away and see how it would look if you were a supplier. Then do the same thing from the perspective of a customer. Be aware of industry trends, and where your organization fits into that. Stay abreast of relevant technology facing your industry.

A key quality of effective leaders is the ability to see reality without blinking. It is hard to lead an organization in the best strategic paths if you are unwilling to face the reality of where you are now. Being brutally frank with yourself, and encouraging total candor from others, is the best safeguard to keeping in touch with your organization's current reality.

14. Learn to think strategically. One of the frequent complaints heard from executives about their subordinates is that they are completely tactical in their thinking. They simply do not think in a strategic way. For many, strategic thinking seems a complete mystery, and they see no obvious way to acquire this esoteric ability. In fact, there are good books on strategic thinking that help people understand the basics of strategy. They give a roadmap to understanding your own organization's strategic choices, to understanding why organizations choose various strategic paths, and generally to becoming more comfortable in intense strategic discussions.[8]

15. Communicate with stories.   Learn to recount important messages with powerful stories that connect emotionally with those about you. Stories help reduce complexity to manageable simplicity. They are memorable. They connect with the hearer at a more powerful level. The best insight into any organization's culture comes from the collected stories that circulate among the people in the organization. So the beginning point is to collect important stories and examples that can be used in your dialogue inside the organization. Then, practice the skill of recounting stories as the best way to convey an important message. Illustrate the major points you wish to make with appropriate examples and stories.

16. Infuse energy into every situation.   One of the keys of leadership is to understand that leaders bring excitement, enthusiasm, and energy to any endeavor. They ignite other people's passions to move forward. We all know people who are energy absorbers. When they are around, it is as if a giant energy vacuum sucks the energy from a discussion. Seldom is that person seen as a leader, because leaders need to do just the opposite. They need to capture and amplify the enthusiasm of others. The best way to get that started is to inject your own enthusiasm into any discussion or activity. Watch a videotape of yourself. Listen to a recording of your participation. Are you depositing or withdrawing energy from the process or project?

17. Allocate specific time to people development.   A powerful tool in your own development process is to become involved in the development of people who report to you, or anyone who would benefit from your tutelage. We have noted earlier that one of the keys of good leadership is the ability to obtain good results. Along with that, however, leaders also need to build the capacity within the organization to continually improve its performance, and thus be able to produce long-term, sustained results.

The "law of the harvest" talks about reaping what we sow. For the organization to constantly reap high productivity and innovation from its people, there has to be "sowing." That means taking the time, putting forth the effort, and possibly spending the money required to get frontline associates trained up.

Some leaders view people development as a frill—extraneous to their real work. Amidst the punishing workload of today's business climate, finding time for people development seems impossible to them. However, taking the time to develop people is an important behavior of a leader, not only for what it does for the recipient, but equally for the impact it has on the leader. Developing others moves you from being an independent professional person, concerned only with yourself, to the role of the true leader who creates organizational capacity and builds people.

18. Weld your team together.   Great organizations nearly always have strong teams at the top, comprised of people who genuinely like each other and who want their colleagues to succeed. A strong, cohesive team becomes a powerful development tool aiding leaders to constantly improve. Many organizations engage in team-building activities, ostensibly to improve the working relationships of the people on the team, and also to enable the group to be even more productive. What is often missed is the fact that a good team-building exercise is one of the most powerful learning experiences for the leader. First, the team has fresh, firsthand data about the leader's behavior and results. They are in the best position to provide useful feedback to the leader regarding strengths and any areas of improvement. Thus, a good team-building session is one of the most powerful and positive development activities that a leader can undertake.

19. Build personal dashboards to monitor leadership effectiveness.   Good overall measures of leadership do not usually exist in most organizations. How do you know if you are performing well? What objective measures exist that would confirm or deny that? If such measures do not exist now, then an excellent developmental activity is for you to take the initiative and develop them for yourself. These will obviously differ by organization and functional responsibility, but some measures that would be frequently used include:

- Retention data
- Customer satisfaction measures
- Productivity measures (costs to complete a given action, or time to complete an activity)
- Performance against budget
- Results from organizational climate surveys

Having developed your own "dashboard" with which to monitor your leadership effectiveness, it then becomes possible to take a weekly or at least monthly reading of your effectiveness as a leader.

A visit to an Air Force base involved a meeting with a major general, the commander of the base. He was obviously proud of the management information system that had been developed, and offered to demonstrate what information it could provide. The general could call up 846 measures of performance, ranging from fuel consumption to productivity measures, and the number of arrests on the base in the previous eight hours. Most leaders will be content with far fewer measures, but without some information system, the leader is driving with a windshield made of opaque glass.

20. Plan and execute a change initiative.   A powerful developmental activity for any leader is to define a change that should appropriately be made, and then undertake to make that change happen. The change could be as simple as the implementation of a new reporting system, a new work process by which work gets accomplished, or a new organizational structure. Whatever the change, a powerful development process involves planning the change, defining the outcomes that will result from the change, then implementing the change, and finally evaluating the results. The real learning and development comes from comparing the final results with the predicted outcomes, and then attempting to find out what caused the differences. As Machiavelli noted, "There is nothing more difficult to carry out, nor more doubtful of success, nor more dangerous to manage, than to initiate a new order of things." Centuries later, a noted psychologist, Kurt Lewin, would observe, "If you really want to understand an organization, try making changes in it."

21. Become a teacher/trainer. Approximately 80 percent of all learning and development is delivered with live, classroom instruction. In a large percentage of those cases, the organization has purchased learning systems from an outside supplier, or they have developed training programs internally. While the organization often has a training department, a large portion of that development is delivered by hand-picked managers selected from inside the organization. They are chosen on the basis of several criteria, and these usually include:

- Well respected by peers, subordinates, and upper management
- Perceived as a high-potential person
- Articulate and capable of making an engaging presentation
- Practices the leadership or management principles being presented in the development program

The process of being trained on how to deliver a learning and development program to people inside your organization is one that produces real growth in the instructor. Nothing cements a body of information inside someone more than teaching it.

In addition to personal growth, it brings the instructor into contact with many people with whom she would never have had contact. It educates the instructor on the challenging issues the organization is facing, and how the people are reacting to those challenges. From our vantage point of having watched many organizations select and train line managers as in-house instructors, we have seen it consistently enhance their careers and accelerate their development. Stewart Friedman headed up Ford Motor's Leadership Development Center. He wrote, "Every program features extensive use of teachers. Graduates of our programs serve as leader-teachers, a practice that helps participants and the instructor grow and develop new capacities for leadership. The concept of leader-teacher isn't unique, but Ford places a high emphasis on teaching. The lesson begins at the top."[9]

22. Study the high performers and replicate their behavior with others. In every organization there are a handful of people who have figured out how to perform a given job in the best possible manner. That is true of customer service representatives, salespeople, factory workers, supervisors, and corporate vice presidents. It will probably remain a mystery why more organizations do not identify who these people are and then take the time to study what they do and how they do it. Then, armed with that information, it would seem logical to attempt to get others to perform or behave in that same way.

What more valuable process could occur than identifying someone with a job that is a close counterpart to your own, and whose performance is recognized as being outstanding? Through observation and interrogation, find out what that person is doing that makes him or her so effective. See which elements of what that person does could be integrated into your own activities.

23. Volunteer in your community. The ideal leader is one who is complete. Stewart Friedman wrote, "We at Ford are pioneering a new dimension of leadership that seeks to integrate all aspects of a person's life. We call it 'total leadership.' It's different from many prior leadership models because it starts with your life as a whole: your life at work, your life at home, and your life in the community. Total leadership is about being a leader in all aspects of life."[10] It is clear that people's work life, home life, religious activity, and community service are not as separate as they once were. The formerly sharp lines are now murky. People are striving for work-life balance, and one popular approach is to blend them rather than build walls between them. By practicing leadership skills in the other aspects of your life, leadership skills can be honed and perfected. The organization is enhanced financially and organizationally, the community is improved, the church or synagogue gets much needed talent, and the family enjoys the benefits from improved leadership.

24. Practice articulating your vision for the firm and your group.   Leaders describe to a group their vision of the future and often assume it has been understood and internalized. Time passes and people ask questions: "OK, what is our strategy? I don't know where we're going." The leadership lesson is that communication of complex messages must be repeated over and over. This is especially true when it concerns a topic that carries over a long period of time, and one which people scrutinize the leader's behavior to see if it is aligned with the earlier words.

Married people or others in any lasting relationship have learned that you do not express your affection and commitment to the other person once and assume it holds until further notice. With the passage of time, things are said or done that cause the other person to question what was said earlier. And the mere passage of time dims the force and clarity of the words, so they need repeating.

That same phenomenon is at work in any organization. Yes, the leader said we value trust and openness, but look what happened to Ralph when he asked the question in the staff meeting. Or, rumors begin to swirl in the organization and they are quite contradictory of earlier messages. It is for those reasons that messages of vision, values, mission, and strategy need to be repeated over and over. How many times? Some have said that people really do not take a message seriously until the seventh time they hear it. The number is probably different for each of us, depending on the topic and what is happening in our lives. However, it is clear that the message needs frequent repeating. We advocate that you practice repeating those messages frequently to the associates with whom you work.

25. Prepare for your next job. Think ahead regarding the skills you will need.   One mistake that many leaders make is not to start getting prepared for their next assignment or role. Like the chess player who sees two or three moves ahead, so are wise leaders looking into the future for the roles they will be playing, and then preparing themselves with the skills that will be needed in those new roles.

Will the future require more technical expertise? More strategic thinking skills? A different kind of business acumen? Whatever those new requirements may be, it is never too early to be identifying them and taking active steps to add them to your skill set.

CONCLUSION

There are those who argue that all development is self-development. It has been estimated that more that 80 percent of what people learn while working in organizations, they gain on the job, casually and informally. No matter how powerful the classroom experience, it always pales in comparison to the learning that comes from experience. How much people gain from their experience is nearly all up to them. Regardless of the percentage, it is clear that leaders can make huge strides by taking responsibility for their own development. They should not count on the organization to do that for them. The 25 suggestions of things to develop your own leadership abilities were meant to convey the message that all leaders can do a great deal on their own. Do not rely on the organization to make you into an even better leader. There are extensive and powerful steps you can take to move you well down the path to becoming a great leader.

C H A P T E R

THE ORGANIZATION'S ROLE IN DEVELOPING LEADERS

I start with the premise that the role of leaders is to produce more leaders, not more followers.

Ralph Nader

The house shows the owner.

George Herbert

IN THIS CONCLUDING CHAPTER, we seek to summarize our message, and provide the leaders of organizations (as well as human resources practitioners) some thoughts about how to make these ideas operational.

The entire thrust of this book is about leadership development. Our primary concern has been to help organizations rethink their fundamental approach to this important need. We have deliberately avoided any discussion of leadership selection. We have also avoided the debate about the distinctions of "transformational" versus "transactional" leadership. We have deliberately skirted the complex issues of the psychological makeup of leaders.

The fact of the matter is that we are simply not producing leaders at the rate at which they are needed. This will be compounded by the demographic trends in the United States, which will have a shortfall of 10 million workers by the year 2010, with an attendant shortfall of leaders.

Compounding the demographics is the fact that the requirements for leaders continue to escalate. In a study by Andersen Consulting (now Accenture) titled *The Evolving Role of Executive Leadership,* researchers collected data from 75 respondents, worldwide, regarding the skills required to function in a leadership role in the past, the present, and those they believed necessary to function well in the future. One dramatic result was that, across 14 dimensions they analyzed, the differences between the skills required in the past, those demanded at present, and those believed to be necessary in the future were statistically significant. In short, the demands on our leaders are escalating sharply.[1]

ADOPT A MODEL OF LEADERSHIP

We have made the case that leadership on the one hand has been an extremely mysterious concept, and on the other hand has been highly controversial. We have presented a model of leadership that allows people to talk about the various elements with more clarity. Whether the organization adopts our model is less important than the fact that there is some way for people to talk intelligently about leadership.

It is frustrating to have a great deal of rhetoric from senior executives about the need for "leadership" on the part of other people, but to leave the concept ill-defined and nebulous. The consequence is that people are both confused and frustrated because they do not know what is expected of them.

Many memorable phrases have been coined on the subject of leadership, such as:

Managers do things right. Leaders do the right things.

Warren Bennis

Leadership is the art of accomplishing more than the science of management says is possible.

Colin Powell

However, these catchy phrases do not fully satisfy the person who sincerely wants to become a better leader.

Part of an effective leadership development process should require participants to write a short essay on what leadership means to them, and how they have put theory together into a practical, living document to guide their own leadership practices.

DECIDE WHO WILL RECEIVE LEADERSHIP DEVELOPMENT

Our focus has been entirely on how any organization can better utilize the people currently in its employ. We strongly echo the conclusions of Peter Drucker, who argues that "the task [of management] is to multiply the performance capacity of the whole by putting to use whatever strength, whatever health, whatever aspiration there is in individuals."[2]

The main decision appears to be the choice between an elitist approach and a more egalitarian posture. Many organizations in the past have focused all their leadership development efforts on a small handful of people who were currently in senior positions, or who were perceived as being "high potential" because of some psychological testing and interviewing, or assessment center procedures.

In marked contrast are the organizations such as the U.S. Marine Corps and Southwest Airlines, which have concluded that the organization will be stronger if everyone is a candidate for development. This approach is especially appealing to those who believe that leadership is necessary at all levels of the organization—not just at the top. It also appeals to those who believe that many people, not just those who occupy positions of authority or who have multiple subordinates, can practice leadership.

David Garvin, in *Learning in Action,* states, "the best simulations combine realism, variety and low risk." He goes on to state: "Pilots, for example, have long been selected for their technical proficiency and self-reliance—the elusive 'right stuff.'" Yet over the past twenty years, air carrier accidents and incidents have consistently been traced "to inadequacies in leadership qualities, communication skills, crew coordination, or decision making. Today's Line-Oriented Flight Training (LOFT) presents pilots and crews with complex, simulated problems that demand precisely these talents. LOFT also provides the opportunity to experience, in advance, such rare but important events as equipment failures."[3]

We strongly contend that most organizations are tapping only a fraction of the potential of the people currently in its employ. We believe that people in general have the capacity to rise to much higher levels of performance if the organization creates the proper climate.

This decision stems largely from the belief systems of the executives. If they believe that people have fixed abilities from birth and that there is little likelihood of people growing or expanding through their lifetime, then there is less incentive to invest in their development. This notion that intelligence and other personal traits are locked in at birth has been taught in Psychology 101 courses for the past 100 years. It has become a widely held belief.

Recent research, however, contradicts that notion. Instead, it has been found that challenging mental activity creates new neural networks in the brain, and that people actually become smarter over time. This fact is well established by virtue of the increasing IQ scores people obtain as the number of years of schooling they receive increases.

Jon Katzenbach, author of *Peak Performance,* believes that the development of people at all levels, and the equal opportunity given to people regardless of where they are perceived to be on the "bell-shaped curve," will define the most successful organizations of the future.[4]

The Importance of Developing Senior Leaders

Our research revealed an interesting though not surprising fact. The leadership skills possessed by the most senior people in an organization become the leadership ceiling. That is, it is extremely rare to find anyone whose leadership skills exceed those of the people at the top.

We realize that it could be argued that the best leaders are promoted to the most senior positions, and we concur. However, in those cases where senior people had mediocre scores, there seems to be room for some highly skillful young leader to blossom, and that was not the case: the senior people were the cap.

This argues strongly for continued development of the senior people, so that the leadership tent is lifted, making room for others to grow. Maybe it is their example that is so important, or it could be their coaching and mentoring that is needed. Whatever the reasons, great leaders at the top are necessary for great leaders to develop at any level in an organization.

Management Development and Leadership Development

Some organizations make a distinction between leadership development and management development. They define topics such as teamwork, vision, values, clarity of mission, managing change, communication, and culture as part of the leadership development process. You could argue that the emphasis here is on people, both one at a time and in groups. Management development, on the other hand, is all about the "hard" skills. It includes financial acumen, project management, strategy, organizing skills, process improvement, financial control, and information technology.

We understand that distinction and find it to be conceptually helpful, but hard to implement in the real world. First, few people have the luxury of functioning only as a leader or a manager. Most everyone in a position of any authority whom we have observed is pressed into both leadership and management activities. These activities seem to be inextricably mixed together in day-to-day work in every organization. They connect with each other in obvious and subtle ways. We find making a distinction to be a bit like going to a tennis camp and having the instructor focus entirely on the forehand ground stroke, and then being told that we can come back in a month or so and have similar instruction on the backhand stroke. Yes, we understand the difference, but if you want to play tennis, you need them both, and you can never predict when one or the other will be needed.

DEFINE THE RESULTS YOU SEEK FROM LEADERS AND HOW THOSE RESULTS LINK TO THE STRATEGY OF THE ORGANIZATION

Leadership is not an end, but a means to an end. That end needs to be made explicit. If an important part of being a good leader is to produce excellent results, then those results must be clearly defined so that leaders will know when they are succeeding. We have presented evidence that effective leaders produce improvements in productivity, product and service quality, and customer satisfaction, and that the willingness of people to work hard and expend energy invariably rises.

Clearly, those results must flow from the organization's broader strategy. Helping leaders to understand that strategy, and how to think about the main strategic alternatives their organization faces, is a valuable element of a leadership development process. We highly recommend Perry, Stott, and Smallwood's *Real-Time Strategy: Improvising Team-Based Planning for a Fast-Changing World.*[5]

We reiterate the message in Ulrich, Zenger, and Smallwood's *Results-Based Leadership* regarding the importance of results being balanced, long-term, and selfless, and that the necessary balance we seek is between the interests of customers, employees, organization, and the shareholders.[6]

Some executives have come into organizations and immediately imposed massive layoffs, slashed research and development, eliminated employee development, and slowed down long-term maintenance of equipment. For a relatively short time the results look spectacular. Earnings soar—temporarily. There is often enough time for this executive to exercise his stock options, cash out, and be gone before all the damage he did has had time to sink in.

It is also clear that effective results cannot be driven by personal agendas and decisions that primarily feather the personal nest of the executive. The results that count must be achieved with the welfare of the organization in mind.

Some of the most useful development for any leader is to develop crystal clarity regarding what is expected in the way of outputs. Those outputs need to be categorized into "What does the organization expect from my department?" A different question is "What does the organization expect from me personally?" It is usually eye-opening for any leader to go about asking selected peers, subordinates, and a boss for the answer to that question.

SET EXTREMELY HIGH EXPECTATIONS FOR LEADERS

For research purposes we arbitrarily set the 90th percentile as the cutoff point for being "great" on some competency. We would much prefer to have absolute, objective standards by which to make measurements, but lacking those measures, we used percentiles as the surrogate measures.

We contend that by getting your best leaders to excel even more, everyone benefits. Again, we recognize the temptation to focus on the lowest-performing leaders and attempt to elevate their performance. That has a nice logic to it. Instead, we urge helping the best of your current group of leaders to become even better.

Peter Drucker points out that major advances in many fields come when a few leading practitioners break new ground.[7] A surgeon develops a new procedure by which to do less invasive heart surgery. Then, in a few years the technique is being used by a wide group of surgeons. An investment banking firm develops a new approach to financing start-up organizations. In time, a number of other firms follow. One university registrar implements a totally online process that enables students to sign up for classes, go through first-year orientation, and place orders for books and supplies, all on the Internet. Within a year, many other institutions will be doing the same thing.

The point is that when good people or good organizations excel, it does more to lift the entire population than similar efforts by the middle group. Within a firm, everyone benefits by helping the strong to set even higher goals. They blaze the trail. They set the bar to a new height, and many who are currently in the tier below will adjust their performance to the new expectation. On any team, the presence of one or two people who are putting forth Herculean effort, and working to their highest intensity, raises the performance of the entire group.

Many people can learn from leaders who are excelling. In fact, nearly everyone can. They can observe both what is being done and how it is being executed. These excellent leaders seemingly cause the tide to rise, and that tide lifts all boats.

INVOLVE SENIOR EXECUTIVES IN LEADERSHIP DEVELOPMENT

Senior executive involvement gives traction to any development efforts. It is possible to create a spectrum of involvement that should help place where your organization currently is, and where you feel it should be in the future. The spectrum is the following.

- *Tolerance.* Suppose an executive condones the human resources function sponsoring some programs, and approves the budget. However, the senior executives have no knowledge of the content or the objectives of what is being done. The process is totally off the executive's radar screen.

- *Cosmetic support.* The senior executives send memos in support of the development effort, and talk about it in large company meetings. They know they should be supporting this, but it is way down their priority list.

- *Dabbling.* At this stage in our continuum of support, the executives inquire about the targets for the developmental efforts, and they may come to an evening session and deliver a talk. This is a token effort to give the appearance that senior executives are concerned, but their concern is quite superficial.

- *Attendance.* At this point executives will often attend the program as participants, realizing that if they think this is good for other people, they should set the example. So, each executive takes his or her turn attending a session. Clearly, their presence sends an important signal to the organization. Willingness to commit time to this activity is one measure of support. We concur with those who say that key executives need to be spending one-third to one-half of their time in people development activities.

- *Ownership.* It is clear that up to this point, the staff owns the leadership development process and the senior executives are bystanders. Beginning at this level of support, the senior executives feel a strong sense of ownership. They set the objectives. They review and approve the activities. They often come to participate in the development process. A prime example of this behavior is Jack Welch's coming to Crotonville every two weeks for 15 years to participate actively with a variety of managers as they went through parts of their development process. Welch proudly states, "I have never missed a session."[8]

Top-executive ownership is the surefire way to avoid the "snicker factor" in an organization. If people see that the executives are solidly behind the development process, then the snide remarks about "not walking the talk" go away.

One key issue is how the senior team handles people who are openly hostile or who show disdain for the leadership development effort. This is an acid test of leadership.

Senior leaders' willingness to act as mentors to younger, promising staff is another way of displaying serious commitment to the leadership development effort. They can provide useful insight into organization culture, explain unwritten rules of conduct, ensure that the younger person navigates around pitfalls and traps, give encouragement during difficult stretch assignments, and in general provide access to the thinking of the people at the top of the organization.

FOCUS DEVELOPMENT EFFORTS ON STRENGTHS

John Flaherty, in summing up Peter Drucker's thinking, writes:

> Drucker was unashamedly dogmatic and took an absolutist stance on the proposition that human performance capability depended on strengths and not on weaknesses. Of course, weaknesses had to be acknowledged and neutralized, but they were incapable of producing results. In his consulting work he followed the principle of avoiding any discussion of what his clients could not do, emphasizing instead what they were capable of doing and what it made sense for them to do.
>
> Because the only purpose for hiring people was to produce results, employees should be paid only in consideration of their strengths, not their weaknesses. But in reality, the opposite was often the case. The organization had a proclivity to focus on human defects, to criticize and harp on the negative aspects of individuals, to see people as threats rather than opportunities, and to esteem the potential of credentials instead of competency.[9]

Drucker wrote:

> Conversely, the effective executive makes strength productive. He knows that one cannot build on weakness. To achieve results, one

has to use all the available strengths—the strengths of associates, the strengths of the superior, and one's own strengths. The strengths are the true opportunities. To make strength productive is the unique purpose of organization. Its task is to use the strength of each man as a building block for joint performance.[10]

We cannot emphasize enough the positive impact this has on organization culture. Rather than people feeling constant pressure and guilt regarding the things they are incapable of doing, there is a completely different tone to the organization that celebrates strength.

Football teams utilize highly specialized players. One of the key players is the kicker. Very often these individuals are slight of build and not capable of doing many of the things their fellow teammates are doing regularly. Seldom are they great runners or pass receivers. However, they are usually among the high scorers on the team. No one seems to mind these "weaknesses" of the kicker, so long as the kicker completes field goals and gets the points after touchdowns. Everyone is content to focus on strengths and ignore everything else.

Every leadership development process should contain time and vehicles to ensure that the leaders thoroughly and accurately understand their strengths. Along with that, however, the organization must constantly be vigilant about the evolving nature of the strengths that the organization requires. Being technically competent may have been a key strength when the organization's challenge was discovering more oil. But if the company is now a consumer marketing organization with a strong retail emphasis, then new strengths may be required for success.

USE POWERFUL LEARNING METHODS THAT CHANGE BEHAVIOR

In the past we have conducted development programs in which people are given general instruction with one of four objectives:

1. *Theory/knowledge.* In this approach, we pour information into a funnel over the tipped head of the participant. One assumption is that "if people knew better, they'd do better," and all we

need to do is fill their theory bins. Another way to express the assumption is, "The more information the leader possesses, the better will be his or her performance."

2. *Insight.* This approach assumes that leaders are produced through developing greater self-awareness. What is wrong with leaders is their lack of self-insight and their flawed inner feelings and thoughts.

3. *Inspiration.* This approach assumes that leaders need an infusion of enthusiasm and motivation. Performance is deficient because of a deficiency in commitment. This is the one place and time where someone may hint at the opportunity to be great, but the nature of inspirational programs is their short half-life. No mechanisms are built to maintain the enthusiasm or lock into place new resolutions.

4. *Skills.* This developmental approach assumes people need to be able to do things that they have not been able to do, or to do things better than they have been doing. The outcomes of these programs are longer-lasting, but their objective is seldom expressed as "hitting the ball out of the park."

We submit that if our objective is to build great leaders, our developmental processes must undergo major transformation, and be built on a radically different mindset. The mindset must be one of expecting high performance from nearly everyone. With that we should insist on hard work and tenacious engagement in all they do. Hard work will then produce significant improvements in performance.

Developmental practices must hold out the expectation and provide the tools for people to move beyond average to good, and move beyond good to becoming great.

Historically, leadership development programs were conducted by universities on their campuses. Then companies began doing their own in-house programs, but still relied heavily on academics to conduct them. The instructional methods were transported from academia, and mirrored the way professors taught in the college classroom. The traditional learning methods for leadership programs, therefore, were:

- Lectures
- Case studies
- Extensive reading assignments
- Small group discussions
- Speeches from company executives
- Video and film presentations

What we are proposing is a dramatic shift to new learning methods. The principles that should guide the selection of learning methods are:

- Practicality
- Immediate opportunity to apply knowledge or skill
- Concrete versus abstract
- Job-related
- Action-oriented
- Emotionally engaging
- Personalized
- Ongoing versus a one-time event
- Built-in accountability for implementation

In practice, this leads to the use of some markedly different instructional methods.

- *Feedback.* It means the greater use of personalized feedback procedures, such as 360-degree feedback instruments. Most leaders are not good at reflection and self-analysis. The pace of their work does not allow it, and that pace seems to accelerate constantly. Our society and culture has not provided good models of mechanisms for people to give those in authority over them any honest reactions to what they do or how they are doing it. Further, there are strong political pressures in most organizations which block the truth from being passed from subordinates to their superiors. People are subtly told, "Don't rock the boat," and "messengers get killed." That is why any mechanism that unclogs the pipes between people in the organization is of great value. Tools such as 360-degree feedback instruments or skip-level meetings perform that function.

- *Coaching.* Coaching and mentoring are powerful developmental processes. There is a rapidly growing trend to provide coaches to leaders, and not waiting until they are in trouble. Coaches are seen as a way to help the good become much better. They observe meetings, review memos, critique speeches, and in general assist in building behavioral skills.

- *Simulations.* Computer-based simulations meet the criteria established above. Simulations can be extremely job-related. They call for frequent decisions. The consequences become clear immediately. There is accountability, and they are engaging.

- *Team-building activities.* Activities that involve teams actually doing something, such as building a product, assembling a tent while blindfolded, or creating a new advertising campaign, are powerful learning methods.

- *Planning back-home application of new learning.* We recommend time spent in development sessions actively planning the back-home implementation of what has been learned. This greatly increases the likelihood of it being acted on.

- *Creating measurement dashboards.* What better activity could there be than to create simple, effective measures by which to gauge leadership effectiveness?

- *Senior people come in to relate "war" stories.* It is one thing to have an executive come in to deliver a prepared speech on some aspect of the industry or regarding the state of the economy. It is quite different if the executive will come in and relate personal experiences regarding ways to handle difficult customer situations, tough negotiations with suppliers, or challenging battles with competitors. The latter are memorable and powerful teaching devices.

You will hear some people say that leadership development is something that organizations invest in for the long run, and that no one should expect an immediate payoff. We take exactly the opposite stance. You should be able to see results right away, and in that way you will be guaranteed significant long-term results. If you do not see results relatively quickly, we doubt you ever will.

One of the authors was sitting by the head of leadership development for a Fortune 500 company during a lunch and inquired of him, "What are you doing in your leadership development efforts that you feel really good about—something that you can see really makes a difference? The executive unhesitatingly replied, "We don't anticipate seeing any payoff from what we're doing for at least five or ten years." We admire the executives of a firm who are willing to invest in something for which they can see no near-term payout, and for which the long-term payout is totally impossible to measure. However, while admiring them, we question their judgment.

As we noted earlier, if people cannot go back to their jobs and apply what they have learned almost immediately, we seriously doubt they ever will. We do not help ourselves gain credibility by portraying what we do as having no immediate payoff, nor having any way to measure it. That feels like we are purveyors of "fairy dust."

The Power of Better Teaching Methods

It is easy to underestimate the enormous power of improved learning and teaching methods. A group of 19 school districts in the Chicago area have banded together to form the First World Consortium. These schools have focused on improving their teaching methods. The outcome is that if these 19 districts were considered to be a "country," it would rank number 1, 2, or 3 in the world on scores in mathematics and science at several grade levels. The students, many from inner-city schools, perform better than students in Singapore, Korea, and Japan, despite the fact that U.S. students overall are in the lower half of worldwide comparative scores.

How was that accomplished? Teachers act as coaches and facilitators. Students are actively engaged. Lectures are seldom used. The students work on projects that are exciting to them. They are far more emotionally engaged than in a normal classroom setting.[11]

EMPHASIZE ACTION LEARNING PROJECTS—OR WORK ON PROJECTS THAT MATTER

The preceding section described how learning methods can make a big difference. In addition to the methodology, there is a way to focus the development process around honest-to-goodness issues the organization faces. Rather than spending time analyzing a company in a totally different industry, why not focus the development process on the most important, thorniest, challenging issues the organization actually has? This idea, dubbed "action learning," was pioneered by Reginald Revans, a management professor at Oxford University in England.[12] The idea met with such success that it has become widely used in the most sophisticated leadership development programs all over the world.

The Siemens organization gave teams of participants in their leadership development process the problems that in times past they would have given to a high-profile consulting company such as McKinsey, Bain, or BCG. Siemens estimated that the recommendations coming from the action learning teams saved the corporation between $3 million and $4 million in consulting costs, and reaped recommendations that produced $11 million in savings in one year. Thus, their leadership development process moved from being a huge expenditure and cash drain to being a vehicle to improve performance. Add the savings from the team's recommendations and then add the fees they would have paid the external firms, and the payoff was handsome.[13]

The other compelling argument in favor of action learning, however, is the highly engaging nature of it. People generally find these activities to be more involving. Action learning projects meet nearly all of the criteria we described. They are eminently practical, because they have been selected with those criteria in mind. They are very job-related because they spring from within the organization. They lend themselves to rapid implementation. The projects are extremely concrete. Normally the groups spend several weeks to several months working on the project, so that it becomes a long-term learning experience rather than an event. Nothing could be more job-related. Very often the teams doing the analysis of an issue or problem are then asked to be involved in planning for, and actually implementing, their recommendations.

Our view is that the great power of action learning is the fact that it so completely meets the criteria for effective learning methods. It is a perfect way to tap into the enormous wellspring of talent, innovation, and knowledge that exists within every firm. The people involved are energized when asked to address a topic of such obvious importance and value to the firm.

One interesting approach in leadership development involves each participant defining a personal action learning project. Ford Motor Company has used this technique. They call it their QIP (Quantum Idea Project) activity. It is a centerpiece of their New Business Leader Program designed for first-level supervisors of salaried employees.

Stewart Friedman observes the results this had in Ford:

> Action learning creates business impact. The projects' participants chosen must have a business benefit in terms of customer satisfaction, cost reduction, or enhanced revenue. One of the most notable examples is the QIP—the Quantum Idea Project. It's the key to our New Business Leader Program—The QIP, intended to drive revolutionary change at Ford, stretch an individual's capacity to think critically, innovate daringly, evaluate choices strategically, and support business objectives wisely. In the process, a manager begins to develop leadership skills that he/she can use every day. The QIP process is organized according to key milestones, check offs, and evaluation processes inherent to a project. Additionally, our programs instill a sense of accountability. Participants are evaluated on the outcome of their projects and how well they performed as leaders. For example, how did they interact with their peers? Did they network successfully? Did they learn new ways of doing things?[14]

Most action learning projects involve sizable teams, often representing different functional areas of the organization and different countries. They meet face-to-face on some occasions, and supplement such meetings with teleconferences or chat rooms on the Internet.

One key element is the process of ensuring that learning is taking place as the team works on a real issue or problem. Outside resources, such as technical experts, are often made available to the team, but it is the team's responsibility to ask for and use these resources. Participants are often working on an issue that is outside the normal sphere of their responsibility. The teams are nearly always devoid of any hierarchy. Instead they are composed of "organizational cousins"—people at generally the same level but from different "families" inside the firm. Often a facilitator is assigned to work with the team to ensure that time is taken periodically to pause and reflect on what they have learned, and to encourage different approaches in the future.[15]

We recommend the reader obtain Michael Marquardt's book, *Action Learning.*[16] It is a practical discourse on action learning and how to implement it in any organization. There is also an excellent chapter (Chapter 4) on action learning in David A. Garvin's *Learning in Action.*[17]

CREATE A CULTURE OF FEEDBACK

Leadership development is significantly enhanced in a culture in which continual feedback is common. A variety of mechanisms exist to help make this happen, and we think they are highly useful. Some of those are:

- 360-degree feedback procedures
- Frequent performance discussions between bosses and subordinates
- Team-building sessions
- Coaching relationships
- Skip-level meetings

We often think of feedback as consisting of harsh or difficult messages. Nothing is more untrue. Some of the most valuable feedback in organizations is letting people know that what they are doing is appreciated and helpful to others. This is very much in keeping with our basic message of focusing on strengths. People often do not appreciate their strengths because so much of the feedback they have received through their lives has been comments on what they failed to do, deficiencies they have, or mistakes they have made. One way of having people more fully comprehend their strengths is for the organization to provide frequent feedback to them. Most feedback can be framed as suggestions, ideas to consider, or things the person might wish to think about. For many people that is all that is required.

There is, on the other hand, value in people being able to deliver difficult messages to each other in a constructive way. Possibly the most common failing we see in executives is an unwillingness to confront performance issues with people. They are so afraid of hurting the other person's feelings, and so afraid that the relationship will be damaged that they avoid any such discussion. Performance of the person often continues to spiral downward until the time comes when the manager has no alternative but to terminate him. Then comes the weird conversation in which the subordinate says, "Why didn't you tell me that I had performance problems?" To which the manager replies, "I did not want to hurt your feelings."

The healthiest feedback in organizations comes when people can freely exchange views with each other. Max de Pree, the retired CEO of Herman Miller, stated, "I now work with about ten people, all of whom see me as one of their mentors. In order for a mentorship to work, it has to be a co-mentoring arrangement. You can't have a teacher and a student. You both have to be a teacher and a student. That keeps me alive. I keep learning."[18]

TRANSFORM COMPLEXITY INTO SIMPLICITY

We live in a time in which during the day a typical manager receives 34 phone calls, 42 e-mails, 6 faxes, and spends two to three hours in meetings. It is a time of data overload. We have access to seeming warehouses of information on everything imaginable, including most business issues. Rather than being forced to choose between one good alternative and one bad one, most leaders find themselves in the situation of having to choose among at least a handful of good alternatives.

It is no longer the choice between right or wrong tactics or strategy. The choice is among multiple avenues, and trying to figure out which is best. *Fortune* magazine editor Thomas Stewart has written of those conflicts in an article about the Canadian Imperial Bank of Commerce. After interviewing all of the senior management, the people in charge of a new leadership development center identified nine dilemmas leaders face:

1. Acting in a "get out with the troops" approach, versus a strong, charismatic, highly visible manner.
2. Having an independent, entrepreneurial culture versus being a good team player and acting interdependently with others.
3. Managing for the short term versus the long term.
4. Having a culture of high creativity versus one of discipline.
5. Trust versus change. The argument here is that every time you institute major change, you risk damaging the feelings of trust that people have for you.
6. Bureaucracy busting versus working toward economies of scale.
7. Emphasis on people versus high productivity.
8. Management versus leadership. Do we emphasize the technical and administrative issues, or swing to emphasize people, mission, and vision?
9. Revenue growth versus cost containment.[19]

The job of the leader is one of constantly dealing with complexity and ambiguity. Leadership development processes must help them to deal with that. Some mechanisms may be institutional, like the Procter & Gamble practice of limiting all memos to one page. That forces you to move complexity into simplicity.

Our discussion of the U.S. Marines' approach is yet another way of going about it. Insist that every major problem or mission be distilled to three alternatives, about which some analysis is performed and a selection is made of the best alternative. Then detailed plans are made for the final selection. The process of taking any problem or mission and winnowing it down to three alternatives is a powerful procedure.

INVOLVE YOUR LEADERS AS TEACHERS

Involving leaders as teachers has a number of benefits. First, you never learn something more effectively than when you have to teach it. So the process of engaging leaders as teachers is a powerful way to let them become highly conversant with any body of content or new initiative. Second, it is a great developmental tool. The teachers gain new skills, both in teaching and as a role model of whatever it is they are teaching. Third, their presence lends high credibility to what is being taught.

The use of leaders as coaches to action learning teams is one obvious example of this practice. Each action learning team needs someone to be its official sponsor or "angel." The team also needs someone to run interference when required, as well as someone to mentor the group through the process. In such a role, numerous opportunities arise for coaching on leadership behavior for all of the participants.

MAKE DEVELOPMENT A LONGER-TERM PROCESS, NOT AN EVENT

Leadership development activities have long been viewed as events. That event could be a weekend, an entire week, or in some cases, it could stretch to as many as 13 weeks. (We are reminded of the executive who asked his boss about attending a 13-week executive development program, and the boss replied, "If I can spare you for 13 weeks, I can spare you.") What we are advocating is not multiweek-long programs. Instead, we are strongly advocating the practice of making any development process part of ongoing work activities, and that it be viewed as part of "lifelong learning."

In conducting focus groups with senior executives it is clear that they prefer short bursts of time off the job with meaningful activities taking place between such meetings. With the majority of people in leadership roles working more than 50 hours per week, the pressure to minimize time off the job is very real. For example, in the new Goldman Sachs leadership development operation, the longest time anyone is off the job is two days.

One useful trend is toward "blended solutions," or programs that combine Web-delivered content along with facilitated sessions. This allows any conceptual material or content to be delivered over the Internet. When completed, participants then attend a facilitated session in which those ideas are applied to real situations, and during which participants can practice new skills. Afterward, the participants have access to online simulations that again reinforce all the content and the skills they have learned.

The blended solution, by its very nature, becomes an extended process of development. Many of these include the creation of a coaching relationship with another person in the organization, and they may also offer online mentoring for people with questions or issues they wish to address. This combination of multiple learning methods, all provided over an extended period of time, is a good example of learning being a long-term process and not a one-time event.

BUILD ACCOUNTABILITY INTO THE DEVELOPMENT PROCESS

One of the strange anomalies of leadership development programs in the past has been the issue of accountability. There has been accountability on the part of those who were organizing and conducting the process. Some have jokingly described these as the "f" measurements. That is, we have collected data about how the participants liked the facilities, the food, the faculty, and the fun.

Where there has been no accountability has been on the participants' side of the equation. Did the participants learn and retain that information? Did they ever attempt to use it? What results did they achieve? How have they passed it on to people who work around them? Are there any concrete business indicators such as productivity improvement, revenue generation, customer satisfaction, cost reduction, or employee retention numbers to indicate that the participants had implemented what they learned?

Some previous studies of leadership development programs suggested that people liked the experience, but seldom did anything with it. Obviously, this depends a good deal on the objectives of the learning process and what was done. We argue that the time has come for organizations to be clear about the business objectives of leadership development and to measure the outcomes.

PLAN DEVELOPMENTAL EXPERIENCES FOR LEADERS

Leadership development is more than a "training station." Yes, classroom experiences can have value, but the research is clear that approximately 80 percent of what we learn is casual and informal. Time spent in formal learning and development is miniscule compared to hours spent on the job. It is vital, therefore, to put aspiring leaders into environments from which they can learn a great deal in a short time.

The research is so clear about experiences making a huge difference in a leader's development that it is obvious that thoughtful planning about these experiences is mandatory. Each leader should be considered by the organization, and decisions made regarding rotational assignments, which could include moving from one division to another, movement from line to staff, from domestic operations to an international assignment, or onto some special task force that is assigned an important project of vital interest to the firm.

Challenging assignments accelerate the pace of learning. They immerse people in the nitty-gritty of the industry, the company, or some functional area within it. They learn first-hand the enormous value of teamwork.

We recommend the book *The Lessons of Experience* by Morgan McCall, Jr., Michael Lombardo, and Ann Morrison. It gives practical insights into how work experiences lead to the development of leaders.[20]

CELEBRATE SUCCESSES

When positive results are achieved, they need to be celebrated. The organization needs to see the link between a business result and the development efforts that helped achieve that. When customer satisfaction numbers go up as a result of the actions taken by recent alumni of a leadership development effort, that should be widely broadcast.

CONCLUSION

The success of all of the above recommendations hinges on the bone-deep beliefs of the senior leaders of the organization. Do they really believe that their people can become great leaders? Or do they hold the old view that intelligence and ability are fixed at birth, and people really cannot change a great deal? Are they willing to invest their time in giving leadership to this leadership development effort? We have often focused on the financial commitment the senior leaders must make, but their personal commitment and time are far more important.

Are the senior leaders willing to set the expectations at a very high level, and insist that everyone strive to be an excellent leader? For the organizations that make this commitment, the rewards are extremely high. For those who choose not to, the future is highly questionable.

Why This Approach Promises Greater Success in Developing Leaders

First, we submit that a focus on developing great leaders rather than merely on "leadership development" gives a new perspective to what we do. It raises our sights and creates a somewhat different mindset for measuring our success. Many of the leaders currently in the "good" category seem satisfied with their current level of effectiveness. This is much like the experience one has when climbing a high mountain. After a substantial hike you can look up the mountain and see what you think is the top. As you approach that point your excitement grows because of your accomplishment. If you were to sit down below what you thought was the summit you might never find out that what you thought was the top was only a peak that stuck out from the mountain, hiding the real summit from view. Many of those who profess to be leaders are only halfway up the mountain.

Second, an emphasis on strengths is more palatable than looking for blemishes and weaknesses. Most of us enjoy doing things we are good at. We contend that it is much easier for a leader to find ways to magnify strengths than it is to overcome weaknesses. It comes more naturally. Becoming really good at something is more energizing than attempting to patch flaws. You are getting "rewards" for the behavior you are enhancing from day one. That in turn increases your aspirations, and in turn makes it easier to work on things you do not do well. Fewer people will resist the message to get better at things you are good at, in contrast to get up to average on some perceived weakness.

Third, people are more willing to practice skills they are good at. Recent research on "expert performers" attributes extraordinary performance to diligent practice, not to some unique quality bestowed by deity. Great musicians, sports figures, and chess players got there the same way. Tiger Woods, it is argued, is great because, with the help of a dedicated coach, he has practiced about 10,000 more hours than most golfers, beginning at a very early age. To get really good at anything requires practice. Leadership is no exception.

Fourth, we submit that by measuring the perceptions of subordinates and peers, we have a tool for the immediate and objective measurement of leadership. Frequent and precise measurements are possible and relatively economical.

Fifth, change need not take forever. The authors frequently ask practitioners of leadership development, "What are you doing that seems to be paying off?" As we noted earlier, the most frequent answer is something like, "Well, it is too early to tell." Reading between the lines, the answer really says, "We can't see that anything is changing or has changed." "We don't want to be held accountable for change, but we hope something shows up three or four years from now."

Two things are troubling about this response. Leadership is all about change, so if the leadership development process is not producing change, then it probably is not working. Our experience with change suggests the opposite conclusion from the one we hear about coming in future years.

Two professors at the Stanford business school taught quantitative methods in their executive program. They decided to write participants who had attended the program and ask them two questions: "Did you apply any of the content you learned in our session?" "If so, when did you do that?" The overall number of people who had done something was discouragingly low, but the instructive part was in the second question. If the participants had done something, they did so in the first two weeks after returning home, or it didn't happen at all. In fact, one respondent's reply was particularly interesting. He had left in the middle of one of the professors' presentations. They assumed he thought it boring or irrelevant or both. They were delighted to get the response back that this participant had indeed implemented something. He noted, "I left half-way in your presentation to go out and call my staff and asked them to start that analysis. I knew if I waited, I probably would not have done it."

That squares exactly with our experience. If you wait, nothing happens. To believe that change will show up years after an executive development process is contrary to all the evidence.

Apply Your "Experience" Test
Think of the best executives for whom you ever worked.

- What impact did they have on you and your performance?
- Were their groups a little more productive and creative than others, or were they a lot more productive?
- Did you perceive that they possessed multiple strengths?
- Was their success driven by their strengths, or was it that they lacked any weakness?
- Did their success push other leaders' performance down, or did their success help to elevate others?
- Did they have any dramatic flaws?
- What impact did they have on the careers of the people who reported to them?

We think most readers will confirm the validity of our thesis from their own experience. We began this book by proposing 20 insights about leadership. In the vernacular of the old preacher, we began by telling you what we were going to tell you, then we did our best to tell you, and now we have summarized what we told you. Our hope is that the leadership tents of everyone in your organization will constantly expand as you take these steps.

RESEARCH METHODOLOGY

ASSESSING THE RELATIONSHIP BETWEEN MANAGERIAL EFFECTIVENESS AND EMPLOYEE COMMITMENT (FIGURE 2.1)

A survey was administered to 954 employees from a high-tech company. The survey contained both a 16-item managerial effectiveness form and 12 employee commitment items. The managerial effectiveness and employee commitment items were formed into an index. The two indexes were highly correlated. A Pearson correlation coefficient between the two indexes was calculated at 0.65 (PC 0.000). The relationship between the two variables indicated that 42 percent of the variance in employee commitment could be accounted for by perceptions of managerial effectiveness. To produce the graph in Figure 2.1, the managerial effectiveness index was divided into 10 groups based on the distribution of the data. The groups ranged in size from 67 to 127 employees. The graph shows the raw score on the employee commitment index for each of the 10 decile groups.

EVALUATING THE RELATIONSHIP BETWEEN MANAGERIAL EFFECTIVENESS AND PROFITABILITY (FIGURE 2.2)

A total of 1672 assessments were distributed to employees, who assessed managers in 35 regions of a mortgage bank. Managers had an average of 9 assessments done on them by their boss, peers, and direct reports. The 360-degree assessment was custom-designed to measure specific competencies thought to differentiate high- and low-performing managers. The assessment survey had 65 items. A leadership effectiveness index composed of 15 survey items was correlated with the net profit for each region. The Pearson correlation between the leadership effectiveness index and net profit was 0.40 (PC 0.000). The leadership effectiveness index was then divided into three categories based on the distribution of the index. The three categories were: bottom 10 percent, middle 80 percent, and top 10 percent. Figure 2.2 shows the strong impact of poor and extraordinary leadership.

EVALUATING THE RELATIONSHIP BETWEEN MANAGERIAL EFFECTIVENESS AND TURNOVER (FIGURE 2.3)

An insurance company administered a survey to work groups in which leadership effectiveness was assessed. Eighty-nine groups matched up aggregated survey results with annual turnover data. The leadership effectiveness measured was composed of 10 survey items assessing the effectiveness of the work group manager. The Pearson correlation between the leadership effectiveness index and turnover was −0.29 (PC 0.007). The negative correlation was created because the higher (more positive) the leadership effectiveness measure, the lower the turnover. The leadership effectiveness measure was divided into three categories, bottom 30 percent, middle 60 percent, and top 10 percent, to create Figure 2.3. The cut points on the categories were chosen because of the consistency of turnover within each of the groupings.

EVALUATING THE RELATIONSHIP BETWEEN MANAGERIAL EFFECTIVENESS AND INTENTION TO STAY AND CUSTOMER SATISFACTION (FIGURES 2.4 AND 2.5)

A high-tech communications company conducted a company-wide employee survey and the same year collected 360-degree survey results from 612 managers. The 360-degree survey results were merged with the employee survey data. The 360-degree survey was customized with 50 items designed to measure overall leadership effectiveness. The aggregate of the 360-degree survey items formed the leadership effectiveness index. The employee survey was aggregated and merged with the aggregate 360-degree results. The data set also contained additional demographics. The employee survey contained a series of items measuring customer satisfaction and an individual item assessing intention to stay with the company. Percentile scores were calculated on the customer and intention to stay measures for the 612 managers. Percentile scores for the leadership effectiveness index were calculated and then divided into the bottom 20 percent, the middle 60 percent, and the top 20 percent.

In another study conducted with a high-technology medical equipment manufacturer, 88 managers were given 360-degree assessments with 63 custom-developed items. The survey also asked direct reports to respond to eight employee engagement items. One of the employee engagement items assessed employees' intention to stay with the company (see Figure A.1). The aggregate of the 63 items on the 360-degree survey were put together into an index that evaluated overall leadership effectiveness. The Pearson correlation between the leadership effectiveness index and the intention-to-leave item was 0.34 (PC 0.007). Because of the small number of managers in this sample, the leadership effectiveness index was broken at the 30th and 70th percentiles into three categories representing the bottom 30 percent, the middle 40 percent, and the top 30 percent. These results are very consistent with those shown in Chapter 2, indicating that leadership effectiveness is a significant driver of intention to stay with the company.

In the same study we were able to replicate a similar study done as is represented in Figure 2.1. In this analysis the individual assessments of leadership effectiveness were graphed at each of the deciles against the employee commitment or engagement index. Figure A.2 is based on assessments by 975 employees and is very similar to the results shown in Figure 2.1. The correlation between leadership effectiveness and employee commitment/engagement is 0.521 (PC 0.000).

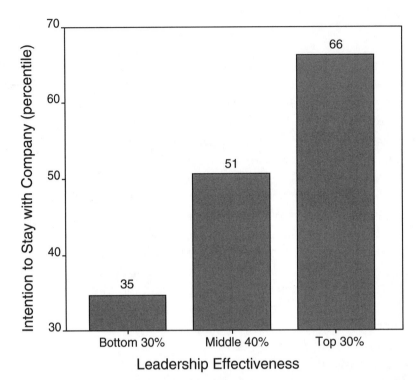

FIGURE A.1   Intention to stay with the company.

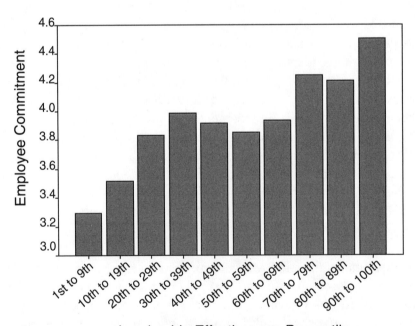

FIGURE A.2   Employment commitment.

SIXTEEN COMPETENCIES THAT BEST DIFFERENTIATE HIGH- AND LOW-PERFORMING LEADERS (CHAPTER 4)

To accomplish this analysis, thirty-two 360-degree feedback data sets were analyzed, containing results from over a hundred different companies. Table A.1 provides a listing of the different data sets used in the analysis.

The analysis was completed using results from 237,123 survey responses on 26,314 leaders. Each of the different data sets represented different customized 360-degree surveys. A total of 1956 360-degree items were used. Very few of the items were repeated in the different surveys. This provided an extraordinarily rich data set of competencies and items from a variety of different organizations.

Extensive analysis was done on each data set. First, data sets were compiled into aggregated format by computing an overall average of all responses (e.g., boss, peers, direct reports, others), with the self-response excluded. This was done for each leader in the data set. Next, an overall score was computed by averaging all 360-degree items into an overall index. We next determined from the overall score the top 10 percent of highest-scoring leaders and the bottom 10 percent of lowest-scoring leaders. Using these two groups, an independent t-test was performed on each item. The t-values from the t-test were then sorted for all survey items. The 10 to 15 items with the largest differences were then selected from each data analysis and put into a combined set of key differentiating items. Once all of the analysis was completed, the combined list was again sorted, selecting only those with the highest t-values. Each item was then put on a 3×5 card. The cards were sorted into groups separately by both authors, and after several iterations the items were grouped into 16 different clusters. Because the survey items crossed over 32 different data sets, we were not able to perform a factor analysis on the overall results, but we did perform a factor analysis on individual data sets, which helped in creating the appropriate clusters.

TABLE A.1   Composition of 32 Data Sets Used in the Key Differentiator Analysis

Data Set No.	No. of Assessments Completed	No. of Leaders Assessed	No. of Survey Items	Organization(s) Description
1	2,872	290	64	Research and Development
2	10,691	762	36	Bank/Investment
3	4,178	639	45	Generic Survey—Many Different Organizations
4	1,346	19	66	Chemicals
5	3,782	486	18	Food Processing
6	6,365	687	54	Food Sales
7	9,395	925	47	Foods
8	137	17	86	Manufacturing
9	2,670	349	48	Foods
10	21,786	3,022	60	High Technology
11	2,573	357	61	High Technology
12	1,502	147	52	Information Processing
13	3,512	259	84	Publishing
14	19,671	2,030	61	Generic Survey—Many Different Organizations
15	7,290	943	60	Oil—Up Stream
16	1,221	180	53	High-Technology Manufacturing
17	2,648	276	91	High-Technology Development
18	2,177	262	73	High-Technology
19	11,048	1,123	88	High-Technology Development
20	12,060	1,175	79	High-Technology Sales/Service
21	1,183	165	51	Automotive
22	9,323	901	50	Foods
23	1,831	210	99	Foods
24	2,001	194	50	Restaurant
25	7,155	1,009	66	Research and Development
26	14,630	2,125	70	Generic Survey—Many Different Organizations

(continued)

TABLE A.1   Composition of 32 Data Sets Used in the Key Differentiator Analysis (continued)

Data Set No.	No. of Assessments Completed	No. of Leaders Assessed	No. of Survey Items	Organization(s) Description
27	62,919	6,716	73	Generic Survey—Many Different Organizations
28	2,300	146	52	Forest Products
29	2,174	196	60	Paper
30	4,083	338	54	Banking
31	1,297	130	55	Mortgage Bank
32	1,303	126	50	Insurance
Total	237,123	26,314	1,956	

ENDNOTES

CHAPTER 1

1. Yukl, Gary, *Leadership in Organizations,* Prentice Hall, Englewood Cliffs, NJ, 1994.
2. Katzenbach, Jon, *Peak Performance,* Harvard Business School Press, Boston, 2000.
3. Weick, Karl E., *The Social Psychology of Organizing,* McGraw-Hill, New York, 1979.
4. Polanyi, Michael, *Personal Knowledge: Towards a Post-Critical Philosophy,* University of Chicago Press, 1958, p. 53.
5. Ulrich, Dave, Jack Zenger, and Norm Smallwood, *Results-Based Leadership,* Harvard Business School Press, Boston, 1999.

CHAPTER 2

1. Rucci, Anthony J., Steven P. Kim, and Richard T. Quinn, "The Employee-Customer-Profit Chain at Sears," *Harvard Business Review,* January–February 1998, pp. 82–98.
2. Johnson, Carla, "Recruitment: Capturing Turnover Costs," *HR Magazine,* July 2000, Volume 45, No. 7, pp. 107–119.
3. Senn, Larry E., and John R. Childress, *The Secrets of Reshaping Culture*, The Leadership Press, 1999.

4. Collins, Jim, "Level 5 Leadership: The Triumph of Humility and Fierce Resolve," *Harvard Business Review*, January 2001, pp. 67–76.
5. Kelly, Walt, creator of Pogo, 1917–1973.
6. *BusinessWeek*, October 15, 2001, p. 114.
7. Ericsson, Anders K., and Neil Charness, "Expert Performance, Its Structure and Acquisition," *American Psychologist*, 1994, Volume 49, No. 8, pp. 725–747.

CHAPTER 3

1. Dalton, Gene, and Paul Thompson, *Novations: Strategies for Career Management,* Harper & Row, New York, 1966.
2. Sandholtz, Kurt; *The 4 Stages of Career Growth,* BT.Novations Publication, Provo, UT, 2001, p. 2.
3. Ulrich, Dave, Jack Zenger, and Norm Smallwood, *Results-Based Leadership,* Harvard Business School Press, Boston, 1999.
4. Frangos, Steve, *Team Zebra,* Oliver Wright Publications, Omneo, Essex Junction, VT, 1993.
5. Gardner, John, *On Leadership,* Free Press, New York, 1990, pp. 3–4.
6. McClelland, David, "Achievement Motivation Can Be Developed," *Harvard Business Review,* Volume 43, 1965, p. 178.

CHAPTER 4

1. Gardner, John W., *On Leadership,* The Free Press, New York, 1990.
2. Spencer, Lyle M., *Competence at Work,* Wiley, New York, 1993.
3. Dalton, Maxine, "Are Competency Models a Waste?" *Training and Development,* October 1997, pp. 46–49.
4. Ibid.
5. Asch, S. E., "Forming Impressions of Personality," *Journal of Abnormal and Social Psychology,* vol. 41, 1946, pp. 258–290.
6. Kelly, H. H., "The Warm-Cold Variable in First Impressions of Persons," *Journal of Personality,* vol. 18, 1950, pp. 431–439.
7. Rosenberg, S. , C. Nelson, and P. S. Vivekananthan, "A Multidimensional Approach to the Structure of Personality Impressions," *Journal of Personality and Social Psychology,* vol. 9, 1968, pp. 283–294.
8. Ibid.

9. Dorsey, David, "Andy Pearson Finds Love," *Fast Company,* vol. 49, August 2001, pp. 78–82.
10. Bronowski, Jacob, *The Ascent of Man,* Little, Brown, Boston, 1974, pp. 115–116.

CHAPTER 5

1. Welch, Jack, *Jack Straight from the Gut,* Warner Business Books, New York, 2001, p. xiv.
2. Sandholtz, Kurt, "Achieving Your Career Best," *National Business Employment Weekly,* July 11–17, 1999.
3. Dalton, Gene, and Paul Thompson, *Novations: Strategies for Career Management,* Scott, Foresman, Glenview, IL, 1986.
4. Sandholtz, July 11–17, 1999.
5. Dalton and Thompson, pp. 218–236.
6. Ibid.

CHAPTER 6

1. Festinger, L. A., *The Theory of Cognitive Dissonance,* Stanford University Press, Stanford, CA, 1957.

CHAPTER 7

1. McCall, M. W., Jr., and M. M. Lombardo, "Off the Track: Why and How Successful Executives Get Derailed," Tech Report No. 21, Center for Creative Leadership, Greensboro, NC, 1983.
2. Zenger, John H., "Responsible Behavior: Stamp of the Effective Manager," *Supervisory Management,* July 1976, pp. 18–23.
3. Drucker, Peter, *Management: Tasks, Responsibilities, Practices,* HarperCollins, New York, 1973, p. 141.
4. Higgins, E. Tory, "Regulatory Focus Theory: Implications for the Study of Emotions at Work," *Organizational Behavior and Human Decision Processes, Special Issue: Affect at Work,* Volume 86, September 2001, pp. 35–66.

5. Dweck, Carol S., and Ellen L. Leggett, "A Social-Cognitive Approach to Motivation and Personality," *Psychological Review,* Volume 95, No. 2, 1988, pp. 256–273.
6. Dweck, Carol S., *Self-Theories: Their Role in Motivation, Personality, and Development,* Psychology Press, Philadelphia, 1999.

CHAPTER 8

1. Kelley, Robert E., *How to Be a Star at Work,* Times Business, New York, 1998, pp. 43–44.
2. Kelley, Robert E., and Janet Caplan, "How Bell Labs Creates Star Performers," *Harvard Business Review,* vol. 71, July–August 1993, pp. 128–139.
3. Kelley, *How to Be a Star at Work,* pp. 43–44.
4. Krames, Jeffrey, *The Jack Welch Lexicon of Leadership,* McGraw-Hill, New York, 2002, p. 123.

CHAPTER 9

1. Katzenbach, Jon, *Peak Performance,* Harvard Business School Press, Boston, 2000, p. ix.
2. Katzenbach, Jon, and Jason Santamaria, "Firing up the Front-Line," *Harvard Business Review,* May–June 1999, pp. 107–117.
3. Freedman, David, "Corps Values," *Inc.,* April 1998, pp. 55–64.
4. Clancy, Tom, *Marine,* Berkley, New York, 1996.
5. Katzenbach and Santamaria, pp. 107–117.
6. Clancy.
7. Freedman, p. 64.
8. Katzenbach and Santamaria, p. 113.
9. Freedman, pp. 55–64.
10. Clancy, pp. 52–53.
11. Ibid., p. 57.
12. Dorsey, David, "Andy Pearson Finds Love," *Fast Company,* August 2001, pp. 49–78.
13. Christensen, Clayton, *The Innovator's Dilemma,* Harvard Business School Press, Boston, 1997.
14. O'Dell, Douglas (Brigadier General), *Newsweek,* November 12, 2001, p. 6.

CHAPTER 10

1. Drucker, Peter F., *The Practice of Management,* Harper & Row, New York, 1954.
2. Kouzes, James M., and Barry Z. Posner, "On Becoming a Leader" in *Growth Strategies,* American Management Association, September 1987.
3. Simon, H. A., *The Science of Management Decisions,* Prentice Hall, Englewood Cliffs, NJ, 1977.
4. Ulrich, Dave, Jack Zenger, and Norm Smallwood, *Results-Based Leadership,* Harvard Business School Press, Boston, 1999, pp. 169–180.
5. Flaherty, John E., *Peter Drucker: Shaping the Managerial Mind,* Jossey-Bass, San Francisco, 1999, p. 335.
6. Ibid., pp. 336–337.
7. Valerio, Anna M., "A Study of the Developmental Experiences of Managers," in *Measures of Leadership* (Kenneth E. and Miriam B. Clark, eds.), Leadership Library of America, West Orange, NJ, 1990, pp. 521–533.
8. Perry, Lee Tom, Randall G. Stott, and W. Norman Smallwood, *Real-Time Strategy: Improvising Team-Based Planning for a Fast-Changing World,* Wiley, New York, 1993.
9. Friedman, Stewart, "Leadership DNA: The Ford Motor Story," *T&D Journal,* March 2001, p. 25.
10. Ibid., p. 27.

CHAPTER 11

1. Andersen Consulting Institute for Strategic Change, *The Evolving Role of Executive Leadership,* Publication 99-0382, 1999, available from Accenture.
2. Drucker, Peter, *The Effective Executive,* HarperCollins, New York, 1967, p. 99.
3. Garvin, David A., *Learning in Action: A Guide to Putting the Learning Organization to Work,* Harvard Business School Press, Boston, 2000, p. 120.
4. Katzenbach, Jon, *Peak Performance,* Harvard Business School Press, Boston, 2000.
5. Perry, Lee Tom, Randall G. Stott, and W. Norman Smallwood, *Real-Time Strategy: Improvising Team-Based Planning for a Fast-Changing World,* Wiley, New York, 1993.

6. Ulrich, Dave, Jack Zenger, and Norm Smallwood, *Results-Based Leadership,* Harvard Business School Press, Boston, 1999.
7. Flaherty, John E., and Peter Drucker, *Shaping the Managerial Mind,* Jossey-Bass, San Francisco, 1999, pp. 329–330.
8. Krames, Jeffrey, *The Jack Welch Lexicon of Leadership,* McGraw-Hill, New York, 2002, p. 68.
9. Flaherty and Drucker, pp. 329–330.
10. Drucker, *The Effective Executive,* p. 45.
11. "Why Johnny May Learn to Add," *BusinessWeek,* December 13, 1999, pp. 108–114.
12. Revans, Reginald W., *The Origins and Growth of Action Learning,* Studentlitteratur, Lund, Sweden, 1982.
13. "Siemens: Building a 'B-School' in Its Own Back Yard," *Business-Week,* November 15, 1999, p. 281.
14. Friedman, Stewart D., "Leadership DNA: The Ford Motor Story," *T&D,* March 2001, pp. 23–29.
15. Marsick, Victoria J., Lars Turner, Ernie Cederholm, and Tony Pearson, "Action Reflection Learning," *T&D,* August 1992, pp. 63–67.
16. Marquardt, Michael, *Action Learning,* Davis-Black, Palo Alto, CA, 1999.
17. Garvin, pp. 89–136.
18. de Pree, Max, "Four Pioneers Reflect on Leadership," *T&D,* July 1998, pp. 41–48.
19. Stewart, Thomas, "Nine Dilemmas Leaders Face," *Fortune,* March 18, 1996, pp. 112–113.
20. McCall, Morgan, Jr., Michael Lombardo, and Ann Morrison, *The Lessons of Experience,* Lexington Books, New York, 1988.

INDEX

ABOUT THE AUTHORS

John H. Zenger, D.B.A., is the vice chairman of Provant, Inc., the world's largest performance skills improvement company. One of today's most authoritative voices on the topics of performance and leadership, he is the author or coauthor of six books, including *Results-Based Leadership*—honored as the best book of 2000 by the Society of Human Resource Management.

Joseph Folkman, Ph.D., is managing director of Novations Group, Inc., a Provant company. He is the author of three books: *Turning Feedback into Change, Making Feedback Work,* and *Employee Surveys That Make a Difference.*

For more information on the authors and the research presented in this book, go to www.extraordinaryleader.net.